Henry R. Pyne

The history of the First New Jersey cavalry

Henry R. Pyne

The history of the First New Jersey cavalry

ISBN/EAN: 9783337814595

Printed in Europe, USA, Canada, Australia, Japan

Cover: Foto ©ninafisch / pixelio.de

More available books at **www.hansebooks.com**

THE HISTORY

OF THE

FIRST NEW JERSEY CAVALRY,

(Sixteenth Regiment, New Jersey Volunteers.)

BY HENRY R. PYNE,

CHAPLAIN.

TRENTON, N. J.:
J. A. BEECHER, PUBLISHER.

1871.

Murphy & Bechtel, Printers.

TO

CHARLES S. OLDEN,

THE WAR GOVERNOR OF NEW JERSEY,

THIS RECORD OF THE BRILLIANT SERVICES OF ONE

OF HER MOST GALLANT REGIMENTS,

IS RESPECTFULLY INSCRIBED,

AS A SLIGHT APPRECIATION OF HIS CONTINUED AND VALUABLE AID IN PROMOTING THE INTERESTS OF HIS STATE, AND MAINTAINING THE PERPETUITY OF OUR NATIONAL UNION.

PUBLISHER'S PREFACE.

In preparing and presenting this work to the public, and particularly to the surviving soldiers of the regiment and their friends, the publisher has aimed to offer an attractive volume that should preserve in a durable form the record of the first regiment of volunteer cavalry that entered the field and was the last to leave it, and whose history from the time it was fairly organized and equipped was one of continuous service and brilliant achievements. This regiment was recruited three times to the full maximum and as often melted away before the enemy's fire, and disease and exposure incident to the campaign. The author was an officer of the staff, and participated fully in all whereof he writes, while his style is exceedingly instructive, abounding in vivid description and entertaining narrative. Desiring to make the book as perfect as possible, the publisher has added an appendix, consisting of the official list from the Adjutant-General's office of the name, rank and promotions of every member of the regiment from the time of its organization to the close of the war, making in all nearly three thousand names, together with a record of casualties of every kind so far as known. This has been done with great care and labor, and it is hoped correctly. There is also given a list of battles in which the regiment was engaged, with the date and place of action.

A novel and interesting feature is a fac-simile of the battle-flag of the regiment as it now hangs in the Adjutant-

General's office, after passing through ninety-two (92) of the ninety-seven (97) actions in which the regiment was engaged. Though soiled and tattered, it has a glory that belongs alone to itself and the men who carried and followed it so bravely; and it will not be strange if their blood is stirred as they look upon it.

The book is dedicated to as true a man and as noble a Governor as New Jersey ever had. Standing at the head of affairs at the breaking out of the rebellion, and holding the helm with so firm and loyal a hand, we believe the men who supported him in the field will be glad that this recognition of his worth has been given, and so beautiful and correct a portrait of Governor Olden presented.

In justice to himself and others, the publisher begs leave to make a statement, which if consistent would have been omitted: At the time Mr. Foster was preparing a work entitled "New Jersey and the Rebellion," he obtained for reference the MS. of "Pyne's History of the First New Jersey Cavalry," which was mostly written in the field, and completed long before that work was projected. Those who have read the work alluded to will doubtless observe a similarity between that portion of it which gives some account of the Sixteenth Regiment (the First New Jersey Cavalry) and the complete history now for the first time published. This is accounted for by the fact that it was taken almost bodily, chapter headings and all, from the author's MS. of this work.

TO CHARLES P. SMITH, Esq.,

TRENTON, N. J.

My Dear Sir: While the regiment whose history is here presented to you, and to the citizens of New Jersey, was lying in winter quarters at Warrenton, Virginia, Colonel KESTER, then in command, suggested to me the idea of employing that season of comparative rest in the composition of a record of our achievements and sufferings. He mentioned your name as that of one who had from the beginning taken a lively interest in our welfare, who would enjoy the perusal of the work, and, he confidently believed, render me valuable assistance and facilities for its accomplishment and publication. My own experience has more than justified his words; and I cannot permit these pages to pass from my hand without connecting with them some public acknowledgment of my obligations to you. In bringing into the regiment some of its most efficient officers (among whom may be included Colonel KESTER and Major YORKE); in promoting enlistments, and favoring, on all occasions, the acceptance of the regiment among the troops of the State; in being always prompt to further any effort which tended to its advantage, you have earned its regard and gratitude as a body; while my own personal obligations are illustrated to myself on almost every page.

This work, as you know, was almost entirely composed in the field, and as such, can pretend to no literary merit beyond the interest of the incidents which are contained, for which I am indebted to the heroes who performed them. If I have succeeded in preserving to them and their countrymen some memory of duty accomplished and hardships suffered in the cause of the nation, I shall feel that I have written for a good and sufficient end. Beyond this I have nothing to offer, nothing to excuse, and therefore nothing to say.

Very truly and respectfully,

ONE OF THE REGIMENTAL STAFF.

CHARLES S. OLDEN,

THE WAR GOVERNOR OF NEW JERSEY.

The history of New Jersey's participation in the war for the Union cannot be impartially written without according especial honor to the Chief Magistrate who during that momentous period wisely presided over her interests. So indelibly was Governor Olden's influence impressed on every branch of the public service, that no hesitation is experienced in designating him as preëminently the man to whom this work should be inscribed; or assigning him a high position among New Jersey's distinguished sons. The earlier portion of Governor Olden's career was devoted to mercantile pursuits in Philadelphia and New Orleans, from which he retired with ample fortune to his home on the battle-field of Princeton. But he was not long permitted to maintain his coveted seclusion. His financial experience and practical business qualifications were appreciated and secured in various directions. He was twice elected to represent his county in the State Senate, where after six years' service he left a record without blemish. While a member of that body, his ripe judgment and proverbial integrity, clothed him with an unusual degree of influence, which he ever exercised for the public good; and the State is far more indebted to his foresight and well-directed efforts for its noble Lunatic Asylum and State Capitol, than to any other man. The gubernatorial nomination sought him, and he was only prevailed upon to accept through urgent representations, placing it clearly in the light of duty. The dark cloud of civil war which spread over the land soon after his inauguration, suddenly required him to assume onerous duties as the head of the War Department. This, after more than forty years' disuse and neglect, was almost obsolete. But Governor Olden was not to be deterred by obstacles however formidable. Fully appreciating the gravity of the occasion, he never for a moment faltered, but proceeded to raise troops, provide munition and transportation, and in all matters pertaining thereto, acted so wisely and efficiently as to elicit profuse commendations from the National Executive. He not only organized, but with unsleeping vigilance endeavored personally to inspect the carrying out of details to their utmost extent. He devoted much time and patient inquiry to the selection of competent officers, preferring wherever possible, those whose experience and acknowledged ability best fitted them for the various positions; and to this, and his careful oversight, may be attributed in a great degree the superior handling and veteran-like steadiness which conspicuously characterized the New Jersey regiments in the field. His labors in the Executive Department were almost incessant—the first at his post and the last to retire—through all the trying years of his administration, it was a matter of astonishment to those who had opportunity for observation, that his physical organization did not succumb.

Governor Olden's financial experience peculiarly qualified him to grapple with the greatest difficulty of his position, an empty treasury. He not only triumphed over all obstacles in securing the necessary means to meet every requirement of the occasion, but put into successful operation the present admirable system of managing our finances under the pressure of public debt, which no one has ever called in question. Aside from this, his careful and intelligent supervision saved to the State an immense amount of money, which in a more confused administration might have been hopelessly squandered. The troops called for were raised, armed and equipped within a surprisingly brief period; and the first four regiments were dispatched down the Chesapeake Bay to Annapolis, and marched into Washington, as complete in all their appointments as regulars. They arrived at the darkest period of the rebellion, and were hailed as affording the first substantial feeling of security experienced at the National Capital. Governor Olden's duties to the close of his official term were equally unremitting. Regiment after regiment was raised and dispatched to the seat of war, and his system continued to work as noiselessly and well as a nicely adjusted piece of machinery. When he retired, every department of his government was settled to its bearing.

Governor Olden still resides within the borders of his native State, and, in addition to other public duties, is filling most acceptably the position of Judge of the Court of Errors and Appeals. He is an intelligent observer of events, and eminent among his fellow citizens for practical wisdom, probity, unostentatious charity, loyalty, and in short, all the qualities of mind and heart which constitute a true man. Most fortunate was it for New Jersey that in such an emergency she could command the services of such a Governor. His name is inseparably connected with many of the most brilliant pages of her history, and his patriotism, integrity and republican simplicity will be perpetuated in the memory of a grateful people.

CHAPTER I.

ORGANIZATION.

While the memory of Bull Run battle was fresh, when there was still a vivid recollection of the panic created by the mere apprehension of rebel cavalry, and a strong conviction that a few effective squadrons of horse might have materially changed the fortunes of the day, or at least, by covering the retreat, have prevented the rout and confusion that spread from the battle-ground into the very streets of Washington; the Secretary of War granted freely to prominent men in various sections of the country permission to raise mounted regiments for three years' service. This authority was granted, among others, to the Hon. WILLIAM HALSTED, of New Jersey, who had been for many years a prominent member of the bar of that State, and also attained considerable political eminence. The State at this time having no authority to organize regiments of cavalry or artillery, the Governor declined to recognize "Halsted's Horse" as part of the State contingent of volunteers, and it therefore remained on an independent footing. Besides this, the colonel was approaching his seventieth year, and scarcely possessed the strength and endurance requisite to fulfill the arduous duties of his new profession.

But whatever judgment may be pronounced upon the capacity of the colonel to command, he certainly proved that he possessed the ability to raise the regiment. It was in August that he had received his authority; and in the early part of September ten full companies were encamped in the vicinity of Washington, there awaiting the orders of the Commanding General. Halsted's Independent Cavalry had come into existence.

While the energies of the nation and its generals were severely taxed in the effort to reduce to order the enormous mass of infantry encamped irregularly in the suburbs of the capital, the cavalry, in the helplessness of its infancy, could secure little attention and less care.

Many officers had seen bodies of foot soldiery in camp and in the field, and had some experience in their management; but all their experience of cavalry service had been acquired in command of squadrons scattered over the prairies in practise of Indian warfare. It is no wonder, therefore, that a Chief of Cavalry, formed in such a school, with a staff, some of whose members had never manœuvered a platoon, posted a picket, or even seen a camp, found some difficulty in organizing, equipping and disciplining thirty regiments of men, ignorant how to groom a horse or to ride him properly when accoutred for the field.

When it is furthermore remembered that these regiments were commanded by lawyers, farmers, merchants and politicians, entirely unacquainted with the details of that difficult organization which they had undertaken to manage, it may be conceived that the early experience of a cavalry regiment was not likely to be of calm regularity or well ordered system. As a type of the history of all, that of this one regiment may prove interesting and instructive; and a brief space shall therefore be given to the incidents accompanying the formation of the First New Jersey Cavalry into an effective regiment.

On the grounds of Kalorama, just without the corporate limits of Washington, between the old tomb of Decatur and the steep banks of Rock Creek, the regiment was put in camp. The hot September sun shone upon ground from which the movements of successive regiments of militia had worn away the soft green turf; and the yellow soil reflected a sickening glare into the closely crowded tents. Beyond the supply of the evident needs of food, shelter, and clothing, which, owing to the surprising energy of the Quarter-Master General, was fully met, notwithstanding the frequent extravagance of the demand; there seemed to be little investigation into the requirements of the men or care for their provision.

The commanding officer had never had an opportunity of studying the complicated discipline of camp life, or the proper manner of meeting its requirements; and the men accustomed to the independence of home, did nothing except what they were told, and often questioned the propriety of the orders which they received. The most ordinary precautions of sanitary police were neglected, and the accumulating filth of the camp, festering in the scorching sun, combined with the pestilential damps that exhaled at nightfall from the creek and river. Some acquaintance with militia training suggested the performance of the parade portion of military life. There was a formal guard-mounting every morning, of men who appeared upon parade with sticks as their only substitute for sabres, and who were placed upon their posts with no distinctly defined idea of what they were to do there. There was also a dress parade every evening, when a crowd of men, not yet trained to stand or step like soldiers, was brought out in line and ordered to go through some complicated evolutions, the proper mechanism of which could only have been attained by weeks of previous drill. Drill, however, there was little, and that little almost a voluntary matter with officers and men; and there was no distinct authoritative announcement of duties, no promptly enforced penalty for disobedience. There was, above all, no care to occupy the long hours of the day in the regulated performance of professional labors, the only thing that can form in the citizen the habits of the soldier. Officers who sought for some advantage or indulgence applied to the colonel, with no consideration whether the favor ought properly to be asked by a subordinate or granted by a commander. If in his endeavor to administer his government faithfully, the colonel refused their petition, they persisted, even to angry remonstrance; finally overpowering his objections, at the cost of all respect for authority. Two lieutenant-colonels were contending for the position to which *both* had been appointed; and the officers were divided into cliques, supporting one or the other. When officers, who knew something of their duty, tried to do it, their men drew invidious comparisons between them and other easy-going company commanders; and without any energetic superior authority to support them, the officers found themselves forced to succumb to the tide of popular opinion.

The regimental commander, in the midst of a throng of duties all strange and peculiar in their character, found himself unable to concentrate his attention upon any one. Called to labor constantly beyond his strength, harassed by responsibilities for which he was unprepared by military experience, and to bear which he was untrained in military habits, he found the confusion around him defying all his efforts and regulation, and could only by slow degrees begin to grapple with the difficulties of his situation.

Still, in one way or another, things dragged along. The regiment passed from camp to camp, and at length, crossing the river, was placed in a brigade. Here the difficulty as to the lieutenant-colonelcy was terminated, and Joseph Kargé, formerly an officer in the Prussian service, though for many years a naturalized citizen of the United States, was permanently established in that rank. When this result was accomplished, the colonel, wearied with the labor which had been imposed upon him, and becoming ill from the effect upon him of camp life, took a sick leave, and retired for a time to Washington.

As the lieutenant-colonel was bending all his energies to the performance of his duty in perfecting the military character of the regiment, a result, the details of whose accomplishment he clearly understood, he encountered a difficulty in procuring those supplies which were essential not only to efficiency, but even to continued existence. The last raised company had just reported to camp without uniforms, without blankets, without tents to shelter them, and the constantly increasing number of horses was insufficiently supplied with forage and the appliances for the preservation of their health, strength and equipments. As these things occurred within sight of the immense granaries and overflowing storehouses of Washington, Lieutenant-Colonel Kargé promptly called the regimental quartermaster to account without obtaining any satisfactory explanation; and though that officer was warned to perform his duty, the supplies were still unprovided. The matter was reported to the brigade commander, who, finding on investigation, that the quarter-master had been irregularly mustered in, had his name without further ceremony removed from the rolls of the regiment; and his place having been supplied by another officer, the needed rations, forage, arms and clothing were without difficulty obtained.

The colonel, who was in Washington, felt that as the ranking officer of the regiment, he should have been consulted before such a change had been effected, and he naturally interpreted the removal of the quarter-master as an infringement of his prerogative and an attack upon himself. He consequently hurried back to camp in indignation, and signalized his resumption of command by an unseemly altercation with the lieutenant-colonel.

The colonel naturally took the part of the men in their complaints against the late executive; and the reforms in drill, discipline and camp routine, at once fell into abeyance. At the same time, the officers of ability and zeal, *though they might question the propriety of the lieutenant-colonel's manner*, could not but perceive that his course tended to the improvement of the regiment, *while the present state of things must result in its dissolution.* They therefore began to draw towards the side of Lieutenant-Colonel Kargé, and were on that account regarded as hostile by Colonel Halsted. Hence there were two prominent parties in the camp, besides numerous petty subdivisions, varying continually, according to the impulses of personal pique and the demands of individual interest: and this state of affairs, by distracting attention and zeal from the good of the regiment, left it still unprepared for service.

During the month of November, the regiment was assigned to the division of General Heintzleman; and in the beginning of December another change of command took place. Owing to misconstruction of certain regulations, Colonel Halsted became involved in difficulties with the War Department, which resulted in his arrest; and the command devolved in consequence upon the lieutenant-colonel. There was a sudden resumption of energy and discipline. Well seconded by the senior major, who, though young, was familiar with the routine of cavalry service, Kargé set to work to make soldiers of the officers and men. As a first step he sent the most inefficient officers and men before the Examining Board, in Washington, thus startling the rest into activity. Wherever there was any duty to be done either he or the major was to be seen, ready to pour forth vials of wrath upon the heads of the delinquent. Officers grumbled and soldiers swore, but still the routine was inexorably carried on; and before long all awoke to a consciousness that they had never been so comfortable since their first enlistment.

In the five weeks of this *regime*, a soldierly spirit was implanted in the men, which preserved its vitality through all the ensuing trouble. Colonel Halsted, by the middle of January, settled his difficulties with the War Department, and was restored to the command of his regiment, which was thereupon removed from General Heintzleman's jurisdiction. This transfer, occurring in the midst of a dismal storm, was undertaken without due preparation; and for two nights the men and horses bivouacked in the streets of Washington, exposed to the inclemency of the weather. A new camp was then laid out near the road leading out of Seventh street towards Rockville; and in a contracted space the troops were crowded into quarters. Knee-deep in the mud, with no provision for their comfort, no duty to employ them except the harassing work of furnishing a double camp-guard, the men began to sicken and desert by scores. Rumors began to float around that in the proposed reduction of the cavalry, the regiment was to be disbanded; and the men began to calculate that it was better to hurry home at once than to linger in discomfort for no purpose. The lieutenant-colonel and major were in arrest. Many of the best officers were in disgrace, and many of the poor ones gave themselves up to intoxication. The colonel's time was engrossed by pursuing the cases of his officers before the Examining Board; and no one seemed to have a hope or a care for the well-being of the regiment.

So the month of February came in and wore half away. Suddenly other rumors were whispered through the camp. The regiment had been recognized by the State, and the soldiers' families were to receive State pay. Colonel Halsted had been mustered out, and Percy Wyndham, an Englishman by descent, colonel in the Sardinian service, a soldier of Garibaldi, and Chevalier of the Military Order of Savoy, had been commissioned colonel by the Governor. The regiment was safe and its prospects brilliant. On the heels of the rumor came its confirmation. Colonel Halsted one morning left the camp and never returned. That evening, an officer, young, dashing, handsome, every inch a soldier, quietly walked in and introduced himself as colonel. The regiment was transferred to better ground; and the mud was dried up by clear frosty weather. Every body was released from arrest, and the spirits of the regiment brightened with the sky. "Halsted's Horse" became the "First New Jersey Cavalry;" and with a change of name there came a change of character.

Once more the regiment returned to its old camp under Heintzleman. Under the active superintendence of the three soldiers now at its head, drill went actively on. Everything superfluous in the clothing and equipment of the troopers was taken away and every deficiency carefully supplied. Several times the regiment was ordered out as if for the march, until the men became accustomed to pack and saddle well and promptly. The regiment was perhaps more perfectly prepared for the field than any other in the army, when to its dismay, McClellan moved, leaving it behind.

The colonel consoled himself by going out to sweep the country in the direction of Dumfries, picking up straggling scouting parties of the enemy. There was enough show of danger to make the work exciting and to give a sensation of success and a feeling of enterprize; so that these expeditions were of great value in their effect upon the men. They also taught lessons for the bivouac if not for the battle, brought to light what faults there might be in the disposition of the equipments, practiced men and officers in their duties, and suggested to them the labors of the campaign. Thus passed the days which closed the period of preparation and initiated the First New Jersey Cavalry into the real work of war.

CHAPTER II.

A DASH ACROSS THE RAPPAHANNOCK.

Early in the morning of Friday, the eighteenth of April, eighteen hundred and sixty-two, the *générale* was sounded at the head quarters of the regiment, in Camp Custis. Nine hundred horses, the saddles packed with every necessary for the march, stood in the streets, equipped for the journey, and the men were busily engaged in providing themselves with rations and ammunition. In obedience to the successive calls of the bugles, the first battalion assembled, led out, and formed; with one impulse the men lifted themselves into their saddles, the ranks were dressed, and with fluttering guidons the troops moved off, giving a farewell cheer to the spot which had gathered around it many of the associations of a home. At regulated intervals the other two battalions followed; and by ten o'clock the tents stood tenantless with that air of desolation which so quickly attaches itself to a deserted dwelling.

By the well-known road past Pohick Church, the scene of many a scout and many a skirmish, near which Lieutenant Janeway had achieved the unenviable distinction of being the first officer in the regiment to make the personal acquaintance of rebel bullets; across the sinuous Accotink, and by the house of the noted Widow Violet, where for the winter months had been the head quarters of the Southern pickets; the road led across the dangerous ford on the Occoquon, into the thoroughfare to Dumfries. For the first fifteen miles, with the exception of occasional spots of mire, the road was tolerably firm. Then, crossing

Neabsco Creek, and making gigantic bonfires of the winter quarters of Wigfall's and Whiting's rebel brigades, we entered upon the route by which supplies had been hauled for the Southern troops from the nearest station on the Acquia railroad. Here there was a depth and consistency of mud for which even the experience of a Washington winter had been unable to prepare the mind. How deep it had been during the winter, how many horses had died there, how many wagons had broken down, it is impossible to estimate; but in the middle of the month of April, when the ground had been settling for six weeks, and the road had been untraveled for the greater part of the time, the troopers did not dare to venture into the middle of the track. In files to the right and left, winding among the trees, or breaking through fences into the adjacent fields, the long line of horsemen picked its way, with every now and then a stumble, an imprecation, and a laugh, as some horse would lose his footing and roll his rider in the quagmire by his side. Thus a dozen miles were traveled, the sun meanwhile declining into a bank of black and sullen clouds; and at last, simultaneously with the rain, the regiment entered the dismal village of Dumfries.

Long ago, in the time of Colonial dependence, Dumfries had shipping at the doors of its houses, and contested commercial supremacy with Alexandria; but year by year the rains brought down the soil from the hill-side, and deposited it in the harbor, until now more than half a mile of meadow land stretches between the few handsome houses of old time and the majestic current of the Potomac. Now the fine old brick mansions are surrounded by a dozen or two tumble-down structures of clattering clap-boards, and the inhabitants are ignorant that there is any world beyond Virginia, except the opposite shore of Maryland.

In this region, so benighted as to refuse the currency of the United States, while the notes of the Confederacy were accepted at their nominal value, with no shelter at hand, and the soft rain soaking through overcoats, clothes and boots, with mud knee-deep everywhere and deepening every minute, with no clear idea where any other National troops might be, nor what rebel force might be in our immediate neighborhood; we passed in dreary bivouac the first night of the campaign.

At length it was over, and morning dawned upon the mud. Rather disappointed at having camped in the enemy's country without the excitement of an alarm or the distinction of a fight, the regiment resumed its march to Falmouth. Through Stafford Court House with its two or three white houses and its pitiful-looking jail, we filed along, traversing a country on which was everywhere impressed an aspect of desolation. Here and there were some cleared fields surrounding a comfortless-looking house; but no travelers were on the road, and only now and then could a negro be discerned, staring from his quarters at the seemingly interminable line of troopers. Late in the afternoon a vidette was passed. Then picket after picket became visible, and we learned that King's Division had already occupied Falmouth, that the rebels had burned the bridges, that the First Pennsylvania and Second New York Cavalry regiments had in a brief skirmish with the enemy lost a few men, and that there were no signs of any further immediate fighting. Defiling through the steep streets of the little town of Falmouth, situated, like all the rest of Virginia during that spring, in an abyss of mud, the regiment encamped in a clover field adjoining the beautiful Lacy mansion-house; and lying within hearing of the shots exchanged between the hostile pickets, realized that it was at length in the field before the enemy.

On the other side of the narrow river stood the picturesque old town of Fredericksburg, with its houses of blackened brick, or weather-stained and dry-rotten wood, from among which a few church spires rose gracefully into the air; the whole resembling rather the pictures of some quiet mediæval town of Europe, than the rapidly growing, unromantic cities of our cis-Atlantic civilization. Behind the buildings, the ground, green and wooded, swelled gradually up into the memorable Marye's Heights, whose slope before the year was ended was stained with the blood of so many heroic regiments, and whose summit was afterward triumphantly crowned by the bullet-torn standards of Sedgwick's stalwart infantry; and here and there were dotted the pleasant residences of the fine old Virginia gentry, who have bequeathed their homes and the honor of their State to the keeping of such degenerate successors. In line athwart the stream stood the abutments of the ruined bridges, supporting a few fragmentary beams still smoking with the embers of the conflagration, and in the water near the bank lay the charred remains of projected gun-boat, consumed by the rebels in anticipation of our approach; the only evidences of war in a scene which seemed by nature devoted to uneventful and calm repose.

Literally, if not figuratively, in clover, the regiment lay at rest for twenty-four hours, which was as long a period of quiet as could be endured by the restless nature of the colonel. On the afternoon of Easter Sunday, in one of those tremendous showers which are a characteristic of the climate, it took the route to King George Court House, a distance of nineteen miles, picking up on the road several parties of rebel soldiers, who had stolen across the river to visit their families and friends. Into the place we poured, wet and weary, quartering ourselves in the public buildings or accepting rather extorted invitations into private families; and soon all except the pickets were finding rest and comfort in well-earned slumber.

The next day the head quarters were transferred to the comfortable country house of Edward Taylor, situated by a noble elm, beneath whose shade, according to tradition, the father of Pocahontas had often gathered his court; in honor of whom the place was entitled Powhatan Hill. The regiment encamped near the house of the overseer, to the ill-concealed disgust of that dignitary, and to the great delight of the negroes who had been subject to his domination. All their little store of poultry, pigs and vegetables was eagerly offered to the troops, who honorably paid for the property of the negroes, though they were not so particular with respect to the stock of the overseer and the farm. The slaves welcomed the army as their liberators, and in every way exerted themselves to supply their wants and to provide for their comfort.

Now commenced an exodus which paralyzed the deluded Virginia gentry, who had argued themselves into a conviction that their slaves were too contented and happy to seek for freedom from their state of bondage. Shutting their eyes to the constant laceration of all the domestic affections, the perpetual state of uncertainty as to the future, the hopelessness of any improvement of their condition, which had been forever hanging over the heads of the unfortunate negroes, their owners had regarded the satisfaction of their material wants as sufficient to reconcile them to their lot; and now they were to learn for the first time that no human being is without some of those higher aspirations with which God has endowed the race. Hour after hour long trains of negroes, men, women and children, came trooping into camp, some carrying their little store of clothing in bundles on their heads, some in carts borrowed without leave from their masters, many mounted on their owners' favorite steeds. With shouts and exulting laughter they swarmed into the lines, hailing the prospect of freedom, and the privilege of possessing the wages of their own labor. Eager for work, as many of them as could obtain places took service in the regiment, so that for a day or two every private rejoiced in the possession of a groom. Then, in self-defence, the camp was cleared of them, and all, except those retained by the officers, took up their march for Falmouth, from thence journeying to Washington, and further North.

The fugitives were not confined to those living upon the north bank of the Rappahannock. Night after night, in canoes, on rafts, by swimming, the slaves beyond the river made their way to us from their thraldom. No difficulty nor danger seemed sufficient to deter them from the path to freedom; and escaping every man, they brought in to us many valuable pieces of intelligence. The farmers at last organized a general rendezvous for the deportation of neir slaves to the neighborhood of Richmond. The slaves were not long without an intimation of the design; and now men, who had before been reluctant to leave their families, felt themselves "forced away." Hurrying to us with a sense of injury upon them, they were eager to punish in return those who had intended to kidnap them; and, in consequence of their reports, an opportunity was soon offered to inflict a considerable surprise upon the people of that locality.

A negro, called Humphrey, in relating the story of his escape, alluded casually to a party of Confederate cavalry stationed in the neighborhood of his home. Captain Virgil Brodrick was within hearing as he spoke, and the reference was not lost upon him. Questioning the negro, he learned that a small body of mounted men acting as couriers and videttes, and without immediate connection or support, was stationed at the house of a Dr. Goulding, about ten miles from the river bank. Though they were isolated from military connection, and had no adjacent post from which to expect prompt reinforcement, still, in a friendly neighborhood, with a broad river and eleven miles of land between them and the nearest enemy, they were not particularly vigilant or apprehensive of attack. It was to this post that the slave owners intended to gather all their active and doubtful slaves, arranging with the rebel general, Anderson, to have them escorted thence to the nearest station on the railroad, to be employed in military labor there, or else transported to the South for similar employment. The negro's face brightened at the idea of seizing these soldiers, so particularly obnoxious to him, and he promptly volunteered to guide any party who attempted such an exploit.

Captain Brodrick had resolved to try to surprise the post as soon as he had heard of its existence; and he applied at once to the colonel for permission to take a party across the river to accomplish that object. The colonel had been too distinguished a partizan leader not to relish the character of such an adventure; and he at once gave Captain Brodrick leave to take as many volunteers as he needed from his own company, and to start that night. From his own experience, the colonel imparted to Captain Brodrick many valuable suggestions, and prepared him for the probable risks that he might encounter.

It was the latter part of April, and during the whole month the rains had been unusually heavy. All the day there had been a steady down-pour, which increased at night, making the air raw and cold, and the darkness extraordinarily intense. The sky was an unbroken black, and the obscurity so great that only a practised eye could distinguish the most prominent object, when, as the bugles sounded tattoo, Brodrick, his orderly sergeant, Henry Darris, sixteen men, and two negro guides, issued quietly from the camp. Through the dripping wood and tangled copse which covered the approach to the river bank, at each movement shaking from the heavy leaves a shower of suspended rain-drops, they forced their way to where, hidden beneath the drooping branches, two old and clumsy canoes had been secreted by the negro fugitives. An attempt to employ the larger of these boats occasioned so much noise that Brodrick was obliged to content himself with the other, in which by twos and threes they were in several voyages ferried across the stream. Sending the boat back across the Rappahannock, the little band of twenty climbed the bank and started on their journey. As they turned away from the river, the plaintive tones of the bugle bidding their comrades to repose, breathed out to their ears like a farewell. Instinctively they halted until its last echo died away, and then tramping over the oozy surface of the fresh-ploughed fields, they stoutly began their march.

The habits of the negroes, accustomed to steal from farm to-farm, evading under cover of the night the vigilance of the patrols, stood them in good stead through the present darkness. The guide had on a light-colored coat of the common negro cloth issued by the farmers to their slaves; and by fixing his eye on this, Brodrick was able to follow his various turns and changes of direction. By unremitting attention, the others kept their places in the file; and through the silence of the night, every now and then a trip, a stumble, or a splash, indicated to him their proximity. Their course was along plantation roads and devious bye-paths, through ploughed fields, knee-deep in mud, and woods strewed here and there with the rotting trunks of fallen trees, until at last they came upon a plainer road, across which it was necessary for them to proceed. Just as they reached it the negro suddenly stopped short, and listening with suspended breath, they heard another party moving along the road, venting a low murmur of suppressed conversation. With hearts beating so violently that they sounded in their ears, and every limb stiffened into stillness, the men listened as the other party passed them without a suspicion of their vicinity. When the sound of footsteps had died away in the distance, and all once more was still, the negro guide again advanced.

After hours of cautious marching, Humphrey halted, and with intense excitement pointed before him, whispering to the captain, "Dar 'tis!" and in the direction indicated Brodrick could faintly discern a deeper darkness of the atmosphere, filling in the outline of a house. A few yards apart from the main building there was a smaller edifice of the character of an office, and it was to this that Humphrey called his attention. Here it was that the soldiers were quartered whom it was his purpose to surprise. Brodrick questioned the negro as to the ground between him and the building, and the arrangement of the interior, but partly from ignorance, partly from excitement, Humphrey gave confused and erroneous replies. Sending a party under Sergeant Darris to the rear of the building, Brodrick himself headed a rush upon the front. At the height of his speed he found himself violently checked by a paling-fence, which struck against his breast. Laying one hand on the top he vaulted over, and drawing his revolver, rushed forward to the door.

While all this was going on, the party of Confederates, as we afterward discovered, were, unsuspicious of danger, carelessly enjoying their easy post. Young men of the neighborhood, members of a local company that had volunteered into the rebel service, they found themselves enjoying all the excitement of military life without needing to abandon their homes, and were naturally recipients of especial attention from the families with which they had been long acquainted. The sergeant of the squad, in particular, found his post uncommonly agreeable, since it secured him a large share of the society of a young lady belonging to the family, for whom he had a great regard. That afternoon, before starting to take a look at our camp and to scrutinize our proceedings, he had nominated her commander during his absence. Laughingly accepting the commission, she had issued orders to him for his guidance, commanding him to report to her before a certain hour. The hour passed without his making his appearance, and when he came he was called to account for his disobedience. All his excuses were rejected as insufficient, and he was sentenced to pass the evening in close confinement in her parlor, with the extra duty of entertaining her, and the slight alleviation of a very nice supper. Accompanied by her cousin, a member of his party, and with the additional aid of some young lady friends who were staying in the house, the sergeant resigned himself very easily to his sentence; and the hours passed away more rapidly than he imagined, while he was enjoying the delights of her society. It was long after midnight when they parted, she warning him gaily to beware of the Yankees, and receiving in answer a mocking depreciation of their ability and enterprise.

Meanwhile the videttes, one posted near the door, the other on the hill beyond, had been left without relief much beyond the limit of their time of duty; and with a carelessness indicative of their sense of perfect security, both had come in together to rouse up their successors. The sergeant saw the men ready to proceed to their posts, and took no further care, and all in the room threw themselves down preparing for sleep, as one of the fresh videttes walked toward the door.

He opened it and stood face to face with Captain Brodrick, whose hand that moment touched the latch on the outside. Slamming the door, the rebel darted backward, followed by the captain. Instead of entering at once into the room, as the latter had expected, he was confused by finding himself in a dark and narrow passage; but a flash of light, as the rebel sprang into the place where lay his comrades, revealed the proper course. As, pistol in hand, he sprang into the room, he saw the man who had preceded him with his hand upon a weapon. "Surrender!" shouted the captain, involuntarily touching the trigger of his pistol. There was an explosion, and, wheeling half-round, the rebel soldier exclaimed, "You've shot me, sir!" Three men were lying on a bed together, one of whom made a motion as if to rise. With one bound, Broderick was upon them, his knee on one, his arm against another, and his pistol at the head of the third. At this moment the sergeant's party reached the window.

Alarmed at the shot, and seeing the captain apparently struggling with odds, one of the men discharged his carbine. The ball struck the cousin of the lady of the house, and stretched him, mortally wounded, upon the floor. There was no more firing. The surprise was complete, and the party, nine in all, surrendered.

It was sad to see the young soldier who had last been shot, writhing in mortal agony, and it was the first time that any of the men had seen such a result of their work. To relieve his pain was the first thing that they attempted, and a message was at once sent to the main building, requiring the attendance of the doctor. In the meantime the shots had excited an alarm, and the shrieks of the ladies were chorused by the yells of the negro women. Another message, more peremptory than the first, ordered the doctor to hasten his coming and silence the noise, or else the captain would be obliged to attend to the matter in person. This produced the desired effect, and in comparative quiet the necessary attention was given to the wounded men. The broken arm of the first one shot was set and bandaged, the dying man was laid upon a couch, and then, leaving the last behind them, the party, with the prisoners, their arms and horses, started upon their return. Moving more rapidly than when they advanced, they retraced their steps in safety; and, as the cheerful notes of the *réveille* rang out over the camp, the exulting troopers were ferried across the river with their prisoners, while the captured horses swam beside the boat.

By this bold adventure, a spirit of enterprise was infused into the whole command, and there were many smaller dashes into the enemy's country. Captain Kester brought off a rebel mail and a number of horses, and others picked up a few occasional prizes. The rebels were obliged to connect their posts and keep as careful guard as were we, thus being deprived of liberty to annoy us as they chose; while our men were eager for any opportunity of engaging an enemy against whom they had already obtained a success.

Sweeping across the country from river to river, and receiving back Lieutenant Robbins, who went to Lancaster county with twenty men and returned with about two hundred negroes and horses, the regiment marched to the estate of Captain Seddon, of the rebel army. Here it was combined with the First Pennsylvania Cavalry into a brigade, under the command of Brigadier General George D. Bayard, an officer whose name, associated with the two regiments which he commanded, was to become as familiar to the ear of the nation as his memory is endeared to the hearts of those who served under his authority.

For a long month we lay there upon the banks of the Rappahannock, steadily improving in drill and efficiency, and astonishing the Mississippi Riflemen, who picketed against us, by the effects of our carbines, while their rifles, from a superior position, only disabled one horse. After a time, they were relieved by a Texan regiment, who proposed a cessation of firing, and with whom we continued on good terms.

After a delay, incomprehensible to the army then, and uncomprehended still by the majority, at last, on Sunday, the twenty-fifth of May, Bayard's Brigade moved across the river, and, passing through Fredericksburg, advanced on the plank-road as far as Salem Church. On the afternoon of Monday, crossing to the Richmond road, it went to the front of the army; and on Tuesday, penetrating through a barren country, and fording with difficulty streams whose bridges were still smoking, it pressed forward, meeting with no enemy, and hoping soon to unite with the Army of the Potomac. Halting upon a rising ground, we heard, far in our front, a dull, thunderous sound, notifying us that a mighty conflict was going on between two distant armies. Nor did we err in our comments upon the reverberation.

In a far-off quarter of Virginia, after a series of events which made the intervening days seem like months in their thick, thronging memories, we received the news of that day's operations, and learned that we, in the advance of McDowell's Corps, had listened to the cannonade of Porter at Hanover Court House. No nearer then were we to approach those victorious troops. It was after months of disaster and many a bloody field, that McDowell and Porter were to make a junction, fatal to them both as soldiers, on the bloodiest plain of all, the twice stained soil around Manassas.

CHAPTER III.

IN THE VALLEY OF THE SHENANDOAH.

On the morning of Wednesday, the twenty-eighth of May, the brigade turned its back upon Richmond, and retraced its way to Fredericksburg. The bivouac of the night before had been dismal and rainy, and the disappointment at the retrograde movement did not contribute to our enlivenment; so that it was with rather diluted spirits, that we passed through the time-worn streets of Fredericksburg, across the pontoon bridges, and over the Falmouth hills. Under a scorching sun, which soon dispersed the damps of night, converting in an hour the clinging mud into a cloud of torturing dust, officers and men, sometimes bestriding their reeking steeds, sometimes marching for hours on foot to ease the horses, fagged on for an unknown object over an unknown road. After a march of thirty miles in the exhausting summer weather, the brigade halted at a place which seemed to have been at one time the residence of a well-to-do farmer. Now, the fields were untilled, the corn cribs almost empty, the men all away, and only a very bitter woman with a swarm of children, remained as occupants of the house. The two eldest daughters, half-curious, half-timid, hovered around the table where the leading officers obtained their meals, evincing the bashfulness of ignorance, and the bitterness of inculcated prejudice in every look and word. But little more than a year afterwards, as the regiment passed in the vicinity of the house, two brazen women, tawdrily attired, rode up, and deliberately scanned the column with bold faces and unseemly laughter. They were the same girls, hardened and corrupted by experience.

The poor horses had but a scanty feed that night, and the sweeping of the barns next morning procured them little more; yet very early they had to start on a march of equal severity to that of the day before. Over bad roads, under a summer sun, the horses labored forward, many of them, but poorly shod at the start, beginning to cast their shoes. At Cattell's Station, on the Orange and Alexandria Railroad, grain and rations met us, sufficient for the day's supply and a load for the wagons that were to follow us; and we learned that it would be necessary to economize that little store. For we knew now that Banks, weakened by the withdrawal of Shield's Division, had been attacked and terribly defeated; that Stonewall Jackson was in the valley with little between him and Washington; and that the troops from Fredericksburg were pressing onward to thrust themselves between the capital and the assault upon it apprehended. There was need therefore of speed on our part, if we were to accomplish our design of falling upon Jackson's flank.

Again, we marched quickly forward, through a country of barren hill-sides, seamed by ravines, and covered by lonely woods, the scene of many a future manœuvre, the lurking place of many a guerilla and unlicensed plunderer. Crossing the macadamised road from Warrenton to Alexandria, we halted to let the hungry horses feed upon the rich crop of clover which grew in the fields by the road, where the cattle driven from the West toward Washington had been wont to pasture; and sheltered by our india-rubber ponchos endured the pitiless beating of a mountain storm. Then passing through the town of Haymarket, we saw before us the gorge of Thoroughfare Gap, into whose narrow pass we entered as night came on with the darkness of another storm. On a rocky hill-side, among the trunks of trees but lately fallen before the woodman's axe, the regiment clambered into camp, casting many a longing eye behind in the direction of our expected train. A few scattered teams struggled through the swelling mountain torrent, and passed on; and then we learned that the obstructions in the road prevented the approach of others through the darkness. As the weary men lugged on their shoulders the needed supply of grain, murmuring at the toil, they little thought how soon they would have welcomed an opportunity for such labor; for from that night we saw our train no more until the termination of the campaign.

When the brigade, the next morning, defiled along the hard macadamised road, the effect of the severe work of the last week began to display itself among the horses. With increasing frequency men would be seen to dismount and attempt to lead forward their enfeebled animals, which with drooping heads, lack-lustre eyes, and trembling knees could scarcely support the weight of the saddles and equipments. The rate at which the brigade marched, and the very few halts which were permitted, increased the number of these stragglers, and left them far in the rear. Hours after the troops had encamped, small parties of two and three came dropping in, and threw themselves wearily down by their comrades. The little grain that could be carried was soon consumed, and the horses munching eagerly the rich clover of the meadow lands, gained from it little strength for the toils of the future.

As the next day's march led us through the Piedmont region, the limestone rocks, cropping out in the noble fields of wheat, gave indications of the roughness and fertility of the glorious valley into which we were to enter. The hills rose on either hand with a fuller sweep, the vales between them narrowed, until at last the wall of mountain seemed to open before us, and we entered the winding defiles of Manassas Gap. Passing the house of Turner Ashby, in a beautiful valley among the mountains, we came upon a road swarming with moving infantry and artillery until there was no room for further travel upon it. With no pause, however, to attend their dilatory motions, Bayard forced forward his brigade. Down went walls and fences on the hill-side, and along declivities which scarcely afforded foothold for the horses, down hill-sides, where they slipped and staggered, over ditches, which they leaped, scrambled through, or fell, the dashing leaders, Wyndham, and Bayard, side by side, led the way. Through the fragrant clover, and the waving sea of thick-growing grain, the troops swept along like a gallant fleet, leaving a wide wake of trampled verdure marking where they had passed; while the hills grew steeper, narrowing the gorge, until we wheeled around an intervening bluff, and saw before us the glittering ranks of Ricketts' infantry passing into Front Royal.

Far off among the mountains, with multiplied reverberations that shook the air around us, the sound of artillery struck upon our ears, in a continuous roar of battle. For the first time we heard the sound that heralded our entrance into action, and with one impulse the men erected themselves in their saddles, their eyes lighting up with the new excitement. The first fight was at hand, and the men longed for it, as they never desire the second.

It was still early in the afternoon as the brigade at a trot, passed out upon the road to Strasburg. Excited by the rapidity of their motion, the men became nervous and anxious, when they were unexpectedly brought to a halt,

The road was narrow, and except among the front files nothing could be known of what was going on. Naturally, therefore, the men in the rear, with their minds full of fight, imagined that the delay was occasioned by some collision with the enemy.

There had been added to the brigade, not only the valuable acquisition of Kane's noble battalion of Bucktail Rifles, but the more questionable re-enforcement of a one-horse battery of mountain howitzers, remarkable chiefly for the facility with which they turned upside down on the smallest provocation. It happened to strike some one at the front that our slapping trot over that uneven road must have brought this battery to grief; and the colonel, sharing the conviction, asked carelessly, "Where's the artillery?" The words were taken up with a laugh, and the question passed from man to man. Before it had traveled very far it had assumed a serious character, and when the men at the rear heard the cry, "Where's the artillery? Bring up the artillery?" they imagined that the guns were needed for immediate action in the front. Opening their files, therefore, to the right and left, they repeated the cry in a tone of command, and looked back to see if the guns were coming.

Behind the regiment, and between it and the rear-guard, were gathered the negro servants and led horses of the officers, with the cooks and other non-combatants of the companies, forming a column of very formidable length, though of no great gallantry. As these fellows saw the movement among the troops in the front, and heard the word, *artillery*, they were seized with an idea that it meant the commencement of a retreat. With the electric speed of panic the impression was conveyed from one to another; and with one accord, the whole body of negroes turned about in the road, and, sweeping the rear-guard away with them, poured back through the town of Front Royal. Thus, from this stampede of negroes, there arose a generally credited report that Bayard's Brigade had turned tail to the enemy and fled back in panic and confusion.

The incident is only worthy of record as an illustration of the origin and spread of a panic, and also how an accident may imperil a reputation; for all through the troops in Front Royal it was fully believed that the First New Jersey had run away.

Word had been sent to General Bayard that only one regiment was needed in the front; and the First Pennsylvania having the advance on that day, it alone was sent forward. There was, however, no action in the direction of its course. Examining the position near Strasburg, and being at once confronted by a superior force well arranged for resistance, its colonel wisely withdrew, reporting to the General the result of his observations.

The night had then set in, and it was intensely dark, as the brigade literally felt its way into camp. Through the latter part of the evening there had been a steady downpour of rain, which continued on through the night. As the different battalions filed into the swampy field which was allotted to the Jersey troops, the obscurity was increased by the shadow of the adjacent hills. So difficult was it to distinguish one party from another that squadrons time after time circled round the field looking vainly for their proper station, and the whole of the second battalion started off after a detachment for picket duty, imagining that the regiment was changing camp. Some of the men got into the soft soil of a cultivated garden, and, afraid to move in the darkness, remained there with their horses, knee-deep in mud and water. Lucky was the trooper, or even officer, who could secure a few rails laid together at an inclination, upon which he could perch, above the reach of the pools of water which soon stood in every part of the field; and the fences, which we were forbidden to use for fire, lest our camp might be revealed to the enemy, became serviceable as bed-posts.

Munching in the dark such fragments of wet crackers as remained in their haversacks, the men, cold, wet, and miserable, lay down in the continuous rain to sleep upon the soaking grass, and in deep discomfort waited for the dawn.

A glorious sunrise dispelled the gloom of night, and after a hurried meal all leaped to horse. In four columns the brigade pressed forward, each eager to be the first engaged. The waters of the Shenandoah rolled turbulently across the road, each moment augmenting the strength of its current and the volume of its waters, which even as we approached swept away the trestle-work that upheld the railroad bridge; but the men forced their horses through the doubtful ford, and scarcely waiting to re-form rode at a trot toward Strasburg. Some hastily constructed earth-works showed themselves above the town, but they were silent and deserted. As the troops wheeled with a cheer into the muddy streets an answering cheer came back from a little church on whose steeple waved the red flag of a hospital, and in its doorway stood a few figures in the blue coats of our infantry. They were sick and wounded men who had been paroled and left behind by Jackson's column, and who now welcomed the opportunity of obtaining sympathy and care. In the main street near the hotel, were clustered together men in the shabby uniform of the Confederacy, dusty, haggard and footsore, stragglers from the hurrying force that was pushing up the valley.

Without a pause, the second battalion of the Jersey dashed on along the road to Woodstock, each moment overtaking more and more of the fugitives, until the prisoners numbered several hundred. Leaving only a provost guard over the prisoners, Bayard hurried his brigade onward in the pursuit. Just as the rear departed from the town, the sound of cavalry in motion was heard upon the northern road, the head of a long column appeared, and an officer rode up, wearing on his shoulders the stars of a major general. He could not realize the truth that the town had been taken before him, and that McDowell's troopers were leading the Pathfinder in the chase of the enemy; and he seemed scarcely pleased to find it so. When Captain Gray, the provost marshal, told him that we had come from Fredericksburg, his astonishment was by no means lessened. Though his own march had been astonishingly rapid, ours had far outstripped him, and he had to be content with the second place in the field.

In the meantime, Kargé was pressing upon the heels of Ashby, thundering down upon all who in fancied security had for a moment lagged behind. Shots were from time to time exchanged with the rear-guard, and a few mounted men and officers cut off. At length, covered by a little stream, whose bridge had been hastily destroyed, a line of cavalry appeared drawn up across the road. At this moment Wyndham brought the rest of the regiment up at a gallop, and, without a pause, the three battalions, in different columns, were thrown across the streamlet against the enemy. The fourth squadron, Companies D and F, covering their advance by a deep ravine, struck the road close to the enemy, and in close column of fours wheeled into it to charge them. Just as they debouched upon it, a deep voice in the tall wheat of the adjacent field called out, "Ready! Aim!" and a regiment of rebel infantry rose up from their concealment. "Down on your saddles, every man!" shouted Captain Boyd, as the word "Fire!" issued from the hostile commander. Each man stooped to the horse's neck, and the whole volley whistled harmlessly over the heads of our men, riddling the fence behind them. As the fire was given, the rebel cavalry in the road opened right and left, uncovering a section of artillery in position. "Right about wheel, March! Trot! Gallop!" shouted Boyd, with a strenuousness proportioned to the emergency. As the column dashed round the bend of the road, a few scattering shots from the infantry were sent after it, killing Company D's blacksmith; and as its rear got out of range, the canister of the artillery tore along the causeway, just too late to hurt them.

While the rebel battery continued to fire, the first battalion took a wider sweep, and now came toward the road in its rear, while a portion of the third, under Haines and Janeway, strove to take it more in front. As our men set up their wild cheer, the supporting rebel cavalry broke and retreated in disorder, leaving the guns without protection. The artillerists and drivers began to waver and look behind them, but by each gun sat the officer of the piece with his pistol in his hand. Deserted by their supports, our troopers coming on, and their pistol-shots whistling over them, these gallant fellows forced their gunners to limber up as accurately as if on drill; and then, at a gallop, the pieces were whirled along to the rear. Major Beaumont and Captains Bristol and Kester, with Sergeant Fowler, of Company E, and half-a-dozen men, were dashing through the field by the side of the road, firing their pistols as fast as the chambers would revolve; but the severe marches of the past week, and the desperate speed of the morning's chase, told now exhaustingly upon the horses. In spite of all their efforts they were left behind, though Fowler, one of the corporals, and a private named Gaskill found their horses so crazy with excitement as to be unmanageable. After the flying battery they raced, plunging into the ranks of the enemy, who were obliged in self-defence to fire at those who were thus riding them down. Within a few yards of Ashby himself, Fowler was shot dead, the corporal wounded, and Gaskill unhorsed and taken prisoner.

All the rest of the battalion were straggling far behind, trying in vain to urge their horses into a charge, and the three officers were forced reluctantly to pull up, abandoning the prize which they so nearly had obtained.

Our Maine battery had now come up, and its shells, which dispersed the lurking infantry, fell thickly around our troopers returning to join the rest of the regiment, formed under cover of a wood. The fight now was between the opposing artillery, and the missiles shrieked through the air, or came crashing among the trees which sheltered our men. The explosions were startling, but inflicted little injury, a few men being slightly wounded, and one or two horses killed. One of these missiles struck beneath the lieutenant-colonel's horse, as he stood in his place in line. The explosion threw horse and man into the air, tearing the animal to pieces, but the rider came down unhurt, and emerged from the cloud of smoke with no blood upon him but that of the horse.

A strange instance of poetic justice occurred during this fire. Two women living among the hills, leaving the safe retreat of their homes, came down into the valley to see Stonewall Jackson defeat the Yankees. As they sat in a room looking toward the scene of action, a shell from the enemy's battery struck the building and exploded, tearing off a leg from one and seriously injuring the other. Crippled for life by their friends, they had to depend upon the surgery of the hated foe for their rescue from immediate death.

Now the night began to close in, and the infantry of Fremont, soaked through by another tremendous thunderstorm, came panting with their rapid march upon the field of battle. It was too late for further action, and pursuit was evidently impossible. Under cover of the night, Ashby, without loss, drew off his men, and our exhausted troopers bivouacked upon their first field of battle.

With trumpets sounding and waving banners, Bayard's Brigade marched the next morning through the town of Woodstock, pressing upon the rear of Jackson. Keeping up with the cavalry through all its heavy marching, Kane's gallant Bucktails stepped out actively beside us, and Hall's First Maine Battery followed in our rear. Through the swollen waters of the river at Edinburg we forced our way, the ammunition of the guns being carried on the backs of horses, and the riflemen skipping like rope-dancers across the shaking beams of the ruined bridge. As we ascended the hills above Mount Jackson, we saw in the distance the long line of rebel wagons, with their army drawn up to protect their passage. Between them and us rolled the swollen waters of a branch of the Shenandoah, over which even Wyndham failed to force his horse; and as we looked, a cloud of smoke arose above the burning bridge. In vain did the gallant riflemen plunge into the thickets that lined the river bank, and vainly did Bayard press his

Pennsylvanians forward to the charge. The bridge, raked by artillery, had been too well ignited to permit its tar-smeared timbers to be extinguished, and we had to gaze helplessly on the destruction of the only means of crossing. Our guns came clattering up and opened an angry fire upon the enemy, forcing them to retire out of range, but they did it with an air of triumph that enhanced our mortification: and we camped, hungry and disappointed, by the river's side, watching its constantly increasing volume, and soaked by the incessant rain.

It was now Tuesday night, and the last regular rations had been issued on Friday morning. Once, since then, a handful of crackers had been given to the men, but no other supply had been attainable. On every side, Fremont's marauding soldiery had been plundering and shooting; but our men, controlled by the habits of their discipline, had not participated in the work. Now, when there was a little rest from the pursuit, Bayard could not endure to see his men suffering from hunger, and permission was granted to the brigade to supply its pressing wants. Before nightfall each mess-fire had its smoking joint of meat, and enough grain was gathered from the neighboring barns to keep a show of life in the starving horses, and then the whole command enjoyed a period of brief but sweet repose.

During the next day efforts were vainly made to bridge the swollen stream. Once the pontoons were fairly in position, and there seemed a prospect that the bridge would be completed, but a fresh flood brought down trees, logs and fragments of the half-burned trestle-works above, sweeping the boats from their moorings. It was not until Thursday afternoon that the crossing was effected and the march continued to Newmarket.

About noon on Friday, the sixth of June, the army arrived upon the hills near Harrisonburg. Brodrick, with his company, in the advance, dashed through the streets of the town, chasing some mounted men who had lingered there for observation. As he emerged into the open road, a body of infantry, lining the stone walls on either side, rose and fired into his men. Brodrick drew up and coolly scanned the numbers of the enemy. Then, seeing that the force was too great for him to charge, he wheeled and retired with a deliberation that, as we afterwards learned, was the object of high admiration among the enemy.

Then, in column of fours, Wyndham trotted through the town and took up a position beyond it, sending out skirmishers through the woods in front. About three o'clock, after a colloquy with one of General Fremont's scouts, the regiment, accompanied by a battalion of the New York Mounted Rifles, advanced at a fast trot on the road to Port Republic. The regiment, which had left Fredericksburg about eight hundred strong, was now reduced to less than half that number; but those who remained were as full of daring as was their gallant leader. As Shelmire, with the leading squadron, passed the line of Sawyer's skirmishers, the latter called out to him to take care for the enemy were in force in the wood beyond. The captain answered in his resolute way, "I have been ordered to charge any force that I may meet, and it is my duty to try and do it," and with these words he continued on. Past the remains of a burning ambulance, Wyndham carried his whole force forward with drawn sabres, all of them wild with the excitement of the race. The narrow road, fenced in on each side, and with the bordering fields also enclosed by strong worm fences, dipped into a hollow through which ran a streamlet with swampy banks, and rising with a gradual ascent, entered a wood that crowned the summit of the hill. On the left, the wood was diminished to a thin belt hiding an open field, strongly fenced in by posts and rails, while the front of the wood was there also lined by an irregular worm fence. Beneath the shadow of the trees, a small body of rebel cavalry was drawn up across the road. "Form platoons!" shouted the colonel, catching, with moistened hand, a firmer grasp of his sabre. While the men were still hurrying their wearied horses into the fresh formation, he gave the orders, "Gallop! *Charge!*" and the whole body, half-arrayed, plunged forward to the attack. The head of the first battalion entered the wood by the road, driving in the squadron of the enemy. The second, diverging to the left, commenced to tear down the fences, Wyndham and Kargé both dismounting to assist in the operation; while the third battalion moved still further to the left to force an entrance there. Shelmire led the first squadron in until he met a heavy column of cavalry blocking up the road as far as he could see it; and at the same moment a force of infantry lying hidden in the wood poured a tremendous volley into his flank. Two men, Charles Parry and William Traughan, fell dead at that discharge, and a lad named Jonathan Jones reeled, mortally wounded, from his horse. Simultaneously with this discharge, two regiments of rebel infantry, from behind the post and rail fence, opened a steady fire upon the remainder of the regiment. Even under these disadvantages, the high spirit of the men sustained them. The first squadron, the only one that could see an enemy, deliberately returned sabre, and, drawing their pistols, commenced a reply to the bullets that were sweeping through their ranks; and at the same moment the heads of the other two battalions forced themselves into the wood, from which issued a steady stream of fire.

Fortunately for our men, the weapons of the enemy threw too high, thus preventing an immediate annihilation of the command; but even when our column had entered the wood, they found the enemy perfectly protected from assault. There was nothing for it but to fall back into the field, and endeavor to form line again even beneath the fire. As the rest of the regiment formed, Shelmire, seeing the cavalry of the enemy sweeping around his flank, was forced out of the wood; and his men pressed by the rebels upon one side, were driven against the right of the line that was just forming. In a moment there was a scene of inextricable confusion. The colonel had entered the wood but had not come out of it; the lieutenant-colonel, only saved by some of his men from being taken prisoner, had not yet regained his saddle; the senior major was enveloped in the rout of the first battalion; while the standard-bearer, unhorsed, had lost the colors. There was thus no general rallying point, and each officer and man had to act on his own individual responsibility. Kester had one little knot of men collected, Lucas another; other officers were hunting for their men; when with a yell, a body of rebel horsemen swept down upon the disordered troopers. The Mounted Rifles, who had not charged, instead of covering the Jersey, turned and left the field; and the regiment, under the terrible fire of the infantry, had no chance of meeting properly this fierce assault. The whole body broke from the field, the officers still keeping toward the enemy, and endeavoring at intervals, and with some success, to check the vigor of the pursuit.

Among the last to retire was Captain Thomas Haines. In the midst of the confusion his slender form was conspicuous, as he called to the men of his company and sought to rally them around him. As he was crossing the heavy ground bordering on the stream, a squad of the Virginia cavalry, led by an officer in a long grey coat, who sat erect and easily upon his bounding charger, came down upon the flank of the fugitives. A bullet from that officer's pistol penetrated the body of Captain Haines, who dropped dying from his horse. Brodrick, in whose company he had been lieutenant, was close behind him as he fell. Reining in his horse, he turned round upon the rebels, and shouting "Stop!" fired his revolver full at their leader. The officer reeled in his saddle, and his men, catching him in their arms, hurried back from the spot. Brodrick stooped over Haines, and called him by his name, but there was no answer, and there was no time to pause. Leaving the lifeless form as the enemy again pressed upon him, he sadly spurred his horse to a renewal of his flight.

If a cavalry charge is glorious, a cavalry rout is dreadful. Pressing upon one another, strained to the utmost of their speed, the horses catch an infection of fear which rouses them to frenzy. The men, losing their places in the ranks, and all power of formation or hope of combined resistance, rush madly for some point of safety upon which it may be possible to rally. Each check in front makes the mass behind more dense and desperate, until horses and men are overthrown and ridden over, trampled on by others as helpless as themselves to rescue or to spare. The speed grows momentarily greater. Splashing through the pools of mire, breaking down fences, darting under trees, with clang of sabres and din of hoofs, officers wild with shame and rage, shouting themselves hoarse with unavailing curses, and the bullets of the enemy whistling shrilly overhead, the mingled mass sweeps on, until utter exhaustion stops them, or their commanders, struggling to the front, can indicate the place to form. Thus the First New Jersey galloped from the field of their defeat, leaving their colonel, three captains, one-twelfth of their troopers, and the regimental colors in the hands of the enemy.

Rallying on the first ground that afforded them a chanee to form, the regiment checked the pursuit before it was relieved by the rest of the brigade, and then dispirited and broken down, it retired into camp. A few of the officers remained on the field, and were spectators of that magnificent fight of the Pennsylvania Bucktails, in which that battalion, unsupported, checked and even drove the whole of Ashby's infantry. Into the woods the little body of one hundred and twenty officers and men, hurled themselves against the enemy. Two regiments that were in their front reeled and retreated before their rapid and deadly fire, Ashby himself falling in the vain attempt to rally them. Assailed in flank by a third regiment, with their colonel and twenty-five men wounded, and no support coming to them from the infantry of Fremont, the little band retired, the colonel refusing to be carried from the field where his men had killed and wounded many more than their own number of the enemy. With this glorious contest ended the fighting for the day.

While the major-general was spending the day in deliberation, Captain Brodrick, the surgeon, and another member of the regimental staff, accompanied by three men of Co. K, resolved to attempt the recovery of the body of Captain Haines. Passing beyond the point where Freemont's scouts had ventured, they followed the road to the battle-ground, discovering and relieving some wounded

Federal soldiers, and some wounded officers of the enemy. They found that a worthy farmer of the neighborhood had decently interred the uncoffined corpse, and that he was the only one of our officers who had fallen on the field. The others were all prisoners and had been carried off by the enemy. In a house a little way beyond lay young Jones, of Co. A, at the very point of death. He was very young, with a face as smooth and beardless as a girl's and with that sweetness of expression which is even lovelier in masculine youth than in the features of a woman. As his captain, Shelmire, was led past him a prisoner, the boy spoke his name. The captain dismounting, took him tenderly in his arms, soothing him and comforting. Then bending down and printing on his pale lips a kiss, the stout but gentle-hearted soldier continued his march to prison.

Removing the body of poor Haines from the earth, and preparing it as well as they could for removal, the party sadly departed into the farmer's house to wash their hands. Here, as they purified themselves from the dust, their eyes fell upon some appetizing pies, which the woman of the house had just drawn out of the oven; and the ever present hunger of campaigners awoke in them with all its rigor. They had just concluded a bargain for these dainties when Sergeant Brooks announced the appearance of the enemy, compelling them to mount their horses and abandon the enclosure of the house. There, under cover of the fatal wood were undoubtedly eight or ten rebel horsemen, maintaining a threatening appearance. But when men have been long on rough fare, a pie becomes a matter of importance, not to be resigned for trivial causes. Showing a firm front to the enemy, therefore, a detachment of the party advanced to the house and received the precious dainties, bearing them off triumphantly in the very teeth of the enemy; and then with dignified gravity of pace, they .commenced their retreat and the consumption of the eatables.

In the Harrisonburg church-yard their lamented comrade was interred on the following day, while the cannonade at Cross Keys thundered out a requiem; and no eye was tearless as the earth was thrown upon his coffin. He was one of those youths in whom centre the affections of a family, who were yet solemnly dedicated to the service of their country; and doing that service nobly, he laid down his young life. What he might have been, who can tell? What he was is the treasured memory of those who have a right to keep the veil drawn over the picture of their love as well as their affliction.

The battle of Cross Keys was fought when Jackson was able at the same time to check Fremont and still keep open his line of retreat by Port Republic. Movements that looked feasible on paper, failed in the field, either from incompetence, dilatoriness or want of harmony in the commanders, or else through those accidents of the weather which had not been taken into account; and the campaign which looked so fair in May, closed in June with a succession of defeats.

It is, after all, a reasonably fair principle to make success the criterion of a general. There are so many accidents and casual circumstances surrounding all military operations; the agencies which sway the fortunes of the campaign are so subtle, and oftentimes so unprecedented, that it is generally an easy task to explain away defeat, and to show that it should have been victory. But while there are adverse accidents, there are also favorable ones to counterbalance them; and it is he who promptly perceives and profits by these latter who proves successful in the grand result; while the unsuccessful man, when he exposes the failure of his plans, and describes the disappointments which he has encountered, is often really proving his inability to seize upon the opportunities presented to him, to so modify his original designs as to gain the end proposed by unanticipated agencies.

As the history of the earlier campaigns of the rebellion has clearly shown, there has never been wanting among our leaders an ability to design; but the experience of that period teaches us as plainly that they sought to accomplish their objects only in the way which they had predetermined, thus placing themselves at a disadvantage when opposed to the quick, versatile, observant officers who were at the head of the Southern forces. This natural defect was of course aggravated and almost made inevitable when to several independent commanders were entrusted portions of a defined plan of operations; each obstacle in the course of one acting and reacting upon the others, until an accumulation of difficulties paralyzed the entire force.

Illustrations of these truths may be easily found by the student of our campaigns. It is only possible for the present chronicler to make this brief digression, while the regiment, returning from the valley, remained waiting a summons to a fresh advance.

CHAPTER IV.

POPE'S ADVANCE.

The hot sun of July was scorching the plains which spread from the foot of the Bull Run mountains into the Northern Neck, parching the scanty grass of the early summer, splitting the earth till it was a net-work of dusty gaping crevices, and transforming the turbid mountain streams into sluggish currents, creeping through deep beds of sweltering mud, when the brigade was summoned from the shelter of the woods, where for weeks the men had been revelling in a rich abundance of blackberries and cherries, by an order to move across the Rappahannock. Hatch's Cavalry had already cleared the way, so there was no exciting prospect of immediate fight; but when a period of rest had softened the memory of hardships encountered, and had allowed the monotony of camp-life to oppress, the mere approach of active service was sufficient to enliven the careless troopers, as with song and laughter they wound through the defiles of the forest, and crossing the narrow ford, found themselves beyond the river which had hitherto limited their operations.

During the few weeks of repose, the stragglers and sick had returned to duty, the worn-out horses had been replaced, new clothing and equipments had been supplied, and the vacancies among the commissioned and non-commissioned officers filled up; and in good and serviceable condition, over six hundred men now followed the lieutenant-colonel.

At the house of an old gentleman, whose leisure hours were spent in superintending the farm labor of his negroes, but whose serious occupation was to hunt wild turkeys, a number of the officers took up their quarters for the night. His wife and daughters not only provided them with supper, but were kind enough to add the favor of their society, and to enlighten the Northern mind with their opinions; though the old lady, uncertain as to the limits of a non-combatant's privileges was often obviously disturbed by the freedom of the language of the younger girl.

The position of the family as to wealth, and the education and refinement which accompany fortune, was obviously far below that of the gentry of the neighborhood, but with all the habits of the second class, they preserved the traditions and prejudices of the first, valuing themselves and others by the dignity of their forefathers, and making that the only standard of recognized superiority. While this lent a slight improvement to their manners, it very greatly narrowed their minds and sensibly cramped their energies. What need was there for one of the W—— family to acquire a careful education or to seek a higher worldly place? Other people might work and grow wealthy or powerful, but this could not give them a royal governor for a great-grandfather, or elevate them to an equality with such as possessed that ancestral distinction, and the W——s would therefore feel justified in looking down upon them. As it was a part of their faith that the North was inhabited by none but common people without great-grandfathers, who had made money, but who were not gentlemen, and as such a race was evidently unfit to associate on equal terms with those who had inherited an inalienable refinement, it naturally followed that they felt a mingled scorn and fear of these busy, progressive, vulgar fellows, who were pushing themselves into all the places of power and profit, and threatening to intrude into the very sanctuary of society itself. Powerless in any individual resistance, too proud, lazy and careless to strive to emulate their aggressive Northern neighbors, this class of Southerners eagerly embraced the first opportunity to combine in defence of their tottering dignity, with an almost pitiable self-delusion as to their ability to defy the world behind its bulwarks. With an unwavering confidence in the perfection of their civilization, and an assurance of their perfect happiness if they could shut out all interference, they sought, like the intelligent Japanese nobility, to force the world to let them alone; and it was this desire, not the more sordid one of increasing wealth from the monopoly of cotton and tobacco, which tempted this large class of Virginians into the embrace of the secessionists.

It was amusing to notice in these people, whose education and accomplishments were as inferior to those of a Northern farmer's family as their dwelling in comfort and elegance was behind a Northern farm-house, the firm conviction of their superiority, their assured faith in the military supremacy of the South. These were not obtruded as points to be proved or disputed, but were quietly assumed as principles from which to draw conclusions. None of the family doubted for a moment that we were only there until General Jackson strove to drive us back, and that in any contest, no matter what might be the odds, we must necessarily be defeated. So, too, our claim to assert the supremacy of the government, the integrity of the nation, the permanence of the Union, could have no force to minds that had never contemplated anything outside the circle of the Virginia gentry; and the whole movement of the North seemed to them merely an unjustifiable invasion of their rights and territory, stimulated by the combined influences of a mean desire for power and profit, and an ignorant fanaticism for the negro.

As a type of their class, the family was perfect. Even to such unwelcome guests their hospitality was courteous and liberal, though they were not foolish enough to reject the compensation that we pressed upon them; through all their outspoken secessionism there was no intention of offence or insult, and in the younger girls there was something like readiness for a flirtation. So, with kindly feelings, Bayard's Brigade departed, receiving a farewell intimation that we would be driven back in a few weeks (which turned out to be correct), and a declaration, not quite so prophetic, that the South would quickly achieve her independence.

The pretty county-seat of Culpeper, with its old jail, court house and hotel, and some neat, new cottages dotted along its streets, was the termination of that day's journey, and we encamped upon the place of a Virginia gentleman of a different school from the family whom we left that morning. A fine old man, with an address of mingled dignity and frankness, who had received a liberal education in times when the phrase implied mental culture as well as a certain extent of information, who had been in the service both of the State and of the Nation, and learned to love the one without undervaluing the other; with strong but kindly prejudices, and slightly pompous, but thoroughly generous hospitality, he was a relic of the Virginians of the past, rather than a type of the present time. He lived in a fine old house that had been in good repair when he was of middle age, and was surrounded by a family of servants rather than slaves, who lived with him after the patriarchal fashion, eating of the food served upon his table, partaking of his sympathy and sharing in his regard. Each one felt a personal interest in his master and his master's welfare, and regarded himself as a shareholder in his master's estate. In consequence of this relation, while the slaves of the whole surrounding region had fled in a body at the first opportunity that was afforded them, not one of this gentleman's servants deserted him, though they knew that he would not have the heart to chase them.

Of course such a man as this had opposed secession strenuously, and held long and lovingly to that nationality of which others around him had thought so lightly; but in spite of his efforts his State had voted herself away. Full of memories of the time when Virginia was foremost of the States in influence and population, the old gentleman could not realize the growth in this country of a present power superior to hers, or a strength sufficient to force her back to the station which she had deserted; and though his judgment was against the South, his heart still clung to Virginia.

Of the last few days, none had been without its shower of greater or less heaviness and duration; and the undrained roads, where the soil had been cut up during the spring by the passage of the rebel trains, became deep receptacles of stagnant water and immeasurable mire. It was along such a track that the brigade, twenty-four hours after its arrival at Culpeper, moved to join General Hatch, who had advanced to Madison Court House. The Robertson River was, when we reached it, swelling into one of those freshets which, in it, have even greater rapidity and fierceness of inundation than in the larger Rapidan, and though the brigade succeeded in effecting a passage, there were few who would, two hours later, have relished an order to return. The region was new to the whole command, the position and forces of the enemy not accurately known, and the chances for success, either in advance or retreat, exceedingly problematical. With a consciousness of this, the officers of the regiment got their men into camp, in a position as little as possible exposed, around a house inhabited by one of the *poor white trash* of the country. A bevy of well-grown, scrimp-skirted, bare-legged girls was driven, like a flock of chickens, by their parents into the house, from the upper windows of which they stared with wonder at the careless crowd of armed men swarming around their home. Small, sun-burned boys, with ragged hair and vacant countenances, dodged around the fires of the men and entangled themselves among the legs of the horses. One or two greasy-looking negro women stared out of the door of their kitchen, their sleek, round faces and figures presenting a strong contrast to the gaunt, care-and-child-stricken aspect of their mistress. There was no evidence in the white woman's face of that superior intelligence which might reconcile the observer to the faded freshness of her prime, no sign of thought, or even of the development of the affections which so often lends a charm to ignorance and poverty. Her nature was plainly reconciled to the kindred sordidness of her life, in which there was no sacredness nor elevated love. She and her husband lived in the labors of the day, caring for little outside their farm and homestead, letting the war pass on with no interest beyond that of the safety of their little stock. Even when that was invaded by our troopers, they looked on with an apathy which almost resembled indifference, though it was merely the result of their dulled sensibilities. The few rumors that reached them of the events of the time were received with equal credence, whether probable or grossly ridiculous, for they had no means of distinguishing their character. A greater contrast to the restless, curious, intelligent character of our Northern people could scarcely be found in the peasantry of Europe, than was here presented in the centre of the great Commonwealth of Virginia. What must be the character of the poor among the sand-barrens of the Carolinas, when such people could be found in the heart of a fertile country?

General Hatch, coming from the neighborhood of the very different people of the Virginia Valley, paid too much attention to the vague reports current among families such as these, and was thus misled as to the forces and movements of the enemy. Their random guesses sounded like positive intelligence to his ears, until he was convinced that the rebel cavalry was actually in our rear, cutting us off from communication with our army, and threatening to deprive us of all means of retreat. His late experience under General Banks had tended to generate cautiousness rather than daring; and he felt more the necessity of getting back than the advisability of pushing forward. Resigning therefore his purpose of seizing Charlottesville, and destroying the rebel communications, he marched his forces along the circuitous route to Sperryville. To cover this movement, Bayard advanced to reconnoitre on the road toward Gordonsville. As we were returning occurred the only instance in which the First Jersey took a base advantage of their comrades of the First Pennsylvania.

While the latter regiment awaited its turn to follow the retiring column through Madison Court House, some of the soldiers, with the marvellous instinct peculiar to the class, discovered a couple of barrels of very old and excellent apple whiskey, which had been, as the owner fancied, safely secreted in the earth. In a very short time the whole regiment was, if not drunk, at least near enough to it to realize a trooper's idea of comfort. Brodrick's squadron of the Jersey had been detailed as rear-guard, and in it were some thirsty souls who smelt the liquor from afar, and hastened to secure their share of the spoil; but alas! the officers had noses too, and discovered the whiskey before the men had reached it. The unfortunate Jerseymen were ordered themselves to destroy the barrels and empty out their contents; and Captain Brodrick stood sternly over them while they watched the rich amber-colored stream mingle with the dust, mocking them with the smell of what they dared not attempt to taste. All their fertility of resource was called into action by this great emergency, and soon they found a means of satisfaction. The Pennsylvanians were hanging around in the amiable stage of intoxication, and their canteens hung as if they were not empty. A strong feeling of fraternal regard sprang up among the Jerseymen, moving them to make warm advances toward their Pennsylvania comrades. As one Jerseyman warmly embraced his suddenly acquired friend another drew up behind him. There was a faint *click* of a knife, and the bewildered trooper found himself alone, able to meditate, when he grew sober, on the inconstancy of friendship and the absence of his canteen. If the First Jersey Cavalry was dangerous to its enemies, it must be confessed that it was sometimes formidable to its friends.

While daylight lasted the line of march was along a good macadamized road, which permitted the column to move with rapidity and ease. There was no sign of the neighborhood of hostile forces, and the only duty performed by the flankers was the pursuit and capture ot sundry domestic fowls, who harassed the passing column by suggestions of *fricassées*. The hens and ducks yielded after a short struggle; but the geese, offering a desperate resistance, were only conquered by a determined charge with drawn sabres. It is painful to be forced to add that no quarter was given by our men, and that scarcely a fugitive escaped with life.

As the sun went down, the column turned into a narrow, broken and difficult road through the steep hills that here crop out from the Shenandoah range; and a storm coming on with the night, wrapped everything in darkness. Late at night the regiment scrambled into camp on a steep hill-side, the horses being picketed to every shrub and sapling that could be found, and the men hunting such dry places in their neighborhood as were not entirely formed by sharp stones with the edges upward. There was little fuel and still less to cook, except by the fortunate possessors of the captured poultry.

Happy it was for head quarters that the men had learned to understand and love the lieutenant-colonel, for he would otherwise have been threatened with starvation. As it was, there was hardly a stew in camp of which a portion was not tendered to him; and of his abundance his staff received a supply sufficient to appease their appetites. But even supper could not banish the sulkiness of the regiment. They all regarded their extra toils and exposure as needlessly imposed upon them; and men who will go through any trials without a murmur when they feel that they are really required, are frequently the most indignant at any wanton infliction. Thus the men refused to believe that a lightly equipped force, consisting so largely of cavalry, could under the circumstances be so completely cut off as really to be endangered; and they felt the whole evil moral effect of such an unexpected retrograde. They were still comparatively new troops, and therefore reasoned more than older ones, and obedience to an apparently mistaken order was not yielded so unquestioningly. Thus the regiment grumbled itself to sleep, quarreling with one another as a safety-valve for their feelings; and the next morning, after a comfortless bivouac, continued their march into Sigel's lines at Sperryville. The succeeding day the troops returned to Culpeper, having accomplished nothing but the destruction of much horseflesh, and discovering that there had not for a moment been any danger to our communications.

At the end of twenty-four hours, General Hatch with a stronger body of cavalry, again pushed down to Madison Court House. Bayard a second time made a demonstration towards Gordonsville, while Hatch took the rest of the cavalry in the direction of Charlottesville. This time he reached the neighborhood of Stannardsville, but was turned back by the report of the enemy in force at that place, whereupon the whole command returned again to Culpeper, having discovered that the country was clear of the enemy on the northern side of the Rapidan.

General Hatch being then ordered to another command, General Crawford, with his little brigade of infantry, was placed in charge of the post at Culpeper, and the cavalry enjoyed a few days' rest. At that time, however, this phrase meant even more than it does at present. Now it only implies that a third of the force shall be kept on picket, while another third is constantly engaged in long reconnoissances. Then it signified that the wagons and unserviceable horses should be put in camp, while *all* the available men were kept on a perpetual scout. Some of these latter were of considerable importance; among others, on one occasion Captain Kester actually went down and took a look into Orange Court House, bringing back valuable intelligence as to the disposition of the enėmy in that neighborhood.

About the twenty-fifth of July, Bayard was thrown forward with his two regiments to hold the line of the Rapidan from Raccoon Ford to Cave's; and there, twelve miles from any support, the hardy troopers kept their station.

It was by no means easy duty for a larger force, as the next two weeks were passed in a series of continued skirmishes, varied by long and venturous reconnoissances, while we found the rebel pickets day by day strengthening along our front. Some detachments of other cavalry regiments were occasionally sent down for temporary duty, who gave a practical illustration of the effect of General Pope's famous order, and the exhortations of Northern newspapers to make war *in earnest.* The New Jersey Cavalry, on some of its early marches, had once or twice attempted wanton destruction and unlicensed pillage, but the practice had been at once and sternly checked, and all necessary appropriations regulated by the proper authorities. Thus the discipline of the regiment had been preserved, while, except the inevitable injury which in spite of an officer's vigilance will accompany the passage of an army, the persons and property of the inhabitants was left undisturbed. Any one who has had experience knows too well that the best disciplined army in an active campaign is like a destructive swarm of locusts, the passage of a conflagration, and the ravages of an earthquake; and to stimulate it to unnecessary excesses is an outrage upon humanity.

We now saw, in the conduct of these troops, what was the natural effect of such incentives. In every direction there appeared a frightful scene of devastation. Furniture, valuable in itself and utterly useless to them, was mutilated and defaced; beds were defiled and cut to pieces; pictures and mirrors were slashed with sabres or perforated by bullets; windows were broken, doors torn from their hinges, houses and barns burned down. The scanty store of food left to women, children and negroes, after the perquisitions of the quartermasters, were wantonly snatched from their mouths and wasted by brutal men; and their few poor articles of crockery, the covering of their beds, the change of clothing necessary for comfort and even decency, were rent in pieces or borne away to serve for a few hours' use in camp. Wherever Bayard's men were not present in force and with authority, the inhabitants were not secure from evils worse than these: for insult and outrage ever walk hand-in-hand with plunder.

On the night of Thursday, the seventh of August, the portion of the Pennsylvania cavalry then picketing at Barnett's Ford was driven back by the rebels, who threw a force across the river. Bayard, after consultation with Kargé, directed him, taking a portion of the regiment, to sweep round the enemy's flank and fall upon their rear, while the general led the remainder, under Major Beaumont, to join the Pennsylvanians, prepared, if circumstances favored them, to make an attack in front.

Before dawn, therefore, the bugles blew "to arms," and the men rapidly equipped themselves and prepared to move toward the enemy. One squadron, Companies D and F, was on picket at Rapidan Station. Of the ten remaining, the colonel took the first battalion and Janeway's Company L, leaving five companies with Major Beaumont. As the detachment filed off upon its appointed route, Bayard rode up and whispered anxiously to Kargé.

"No matter," responded the latter, half-aloud, "I will go on. It may do good;" and then rode forward to the head of his men. Not till hours had elapsed were we made aware that in that short colloquy Bayard had imparted the intelligence that there were fifteen thousand men in that position where we had calculated to encounter less than as many hundreds; and that our resolute commander had engaged to lead his hundred and fifty troopers around the rear of this formidable body, while Bayard as stoutly engaged to face their front with about one-twentieth their number.

The frequent scoutings that we had made now repaid the labor that they had occasioned, for there was not a foot of the ground with which we had not become familiar. By circuitous lanes, through sequestered valleys, and beneath shadowing woods, the little band stole quietly along, no laugh, or song, or shout breaking the silence of the march. Past lonely farm-houses, whose inmates still slept undisturbed by our advance, and ignorant of approaching battle, waited peacefully the rising of the sun; and by the side of a rapid brook, rippling noisily over its rocky bed, Janeway led the dangerous march, until his company was hidden from the view of the main body by the darkness of a wood. When the rest of the column entered it, they saw before them a broad and beaten road, marked everywhere with the print of horses' hoofs. Taking for granted that they were the tracks of the advanced guard, the main body turned into the road; but the colonel quickly observed that no company ever left such traces of its passage. It was evident that a strong column of cavalry had passed over the road before us. Another examination showed that there were no hoof-prints that were not hours old, and that Janeway therefore must have taken the direct road across the fields to Cave's Ford. As with his present knowledge of the rebel force, Kargé did not wish to move so close to the river bank, he sent with haste to recall the errant company, at the same time throwing Bristol forward to examine the road, and another detachment up a diverging road to the right, which also indicated the passage of the enemy. Thus, before us, behind us, on the right and on the left, the presence of the enemy was revealed to Kargé who alone possessed the clue to the interpretation of all the signs. The rest of the party were expecting to surprise a moderate force of the enemy, ignorant that they themselves were in the midst of an overwhelming host. As Kargé spurred his horse up a hill, from whose summit he could see in the direction taken by Janeway, an orderly riding at speed came towards him from the rear, and saluting him, delivered his message: "Captain Janeway has the honor to report that he has ridden into the enemy and taken twenty-two prisoners, together with a rebel lieutenant and a colonel of militia. He is bringing off the prisoners, but would like support, if possible, as he took them in sight of their encampment." Startling as the intelligence was, it was not in any particular exaggerated. As Lieutenant Beekman, with Janeway's extreme advance approached the house of Colonel James Walker, which is a short distance from Cave's Ford, he saw some Confederate soldiers standing in the porch. Never imagining that any but Confederate cavalry could be so far in the rear of their army, they did not take any alarm at his appearance; and with a rush, he and his men were on them before they found out their error. Janeway took the gallop as he saw his advance increase their speed, and in a moment the house was surrounded and all its inmates prisoners. The rebel lieutenant made a desperate rush for his camp, the smoke of whose fires rose just behind the adjacent hill, but the horses of Company L were too swift, and the men too watchful to permit of his escape. The prisoners had come. to the house to obtain a breakfast, which the hostess had just prepared them, and now they had to resign not only their liberty but their meal also.

While the troopers were securing their captives, a little negro wench, chuckling with suppressed enjoyment, could not resist the temptation to communicate the object which had excited it. She had seen her master, who had returned home with the Southern army, and had taken the alarm before his guests, force his way beneath the ground-floor of the house; and as it was rather a tight fit, his struggling into his hiding-place had naturally overcome the gravity of the little negress. There we discovered the portly and dignified colonel of militia, lying overcome by fear and perspiration, in quarters theretofore sacred to wandering chickens and mauraúding cats. Almost suffocated and very dirty, he was uttering suppressed groans, and making silent gestures with his boots expressive of extreme discomfort. Several sturdy troopers, laying hold of those boots, endeavored to draw their wearer from his retirement; but with the heat and his apprehension, he had swelled since he entered it, and a prominent portion of his figure refused to emerge through the space between the earth and the clap-boarding. The tugs of the men became more energetic, as did the spasmodic motions of the colonel's legs, until at length, though his figure would not compress, one of the boards gave way, and, like a cork from a porter bottle, the colonel, sound in person but disordered in spirit, was drawn into the outer air. His hair, adorned with the feathers of moulting hens, and his clothes, revealing other secrets of his prison-house, threw into very bold relief the peculiar majesty of Virginia dignity, which was, however, somewhat modified by a profuse perspiration and a manifest tendency of blood to the head.

The troop could not delay to eat the breakfast now upon the table; but with many compliments to the hostess on the excellence of her provisions, they deposited the portable portion in their haversacks; and, carrying off the host to partake in turn of their hospitality, hurried their prisoners away in the direction of the regiment. As they came up from one road, Bristol sent in two men from the other, who had come to him, supposing his troop to be rebel cavalry; and from them we learned that Robinson's Brigade had passed along that road to Madison Court House, and that Jackson, with four rebel divisions, was advancing directly upon Culpeper.

It was now high time to commence our retreat, for every moment added to our danger. Our prisoners were so convinced that our capture was inevitable, that they made one or two remarks on the probable change in our relative positions; and none of us could be certain that the road on which we had advanced would be still unoccupied by the enemy. As, however, it was absolutely clear that every other path was in their hands, it was necessary to risk the danger. Forced to accommodate our pace to the powers of our prisoners, the way seemed longer than before; but at length we emerged upon the ground still held by our comrades in the face of the advancing columns of the enemy. So close was the calculation, that the rear-guard, which came out a few minutes after us, had to make a considerable circuit, and was even then under fire. For the enemy's skirmish line, rapidly deploying, far overlapped our own; and scarcely had the cheers of welcome to Kargé subsided, when the whole brigade was in a retreat, carrying on the movement with mingled skill and impudence. Taking advantage of every inequality of the ground, of every hill and little clump of wood, our skirmishers threatened the line of the enemy, forcing them to keep within supporting distance of the reserves; while the main body, taking up position after position, prevented a continuous advance in column. So the day was consumed before the enemy had advanced five miles from the river, while the camp equipage of the brigade had been safely transported to the rear. Utterly exhausted by fatigue and want of sleep, the men of the regiment were glad to throw themselves upon the ground, and snatch such repose as could be permitted them, preparatory to the battle that impended on the morrow.

While all this was going on, no tidings had arrived from the little squadron of sixty men picketing the left, far away upon the Rapidan. A dispatch had been sent them warning them to retire, but the messenger never reached their station; so that during the whole of our retreat they remained quietly at their post. Toward evening, Captain Boyd, who had been giving some information to a topographical engineer, found himself cut off from his men and pursued by a party of the enemy. In order to escape, he was forced to take the road to the regimental camp; and, surrounded by the fire of his pursuers, he distanced them and galloped on, intending to obtain some men to chase back these intruders upon his line. As he drew near to the camp, an old negro woman warned him that it was in the hands of the enemy, and as he turned, they caught sight of him, and swarmed out in pursuit like a throng of angry wasps. Dashing into the wood the captain spurred his horse, bent on evading his pursuers; but their number enabling them to spread out upon his flanks, he scarcely hoped to dodge them. It was not until he had ridden nearly to Cedar Mountain, making the circuit of half the camp, that he succeeded in escaping from their view. The moment that he did so, he checked his horse and crouched beside him in a little grove of trees, where he lay through the night, without venturing to move. As the morning dawned, he saw about half-a-mile in front of him, some cavalry drawing up in line of battle; but not recognizing their character, he did not venture to ride toward them. Tormented, however, by a burning thirst, he crept on foot to a little stream that traversed the valley beneath him. As he rose to return, he found that the rebel skirmishers were already between him and his horse, and knowing then that the cavalry must be Union troops, he hurried to gain their line. They were the First Rhode Island, who had that morning been added to our brigade, and he was quickly supplied with what he needed for himself, his only remaining anxiety being for his squadron of which he could give no account.

The squadron, however, was in the hands of Captain Lucas, an officer who never failed in any duty that was imposed upon him. That night, though his pickets were three times driven in, he as many times replaced them in person, in spite of the protests of the lieutenant that the position was untenable. He did not know how much might depend on the maintenance of that post, and he determined to hold it to the last. Morning came, and Captain Boyd did not re-appear. Lucas, writing a brief report of his situation, sent his orderly sergeant, Kinsley, attended by private Gourlay, both well-mounted, to carry the dispatch to camp, and bring him instructions as to his behavior. The two men arrived unobstructed within sight of the camp, and saw the whole place filled with the stragglers of the enemy, while all the fields around were covered with masses of their troops moving into position for the battle.

Kinsley handed the dispatch to Gourlay, who was the better mounted of the two, and ordered him to outride him with it to Captain Lucas, reporting what he had seen. As they turned to go back, a rebel soldier stepped out into the road, confronting them. Without a pause they charged, and he sprang back into the wood, leaving them a clear track toward the picket. Gourlay put his horse to speed and quickly reported to the captain, who immediately sent Sergeant Inglin to call in the different videttes; and by the time that Kinsley arrived the squadron was ready to depart. Seeing that the whole rebel army was between them and the National troops, Lieutenant Sawyer proposed that they should destroy their arms, scatter through the country, and each for himself endeavor to regain our lines; that so, if any were taken, the rebels might not profit by their weapons; but Lucas sternly forbade any such wild proceeding. When they had gone some distance on their way, two regiments of the enemy were discovered on one side of them and another in the opposite quarter; forces that, restrained by the firmness of the pickets, had made a wide detour, hoping to come in upon their rear and capture them. At the time when this discovery was made, the squadron had paused to breathe their horses, and Lucas, instead of springing at once to horse, quietly drew out his map and spent a short time in scrutinizing it. Then, folding it up and rising to his feet, he said, "Now, men, mount, and we will be off." Turning out of the road, he lead them rapidly through the woods, where there was no road nor pathway, keeping steadily the line which he had marked out in his own mind. After some miles of this traveling, they emerged upon a thoroughfare, and inquiring of a man whom they encountered, learned that they were but seven miles from Culpeper, and that the First Maine Cavalry had been out in search of them. With joy at their escape, the squadron made its way to town, having held their position long enough to save the flank of the Union forces from the rebel cavalry at a time when Bayard's Brigade and Crawford's little body of infantry were all that were yet upon the field. The daring that ventured this was equalled by the judgment which brought off his men in safety, and without discovery by the enemy.

To this, and to Kargé's manœuvre of the previous morning, was no doubt due much of that over-caution on the part of Jackson which enabled Bayard to check the rebel advance so far from Culpeper, and to secure time for the concentration of our scattered troops. It was not until noon that Banks arrived upon the field with the little corps that fought the battle. It was not until night that Pope brought up portions of McDowell's and Sigel's troops from their positions along the line from Fredericksburg to Sperryville. If the night before, Jackson had pushed on into Culpeper, he would have cut that line in two. Even if before twelve o'clock that day there had been that terrible assault which was made at half-past three, night would have seen our shattered divisions struggling on the route to the Rappahannock. To Bayard's Brigade and to General Crawford belong the credit of having saved the Army of Virginia, and of having enabled General Banks and General Pope to close the door which would have otherwise been opened into Washington.

CHAPTER V.

CEDAR MOUNTAIN AND BRANDY STATION.

The sun was rising brightly out of the white, low-lying mists of the summer morning, as the First New Jersey Cavalry moved to its place in the line of battle. The tops of the well-grown maize waved all around us, save where a battery, drawn up in sections on the rising hill, had trampled it down in passing to its position on our left; and on our right lay the road to Barnett's Ford, emerging from a wood some hundred yards in our rear, and entering another somewhat further off in our front. This timber on the right of the road spread out until it connected with a larger forest which lined the range of hills toward Thoroughfare Mountain; but on the left, in front of us, it thinned away and ended in cultivated fields, across which we could see the enemy gathering upon the distant hill-side. To the left of the battery, and well advanced beyond it, the First Rhode Island formed almost at right angles to our line; and across the road, partially hidden by the intervening wood, was the Pennsylvania cavalry, supporting another battery of artillery. This was the centre of our line of battle, and comprised all that we knew concerning it. Equally interesting to us, however, was the study of that of the enemy, whose infantry we could observe filing steadily toward our left, and skirting the line of woods near the foot of Cedar Mountain. Along the crest of a gently-rising eminence, to the left of our front, were seen the ominous clusters of men and horses that indicated a battery in position, commanding our line, and seeming to threaten us with destruction. Well upon our left flank rose the conical summit of the mountain, its sides partially marked off into cultivated fields, partially still covered by its ancient forest trees, and beyond the mountain lay the railroad. Along our front, watching the movements of the enemy, stretched the carbineers of the first battalion, under Bristol; and, secure that no attack could take us unaware, we waited for the battle to begin. The period of expectation is very solemn, if it be not too long protracted. For men to march up quietly into the presence of the enemy, to form within reach of the death which at any moment may be hurled into their ranks; to watch the gathering hosts opposed to them, and scan the advantages in the position of the enemy or secured by themselves; to expect, from minute to minute, the rush of the bursting shells and the whistling of Minie bullets; all the anxieties, hopes and fears that, at such a time, crowd into the mind, have a powerful effect upon the nerves and the imagination. The explosion of the first few shells, thrown by the enemy to try the range and feel the line of battle, causes an involuntary start and shrinking, and forces the eyes of all to watch the course and direction of the missiles, from the first appearance of the thick white smoke above the gun, to the time when the shriek in the upper air announces the coming of the ponderous projectile. But the strain is too great to continue long without a corresponding reaction, and when the minutes begin to lengthen into hours, the attention wanders from the warlike preparations, and seeks occupation in the most trifling incident that may arise. Thus, before long, officers and men were taking their ease, as fully as was consistent with the maintenance of the line, and the same indifferent talking, eating and drinking was going on that characterizes an ordinary halt. Indeed, at the very moment when a shell was whistling above our heads, the discovery of a rabbit scudding through the corn created an excitement which drew the attention of the men entirely away from the destructive missile, and the longing to get it for dinner threatened more danger to the steadiness of the ranks than had occurred from the fire of the enemy. Colonel Kargé, who had, for the past two days, been suffering from the symptoms of bilious fever, and had only been kept in the saddle by the strength of his will, now turned over the command to Major Beaumont, and retired, until the action should commence, to the ambulances of Assistant Surgeon Dayton. Now and then a few shells, thrown more rapidly than usual, would bring him upon the field; but, as soon as the alarm was over, he retired again from exposure to the sun, whose heat scorched his fevered brow and stimulated his throbbing veins.

The hours of weary waiting passed on, the regiment standing in the sun, passively enduring heat, hunger and fatigue, while the poor horses, who, since the previous morning, had received no food, except a little mouldy hay the night before, cropped eagerly such stalks of corn as the men could pluck and lay before them. In the field to the right of the road, the wheat and oats, which had been cut a few weeks before, was thrown together in careless bundles, and the major, as he permitted the battalions to move successively to water, directed small parties to bring in some grain for the animals. While the horses of the first and second battalions were munching their feed as well as their heavy bits permitted, the detachment of the third, which, of course, had to advance somewhat farther to secure a supply, was suddenly fired on by a strong skirmishing party of the enemy. Notwithstanding the surprise, many of the men brought in the oats which they had gathered, in defiance of the enemy's assault; but there was now no leisure for their steeds to profit by their excursion. With one burst of thunder, twelve pieces of artillery opened upon our line, while the skirmishers of the enemy engaged warmly with our own. At the same time the Pennsylvanians on our right were attacked, and our own batteries rang out their defiant response to the enemy.

At the first discharge Kargé was again with us, and as the smoke from the guns upon our left rolled down and covered the plain in front of them, he took advantage of the concealment to shift our position, bringing the line a hundred yards farther forward, where the rebel shells would do no harm. With great delicacy, declining to take the command out of the hands of Major Beaumont, who showed himself fully capable of discharging his duties, the lieutenant-colonel retired to the position occupied by the general, where, under the same fire as ourselves, he would be ready, if any emergency should require his presence. There he sat, looking at our steady behavior, though his eyes were dim with fever, and his frame reeled with weakness in his saddle; and not until the regiment was withdrawn to its second position, could he be persuaded to obey the orders of General Bayard, and retire from the field.

Through the roar of the artillery and the scream of the passing shells could now be heard in front the sharp rattle of small arms. Bristol's skirmishers were at it, firing with that rapidity which renders the breech-loading carbine so formidable, and holding with tenacity the ground which had been appointed them. Vainly did the enemy, taking advantage of the fences, throw against them their strong line of infantry skirmishers. Galloping back from time to time to reload, and to tempt the enemy from their cover, they charged up again, with a daring courage and accuracy of aim that shook the steadiness of the opposing sharpshooters; and it was only when canister was poured into their line that they were driven from their position. Then, with the skurry of a flock of wild fowl, the mounted skirmishers were seen racing to the rear, and, gathering upon the flank of the Rhode Islanders, they re-formed and resumed the place in our line of battle. At the same time, the Rhode Island regiment, exposed to the flanking fire of the rebel guns, which were sheltered from a return by the wood interposing between them and our battery, was withdrawn to a new position, and the First Jersey stood alone in front.

It was impossible for the rebels to pass beyond the wood while our regiment was ready to charge them, and the battery could sweep through their advancing line, and the brigade that lay in the rear of the timber, waiting for an opportunity to charge upon the guns, sent forward its sharpshooters to disperse the cavalry that defied the menace of the rebel shells. It was at this time that Brodrick, who was in charge of some skirmishers on the right, performed the feat that won for him his major's commission. While his men kept the line of rebels at bay beyond the wood, he, with some few troopers, stole through the trees, and found himself on the flank of the enemy who were engaging us. In narrow and dense column, to avail themselves of the leafy cover, they lay, waiting for the moment when our cavalry should be broken, and they could dart upon our guns, the shells from which dropped well in their front, as the pieces were fired at random. Brodrick stole to the hither border of the wood, where he could be seen by the commander of the battery, and, by his signals, procured the requisite elevation. As he returned to his post of observation, he could see the result. Shell after shell dropped into the midst of the densely formed brigade, dealing out destruction. As the men scattered in dismay, the captain chanced to observe one little group of a dozen, who seemed to be bearing off a couple of wounded comrades. As they were slowly moving off, a shell burst right among them, and when the smoke rose not a living man remained. The whole brigade was scattered in disorder, and the centre of the rebels remained for a brief space open. As the captain rode back, he met General Crawford, to whom he pointed out the wood, and the advantage of its occupation. From our scanty force of infantry a regiment was ordered forward, but, unfortunately, their colonel occupied the time that should have been spent in marching, in making his men a speech, and before they got on their way the enemy had taken possession of the ground.

In the meantime, the rebel sharpshooters were pitching their lead into our lines with very tolerable accuracy, their aim not being disturbed by any response from us. Like the first drops of a thunder-storm, the shot pattered on the ground around us, each striking up its little cloud of dust, while the air over our heads was vocal with their whistles. "Steady there!" cried the major, sternly, as there was a little confusion visible in the ranks of Company A. Two men, Washington Raisner and Albert Young, drew their horses out of the ranks and saluted, saying quietly, "We are hit, sir," as they moved to the rear. The ranks closed up again like a wall, and in ten minutes these two men, instead of nursing their hurts, had the balls extracted, the wounds bandaged by the surgeon, and, before the blood had clotted on the lint, were once more back in their places. Once the enemy attempted to bring a piece of artillery out of the wood against us; but the men of our battery were too vigilant for them. As they brought it above the brow of the hill, a gallant Dutch gunner squinted carefully along his piece and instantly discharged it. A cheer burst from the battery, as they saw the rebel piece bound upward and topple over dismounted to the ground.

Still the balls of the sharpshooters kept doing their work among us, and every now and then a man would drop out of the ranks, or a horse rear and sink upon the ground; but the line maintained its unbroken front, and the battery was unassailable. The rebels, unable to comprehend why cavalry held the front of our line of battle, and apprehensive that we might design a desperate charge right through their centre, did not venture to make their grand assault, while we maintained our ground. Little did they think that we had held them so long with the mere shadow of a line, and that cavalry had been holding a place which we had had no infantry to fill.

But now, as the balls continued to hail around us, a grave, calm voice in our rear was heard to say, "It has been bravely done. They stand like veterans," and there was the iron face of General Banks, his proud eye softening with a smile of approbation. Just then the major discerned a gleam of reflected light among the foliage of the distant mountain, as the western sun shone upon the muskets of a flanking column of the rebels. At once he communicated the fact to the battery commander, who wheeled his front section to enfilade their line. With beautiful accuracy the shells dropped upon them, and soon there was no vestige of their presence. But our position was fast becoming untenable. A fresh battery of the enemy had been so placed as to command the whole field in which we stood, and its missiles threatened us all with annihilation. Bayard spoke for a moment to the commanding general. "You retire the Pennsylvania," was the answer, "I, myself, will show these where to go." Dispersing his staff with orders, General Banks alone rode calmly in our front as we crossed the summit of the hill behind us. Forming there with the Rhode Islanders, we waited until the battery, with two of its guns disabled and many men and horses lost, had limbered up and retired. Then we also moved to the rear. The ground which we had to traverse was like the flow of a fiery furnace, with exploding shells. Three batteries of the enemy were hurling upon it a converging fire. As we passed their range, two of the platoon commanders fell, Beekman with two pounds of iron in his shoulder, Alanson Austin with his thigh almost severed from his body. With the same discharge, several of the men were wounded, and the horse of Craig, sergeant-major of the third battalion, was struck dead to the earth. Though he was the last man of the column, and there was now no protection against the advancing enemy, he paused in the midst of the fire to remove his saddle and equipments, and bearing them upon his back proceeded on foot to rejoin the regiment. While other hospital attendants were cowering in the rear, or refusing to emerge from the ditches in which they had sought protection, our hospital stewards, Lame and Shaw, brought up their men, who never wavered in their hazardous duty. The wounded officers and men were taken into the ambulances of Proud and McAfee, and borne with tenderness from the field. Poor Austin, the youngest officer in the regiment, was laid upon a stretcher, ready for amputation. "Oh, chaplain, if I could only pray!" he touchingly murmured, as his mind struggled against the dulling influence of the shock to his physical frame. As the exquisite words of the Office for the Visitation of the Sick were uttered by his side, his lips moved in unison with the supplication; and the blessed associations of home worship, and love, and teaching, which cluster around the familiar words of the Lord's Own Prayer, drew from him a sigh of softer utterance amid the low groans of his dying agony. As the leg was removed, the shells of the enemy struck the fence behind which the surgeons plied the knife, and but few moments could he be allowed to lie still undisturbed. As his life ebbed away his mind wandered under the influence of chloroform and in the delirium of exhaustion. He feebly waved his arm, and gave some orders as if still on the field. Then, with a half-articulate cry of "the Star Spangled Banner," his voice was hushed in death.

The obstinacy of the cavalry and Crawford's small brigade had accomplished the vital object, and when they retired it was upon the line which Banks had formed behind them. The First New Jersey Cavalry had no more actual fighting to encounter, though they continued drawn up upon the left flank, ready to charge if it was required. Upon their comrades of the First Pennsylvania was imposed the only duty that afterwards fell to the share of the cavalry. As they prepared to withdraw, two brigades of the enemy were pushed down upon the battery which they supported. Rushing out of the wood upon their flank, the rebels were upon them before the guns could be limbered up. The ground, intersected by ditches and fences, did not admit of an effective charge by the regiment, and a narrower front exposed the charging party to a terrible fire from the flank. But Bayard saw that the guns must be saved at any loss, and he ordered Major Falls to charge with his battalion. Putting himself at the head of McDonald's squadron, the major took the gallop just as the front line of the rebels had clambered across a fence. With a wild cheer the bold Pennsylvánians dashed forward, riding down the rebels within their reach, and scattering the line in disorder over the field; but the terrific fire of the rest of the brigade swept through their rank, and, of the whole squadron, only Major Falls and two others struck the fence. Lying on top of the rebel dead were the killed and wounded horses of half the squadron, with the forms of the troopers themselves strewn all too thick among them, while others, with swaying bodies, rode back to the retiring regiment. McDonald himself, with both arms disabled, caught the reins in his teeth, and, followed by the survivors, succeeded in making good his retreat. One company of the squadron was almost annihilated; but the battery was saved, and the major who had led the charge rode back without a scratch. Late in the day as the battle had begun, and short, therefore, as was its continuance, the number of the wounded was really dreadful. All the night the surgeons were busily employed, and yet there seemed no diminution in the number to be attended to, until, at length, Dayton sank down in utter prostration by the side of the man to whom he was endeavoring to minister. Just then the enemy opened a cannonade in the darkness upon some of our men, who had incautiously lighted fires to prepare some coffee. General Pope, who had but lately arrived upon the field, seeing a battery not far from where he was standing, the balls from which fell into our ranks, ordered Captain Asch, of the First Jersey, who was on his staff, to ride over to it and direct its commander to cease firing. Asch hinted that he thought it was a rebel battery.

"Nonsense!" replied the general. "You go and give them the order." The captain rode boldly up, and exclaimed: "The general directs that you cease firing." "Does the general order that?" asked the surprised artillery officer. "Yes," said Asch, "he sent me with peremptory orders;" and while the wondering rebel obeyed, the aid galloped off, delighted to escape without detection. Scarcely had he left, when a battery of our own opened on the rebels, at short distance, with a raking fire, and the ground the next morning was found covered with dead horses, heaped together as they had stood when waiting to limber up. Captain Asch, however, still maintains that it is going too far when a general sends his aids with orders to the enemy.

The little town of Culpeper was thronged with wounded men, for whom, as the battle was unexpected, there had been no previous provision. Packed in miserably ventilated buildings during the burning August weather, with insufficient medical and hospital attendance, and with very limited supplies, many even slight wounds took an unfavorable turn. With justifiable pride, therefore, can we look at the condition of the hospital under the direction of the assistant surgeon of the First New Jersey Cavalry. Among more than a hundred wounded there was but a single death, and that from a hopelessly mortal hurt; while injuries which had elsewhere cost many a limb and not a few lives, were there treated without the necessity of a single amputation. Sufficient food, wholesomely cooked, was provided almost from the first; beds of dry and clean hay or straw were made up for all the sufferers, and the building kept in a perfect condition of purity and ventilation. As each wounded man was taken out to be placed upon the cars for Washington, a draught of sound light wine was given him, to strengthen him for the journey, and thus they reached there without experiencing that terrible exhaustion which is sometimes of itself a cause of death. So marked was the difference between these men and the patients from other hospitals, that the surgeons in Washington inquired under whose treatment they had been, remarking approvingly the superiority of their condition; and the intelligence of this fact had great effect in rallying Dayton from the depression of his own illness. Any one who has seen the difficulties to be encountered in field hospitals, even where every appliance is procurable, will acknowledge that the result obtained in this instance was a reasonable cause for self-gratulation.

If, on the day after the battle of Cedar Mountain, General Pope had renewed the engagement, it is probable that Jackson would have had to retreat with heavy loss in men and guns; for despite of his superior numbers, the contest had so disorganized his men that they were falling back in confusion. At one time the whole road was choked up with wagons and guns, whose drivers had fled at the rumor of the approach of our cavalry, and the reality would have aggravated the disorder. But General Pope had sad reason to know his own weakness much better than Jackson's difficulties. While keeping up the show of a powerful force so well as to impose upon his own men, he was aware that it was insufficient to watch his front properly, and that he was completely unprotected in the rear, and thus he had to move with a guardedness which shook the confidence of his men in his energy and capacity. The whole condition of our troops in Virginia was one of frightful risk; and that we escaped even as well as we did was owing as much to the difficulties of the enemy as to any efforts on our own part. Under the circumstances of the case, Pope was probably well enough satisfied to have Jackson beyond the Rapidan, and felt no wish to move any farther from his base at Washington. His chief desire was to secure the retreat of McClellan, and to enable the two armies to unite before Lee could concentrate his forces against Washington. With this object he held his ground until McClellan's movements were well advanced, and Lee's army actually *en route* against him; and then, to the indignation of his men, who were expecting a forward movement in conjunction with the Army of the Potomac upon Richmond, he quietly began his retreat toward Washington.

On the evening of the eighteenth of August, Bayard's Brigade, at that time consisting of the First New Jersey, First Pennsylvania, Second and Tenth New York Cavalry regiments, was ordered to be in readiness, and marched from its camp across the battle-field until it had moved a quarter of a mile to the left of its first position of the day of Cedar Mountain. Lying there under arms through the night, with the sickening corruption of the field tainting the air around it and the water which it was forced to drink, it listened to the steady retrograde of the seemingly interminable line of the army trains, as the wheels of the wagons rumbled along the road. For several hours after day had broken, it still held its position, until the heavy columns of infantry were so advanced as to secure the road from any attack; and then, pushing across the fields and through the tangled alleys of the woods, it made its way into the road that led from the lower Rapidan toward Culpeper. Hovering upon that right flank, and scouting far along every divergent road, the Jersey regiment fulfilled its share of the arduous task; and it was not until the sun had sunk behind the hills that it at length entered the uneven streets of Culpeper. As the shadows of the night fell around, it still stood there, waiting the slow progress of the retiring columns; and the darkness was at its blackest before, by yards of advance and half hours of halt, it had crept forth from the skirts of the town. Along a road marked by the little fires kindled all along its borders, where the lingering infantry had cooked its hurried meal, the cavalry rear-guard slowly followed up the line of march; and by the time that it had reached the neighborhood of Brandy Station, midnight had sounded from the clocks of the deserted town. In the intense obscurity, the overworked staff of the brigade commander were long delayed before they could arrange for the final halt; and while the regiment stood patiently in the road, the wearied men drooped down upon their saddles, or sank down in the dust before their horses' feet. At length all but the unhappy pickets received permission to bivouac along the fence that bordered the road, and not waiting to prepare any food, the troopers threw themselves down and slept on their arms beside their accoutred horses.

At the first glimmer of the dawn, the regiment, snatching a hasty meal of coffee, broken biscuit, and corn gathered from an adjacent field, was again under arms, with a detachment under Brodrick scouting back in the direction of the town. While it was still absent on its perilous errand, a rapid discharge of firearms was heard along the line of the Second New York, and a portion of the rebel cavalry, driving in their pickets, skirmished sharply with the reserves. It was a moment full of risk, for if the rebels succeeded in turning the left flank of the rear-guard, they could cut off part of our infantry before it had crossed the river. At once Bayard was at the threatened point, sending orders for the Pennsylvania to advance to the support of Kilpatrick. But the Second New York held its ground without the approaching succor; and Kargé, pushing his dismounted skirmishers forward upon the flank of the enemy, forced them to give way. There was a rapid exchange of shots, several horses rushed riderless across the front of our dismounted men, and then the whole body of rebels hurried back from the scene of action, secure against a long pursuit from us. Then there was a period of anxious waiting, and then Brodrick returning with the third battalion, reported no sign of the enemy in the direction of the town; whereupon the brigade commenced its steady and uniform retreat.

Across a gently undulating country, divided at irregular intervals by narrow belts of open woods, the troops moved beautifully along, the battalions of each regiment alternating in halt, wheel, and retirement, while the skirmishers covering the rear of all, conformed their manœuvres to the movement of the whole body. Nothing but an attack in force could have hurried the regulated movement; and not even an attack in force could have taken the brigade unaware. Two miles had been traversed in this way, when upon the road over which we had passed was seen a vast and rapidly moving cloud of dust, indicating the swift approach of a formidable body of horse. Nearer and nearer it came, until there was on the part of the enemy an evident purpose to force us to engage before we could cross the fords of the Rappahannock. It was Bayard's first time of handling cavalry on a large scale in contest with troops of a similar character, and unfortunately there were but two terribly reduced regiments with whose qualities he was familiar, The other two regiments were as new to him as he was to them, and the strongest of them was now for the first time to engage in a serious conflict. But that Second New York was in fine condition, led, with one fatal exception, by good and gallant officers, giving promise of that future distinction which Kilpatrick was sure to seek for it wherever it might be found. While the First Jersey, therefore, formed upon its right as we faced the enemy, the Tenth New York deployed on its left, and the Pennsylvanians moved into reserve, the Second New York, or Harris Light Cavalry, was held together in the road, ready to charge the advancing enemy.

Down came the enemy, charging along the road, and Kilpatrick was ordered to meet them. In column of platoons, keeping splendid order, with sabres glittering in the sun, the regiment swept over the hill, taking the gallop without a single waver. Kilpatrick, to steady his men in this their first formidable struggle, delayed to take his place in the front, riding by their side until the final moment should arrive for the charge. From this slight incident came the loss of the field. Leading the first platoon was the one man who proved unfit for his important station. As the two opposing forces came in sight of one another, and as Kilpatrick put spurs to his horse to take the front and order the bugles to sound the charge, the leading lieutenant drew rein, and backed his horse right through the ranks behind him. Of course, with inexperienced men, in the nervousness of a first engagement, the instinct was irresistible to follow his example; and the whole front of the column halted in irremediable confusion. At the same moment the rebels charged, breaking the New Yorkers, and scattering them over the field, in a rush that swept with it their own line of skirmishers. Thus the centre of the field was open, and the victorious rebels swept around the flank of the First Jersey.

Those who advanced upon our front did not meet with the same success. As Sawyer firmly held his skirmish line, he discerned a cloud of dust whirling straight against his centre. Rallying his men to that point, he made them aim and recover twice, before he thought the proximity of the enemy and their own steadiness of nerve would give sufficient efficacy to the fire. Then, as the rebels, blinded by their own dust, rushed madly down upon him, he gave the order, "Fire!" and a stunning discharge tore through the charging squadrons. The cloud of dust eddied as if in the circles of a whirlwind, while from its envelopment rose up a frightful chorus of shrieks and groans. As it hovered stationary for a moment, twice more did the breech-loading carbines pour in their fatal fire. Then, from the midst of the dust and smoke, a few staggering men and horses broke away to the rear, leaving most of the charging party bleeding upon the ground.

The defeat of the Harris Light Cavalry forced Kargé to change front with his line, before he could move them into action, and the exhausted horses responded slowly to the command. Before the half wheel had been perfectly made, and the line once more in motion, down upon their front and flank dashed the irregular masses of the enemy. Kargé emptied the chambers of his revolver into their ranks, and then, throwing the weapon at their heads, dashed among them with his sabre, followed by the men around him. The enemy gave way before him, but both flanks of his line had been broken by their circling charge, and all that could be hoped was to regain the reserve and rally under cover of its charge. Skirmishers and main body, with one accord, spurred as rapidly as possible to the rear, fighting hand to hand as they did so, with the foremost of their pursuers. A wide ditch, stretched across the fields, relied on by the colonel to assist the charge of the reserve. Many of the exhausted horses fell as they strove to leap it, and pell mell above them rolled the chasing rebels. As he drew near it, the last man of the Jersey, Lieutenant Robbins' horse fell dead beneath him, a bullet through its brain. Robbins kept his feet, and actually sprang across the ditch on foot. But the reserve, at the time of the Harris Light's disaster, had been drawn back to the wood by General Bayard, where, disordered by the undergrowth, it had not yet re-formed; and Lieutenant Robbins was seized by his pursuers, dragged to the rear, and cut down while a prisoner, though saved from death by a metal plate in the centre of his cap.

The feelings of the troopers may be imagined when they swept past the position of the reserve only to find it deserted. In dismay they were compelled to continue their retreat upon the railroad track through the wood, where the First Pennsylvania were drawn up to cover them. But, at the moment when their rear seemed in the hands of the rebels, Brodrick rushed with what men he had from the bushes upon the flank of the enemy, while Lucas simultaneously wheeled his company upon them on the other side. The unexpected charge cut the rebels in two, and drove back the mass of them with loss into the hollow; and Falls, with his Pennsylvanians, charging upon all who passed the wood, dispersed and cut them down. Kargé, with his adjutant, Penn Gaskell, charged unsupported upon a party of fifteen, and drove them before him; but a bullet from one of their pistols took effect in his leg, and forced him to give up the chase. The fighting was over, but, of the two hundred and fifty

Jerseymen engaged, forty did not answer to their names. Kargé was disabled, Hick hurt and unhorsed, Robbins and Stuart in the enemy's hands. Many others had been captured, but were cut out by the well-timed charge of Brodrick, Lucas, and their comrades.

The few rebels who had penetrated the woods had time only to see the last of our army crossing the Rappahannock bridge, and forming in safety on the opposite shore; so that, in spite of the reverses, the object for which we had fought was gained, and the rebels had nothing but the barren field of battle. Their loss in killed and wounded was treble that of ours, though the number of prisoners, no doubt, in some degree, balanced the account. Their general was much less satisfied with the result than ours, for Robinson was, in consequence of this engagement, removed from his command, showing that their authorities considered that his forces should have accomplished more than they had done. The rebels might well be mortified, for, directly in their face, Pope had moved his army and its trains over twenty miles of open country, and through many awkward defiles, without leaving them a wagon, a horse or a gun, as trophies of their pursuit.

CHAPTER VI.

MANASSAS PLAINS AND CHANTILLY.

Fortunately for the regiment, scarcely had Kargé been removed by his wound from the command, when Wyndham reappeared in the field and took again its head. In the succeeding series of exhausting marches, continual skirmishes, and frequent confusion, without guidance from the chief commander of the army, it would have been a very serious thing to have had no one of experience to direct the movements of the regiment.

Each day saw the First New Jersey hurried to a fresh position, to skirmish with the enemy, who menaced the line of the river; and rarely did night close upon a quiet encampment. An hour or two of sleep was followed by many hours of weary watching or toilsome journeying, until every rood of river bank between Rappahannock Station and the ford at Waterloo had been scouted and fought upon by the vigilant light horse.

Better would it have been for the army had Bayard's Brigade been sent along the turnpike to watch the defiles of the mountains; for passing completely around our flank, Stuart's troopers rode through Thoroughfare Gap down upon the line of railroad, cutting the telegraph wires and seizing the valuable supplies which the government was hurrying forward to the army. After them marched the tireless Jackson, exposing his own flank to destruction from an active enemy, but passing our unconscious troops twenty-four hours before they heard of his presence. In the centre of our converging corps the daring rebel completed the work of devastation begun by Stuart, and then boldly pushed onward to cut himself out by the roads through Bristow Station. But here he was leaped upon by Hooker, with the division which had won laurels for New York and New Jersey on the bloody roads of the Peninsula. With no artillery, the Excelsior and Second Jersey Brigades rushed against the guns of the enemy, took them with the bayonet, and turning them against their owners, swept the rebels from the field. Backward Jackson hurried across the fields of Manassas to encounter the untried troops of King. Driving them back for a little space, yet unable to regain communication with the advancing hosts of Lee, he turned like a lion at bay to confront the hardy Germans of Sigel, and hold the ground until he could be reënforced by his great commander.

Through a long day did the troops who had contended before at Cross Keys, grapple once more on the hills of Groveton ; and before the stern onset of the Germans the wearied soldiery of Virginia, inch by inch, gave back ; but Lee was already in the mountains ; Pope was on the hills of Centreville, looking for the reënforcements from the Army of the Potomac ; the divisions of King and Ricketts were without guidance from their corps commanders, and the manœuvres of the Army of Virginia became one entangled maze of cross-purposes. Of the most fatal part of these, the First Jersey was a spectator, and in their consequences it had a share.

On Wednesday afternoon, Bayard's Brigade, passing the corps of Sigel on the road, was hurried toward Thoroughfare Gap. Two days before, Franklin should have been holding the defile, which Jackson had traversed within the last twenty-four hours ; but a storm had delayed his artillery at Yorktown, and he was awaiting its arrival in Alexandria. Bayard, therefore, without guns and without infantry, went to it to check Lee from following the track of Jackson, until at least our army and its trains should have passed beyond its dangerous vicinity. On Thursday morning that skeleton, which represented the New Jersey Cavalry, rode into the narrow pass and prepared for its defence. Hundreds of stragglers from the hasty march of Jackson were gathered up, who all reported the main body of the rebel army as pressing forward close behind them, seeking to gain possession of the gap; and there were two hundred weary horsemen to oppose their march. Seizing every axe in the neighborhood, Wyndham at once set his men at the trees that hung above the pass, while small parties penetrated to the other side of the gap, looking for signs of the approaching enemy. At each moment more stragglers fell into their hands, Sergeant Brooks alone taking and bringing in seven prisoners as an individual contribution; and as the majority of the scouts turned back with their prizes, Sergeant-Major Craig and Corporal Patterson, of Company L, still kept looking eagerly for the more serious danger of General Lee's advance. Presently, from between the sloping hills rose up the ever-increasing clouds of dust that indicated the approach of a heavy force, and the two daring troopers rode forward to examine it. As the advance-guard halted to rest and concentrate the column, the two men went near enough to reconnoitre its character and composition, and to observe even the movements of individuals. As they watched, they saw an officer and two men, anxious apparently to escape the dust that choked them in their places, leave the advanced-guard reposing on their arms and start forward upon the road alone. Scarcely had a bend in the road concealed them from their comrades, when they were swooped on by our scouts, and hurried away through the gap into the presence of Colonel Wyndham.

In the meantime the work of obstruction had not been neglected, and Craig and Patterson could scarcely lead their horses and prisoners across the barricade. Trees had been felled all along from one height to the other, and immense rocks rolled down the hill-side among them. Earth was cast lightly upon the branches, and ravines converted into traps for the unwary; until no horse could expect to pass with life, and even infantry would be obliged carefully to pick their way, while every cover sheltered a dismounted trooper with carbine ready to open upon the advancing skirmishers. Hidden by the belts of wood, the remainder of the First Jersey stood prepared to charge any body of men who should make their way through these obstacles, and behind them were drawn up the battalions of the Pennsylvanians and some squadrons of the Harris Light Cavalry.

It was not long before the carbines of the skirmishers woke the echoes of the pass as their bullets fell among the carelessly advancing enemy. Then the return fire cut through the leaves of the fallen trees, as the enemy endeavored to push into the obstructions. Firmly, however, the carbineers did their duty, maintaining the post upon which depended the safety of an army. In vain did the rebels strengthen their skirmish line. Our men, protected by the abattis which they had constructed, rendered it fatal for any man to show himself in the open ground before them, and the partial charges of the enemy ended only in heavier loss to them. They strove to bring up artillery to sweep the gap; but the only position was covered by our carbines, which drove the pieces from the ground. At length it became evident that the enemy were profiting by their numbers to throw a force around the hills by the gorges and mountain roads upon our right, and Lieutenant Yorke, with a few men was sent to observe them, and to make the best resistance that he could. He had not been long at his station before we found that the rebels had actually succeeded in their endeavor, and that a strong body was interposed between him and the brigade, and we gave the party up as prisoners or slain.

But in the interval came the cheering intelligence that General Ricketts, with four brigades, was hurrying to our support; and in the soft light of the setting sun a glorious red cloud of dust arose near at hand, from which flashed out the glancing barrels of their muskets. Racing up the hill, the brave infantry opened upon the rebels who were pressing us; while Doubleday wheeled three pieces of artillery into position and swept the gap with canister. Not in vain had we been laboring. Here was the help that was needed to hold the gap, and its rugged defile was for the night impregnable. Pushing back the cavalry who had come through Hopewell Gap upon our flank, the weary cavalry drew back to the rest which they had so well deserved, and bivouacked behind the infantry who had rescued us.

Far away upon our right sounded the heavy guns of King, as his division contested with Jackson the possession of the turnpike. Two of McDowell's divisions were thus between the two wings of the rebel army, in danger of being cut off, while at the same time they threatened the force that was before them with annihilation. Now was the time when we felt the need of a commander and the guidance of a general plan. For over twenty-four hours the generals of division had had no communication with their superior, and were ignorant as to the situation of the remainder of the army. The main body might be in full retreat on Centreville, and they left alone to be crushed by the whole power of the rebels. Through Hopewell Gap, seven miles to the right of Thoroughfare, portions of Lee's forces were beginning to enter the plain, and it was impossible to hold the line of mountains while they were in danger from Jackson on the flank. Had those twenty thousand men only known what they might have done; had they been aware that Sigel was pressing upon the enemy's front, and Pope bringing up reënforcements against his right; that Porter was before day that morning pressing forward his gallant corps from Manassas toward that very Gainesville, where they seemed isolated from all support, and that Jackson, completely surrounded, could be destroyed before Lee could debouch from the mountains in whose defiles he was entangled; the first rays of the morning sun would have witnessed the beginning of a battle whose end would have left Jefferson Davis without an army to defend his capital.

No intelligence reached them to direct their movements in combination with the rest of the troops. They had to decide for themselves, from the study of their own situation, with Jackson barring the road to the Capital, and Lee thundering upon their rear. Rightly, therefore, they yielded the possession of the gap, and fell back toward the railroad at Manassas and Bristow Stations, the only path which opened to them a retreat. The precious hours of that critical day were thus passed by the freshest portion of the army in marching and countermarching. King and Ricketts moved away from that very position which Porter was straining every nerve to reach; and while Sigel alone drove Jackson back at Groveton, the troops that might have completed the success were still miles from the scene of action. When Porter's advance emerged from among the woods and ravines, within sight of the turnpike road, there, in their front, was the whole force of Lee, drawn up in readiness to receive them; and Jackson, in falling back, only made perfect the broken connection. The charge of Bayard's cavalry, which was directed, was not ordered until the darkness had obscured the field, and resulted only in the utter annihilation of a squadron of the Second New York; and, after a day spent in fruitless and exhausting marching, the disappointed troopers stretched themselves sadly upon the dusty ground.

We had marched before daybreak in the rear of Ricketts' division, and, with horses still ungroomed and unfed, were now lying under arms, on the hill-side which had witnessed that officer's gallant fight at the first Bull Run. It was dangerous to move away from the immediate spot, for, in the darkness, it was almost impossible to recover it. Numerous squads of infantry were wandering around, searching for their regiments, and one stand of colors was brought to us, with a prayer that we would guard it till the morning. The horses were as restless with hunger as they were exhausted with fatigue, and, in their frequent struggles to reach a neighboring blade of grass or dangling leaf upon the trees, they endangered the limbs of the men who lay around them. Discouragement universally prevailed. The American soldier is quick to discern when he is badly handled, and there was a universal conviction that a victory had been given away. The long lingering of McClellan's troops, the absence of McClellan himself, in whom the soldiers trusted with a touching confidence, increased the depressing influences. Worst of all, *the army was almost out of ammunition.* Though thousands of boxes of cartridges were destroyed next day by Banks' Corps, at Bristow, the attack which our troops were, at daybreak, to make upon the right, was delayed until wagons went to Centreville and returned, by which time our left had been attacked, and was being shattered to pieces. Under such an accumulation of disturbing influences, the troops formed for battle on the morning of the thirtieth of August, while the commanders, full of mutual jealousy and open discord, felt a fatal lack of confidence in one another; and the corps of Franklin and Sumner were advancing toward the field twelve hours too late for usefulness upon it.

The panorama of the battle ground next morning was magnificent. From the hill, where Ricketts, in the first Bull Run, lay wounded amid the wreck of his battery, looking his enemy in the face, the centre of the line could be seen, as rank rose above rank along the slope of the hill in front of it. Beyond the wood that crowned the summit of the slope, the long array of batteries were vomiting forth their fire, and the bursting shells were visible above the distant position of the enemy. Beneath the shelter of the woods, upon the left of the road, Porter's line extended, glimmering here and there through the leaves of the thick-growing timber, while off to the right the heavy smoke rose like a cloud, from whose bosom burst the continuous roar of the engagement. But on the flank of Porter, which was closest to the enemy, there was no protecting force. Bayard's cavalry, which had been there in the morning, was withdrawn early in the day, to be massed in a hollow by the road, whence they were driven out by shell, at the very commencement of the attack. That left flank was left at the mercy of the man who has never yet failed to throw his heaviest force upon the weakest point of his enemy.

As the eye glanced over the hill-side, ridged by brigade after brigade of infantry, whose regular lines, gleaming with burnished steel, looked like the growth of the dragon-teeth of Jason, with the caissons of the batteries ready to supply the missiles of destruction, it saw, far away upon the road, the dull smoke of the replying cannon of the rebels. The whole woodland nearer to our left lay in an ominous silence. From beneath that clustering smoke there darted now and then a flash, and the hurtling shell came plunging into our line, long before there reached us the muffled roar of the report. Occasionally a squad of men, stepping carefully together, bore into the neighboring field hospital the mangled form of some victim of the battle, or some stragglers crept past, with that languid air which evidences the still present nervous shock of a gun-shot wound. As the lingering hours passed away, the troops, lying by their stacked muskets, began to gather in groups, cooking their little cans of coffee, though every now and then a bursting shell would send some among them to death or to the surgeon. Cavalry and infantry alike took their ease, during the lengthened period of expectation. Suddenly there was a roar that shook the solid earth beneath us, and the air around was filled with all imaginable missiles. Shell, round shot and spherical case tore through the ranks in a terrific cross-fire that left no place of shelter, and long bars of railroad iron struck the top of the ravine, and came humming and whirring down the slope. At once Bayard ordered his cavalry from their useless and dangerous exposure, and, breaking off by platoons, they marched behind the shelter of the further hill-side. As Wyndham wheeled his men, preparatory to the retrograde, some of the troopers betrayed undue haste to come round. Instantly he ordered them again to the right about, and marched them forward toward the fire that had excited them. Then he halted, and made them a few remarks. Twirling his long moustache, he informed them that he objected to confusion and disorder, and disliked their manner of performing the late evolution; that if the next attempt was not more satisfactory, he would be forced to keep them drilling under fire until they had learned the proper way in which a wheel should be performed, and that he would like to see any man try to leave his place in the ranks without permission. The wheel next time was accomplished as if on parade, and, without a waver, the column passed steadily through the fire to its position. The ground was pitted with musket balls by that time, but the twirl of that long moustache was more formidable than a rifle.

The attack seemed to have taken our commander by surprise. He had seen the immense column moving out of the woods upon our left some time before they opened on our men, and the batteries of the centre might have done fearful execution upon them; but the leading regiments were dressed in blue uniforms taken on the Peninsula, and he had imagined them to be a portion of Porter's Corps just coming into position. He was only undeceived by the fire of their guns, as half the rebel army was hurled against the thin line of the Fifth Corps. But gallantly did Fitz John Porter maintain the reputation earned at Mechanicsville and Malvern Hill. As the rebels charged, Sykes advanced to meet them, his batteries opening at short range with canister, while the guns beyond the road poured in an enfilading fire. Regiment after regiment rushed into the fight to be torn to fragments by the artillery or to melt away beneath the fire of that gallant Regular Division. Every gun that the enemy could bring to bear was pouring its contents into that single line of troops, while the solid columns, charging through the fire rushed against them with the bayonet. The result was inevitable and it came soon; there were not enough men to carry off the wounded; scarcely one of Duryea's Zouaves escaped without a scar; the batteries were unhorsed and many of the guns dismounted; and with a triumphant yell Longstreet was in upon our left.

Yet through all the slaughter and dismay, though the broken regiments came pouring to the rear seeking for some opportunity of formation, other troops dashed forward at the double quick to form a fresh line as a protectection for the retreat. Pope and McDowell did their duty gallantly in the terrible crisis that was upon them, and their troops showed the steadiness which had become part of their nature. Most strikingly was the difference illustrated between the gallant but untrained men who fought at the first Bull Run, and those who were again encountering a reverse.

The same tremendous flank attack again terminated in disaster, and was urged this time with greater vigor and even greater success than before; but now with the success of the attack the rout was ended. As soon as one line was broken another was formed behind it to check for a time the progress of the triumphing foe; and under cover of a steady and organized resistance the whole train moved safely from the field. The natural impulse of the stragglers was to regain their colors, instead of making a blind rush in search of individual security; and in its proper brigades and divisions, obedient to the orders of their commanders, the army retreated in a condition to fight again. Who could have got another fight out of the tumultuous rush of fugitives who never halted after the first field until they were within the shelter of the Washington fortifications?

The day was closed by Buford with a crashing charge of cavalry, which ended the pursuit with the day.

During the period of rout, Bayard's Brigade was deployed over the field, checking stragglers and forcing them back into their ranks. At each available point a constant stream of horsemen was kept riding back and forth, rendering unavailing any effort to pass beyond them. Sometimes some officer of rank would attempt to assert his right to go through wherever he desired; whereupon Major Jones would inform him that he could not go beyond his orders, but that by going to the first post he would no doubt be able to obtain the requisite transit. The officer would then move towards the first post. There, smoking his cigar, sat Major-General Pope, scrutinizing all passers by; and the fugitives would generally prefer the dangers of the field to the risk of his observation.

At one point, Lieutenant Allibone with a few men was stationed for purposes of observation. In front of him were placed two guns whose support had been drawn away to some other position, leaving the officer and his artillerymen alone. As they stood there, General McDowell, who was everywhere during the period of defeat, rode up to them followed by a single orderly, and inquired what ammunition was in the chest. "Only two rounds of canister," was the answer, accompanied by a petition for support. The general promised to try to get them a support, but begged the officer to hold the enemy if he could in the meantime. Scarcely had he left before down came the rebels against the artillery. Steadily the gallant gunners waited until they came within range, and then poured into them their little store of canister. The rebels had not cared to deploy their column against two seemingly deserted guns, and the discharges made long lines of death through their closely crowded ranks; but the stoppage was but for a moment. Before the guns could be limbered up the enemy was upon them, and the gallant officer and his men, who stuck bravely by their pieces, sank dead beneath the bayonet.

The guns were taken, but there were no cartridges left to be used against the long line of National troops which was crossing the fords and bridges within range; and before the supply could be sought, the danger, to avert which the heroic soldiers had devoted themselves, had finally passed away.

As the beaten army crossed Bull Run, directing their march on Centreville, they met the advance of Franklin marching toward the field. The reënforcements which six hours before might have secured the weak point of our line, had arrived that much too late.

The hospitals after Cedar Mountain were horribly crowded and miserably defective; but words cannot express the frightful condition of those at Centreville for the first twenty-four hours after the engagements. In the deserted, dilapidated buildings, from which our marauding militia, in the march to the first Bull Run battle, had swept away every comfort and even necessary furniture, and whose broken windows and defiled rooms scarcely afforded shelter from the melancholy rain, were crowded the mangled relics of this mighty battle. There were no bandages, no stores, no nurses, no provision for any of the contingencies of surgical practice. The make-shifts which might have been employed had there been inhabitants protected from violence, were now unavailing. The very wells, from which alone could be drawn water to assuage the agonizing thirst of the wounded, had been broken and rendered useless by a wanton soldiery; and there, on the rough floor, with no beds, no straw, no covering, the poor sufferers had to endure the fever-increasing thirst in aggravation of their paroxysms of pain. Officers and men together were dropped down wherever there was room for them to lie, in order that the over-driven ambulances might return to the field for more. No one knew where to apply for assistance; no one knew how to obtain food; no one knew where to look for orders. The night wore away and the next day dawned through the dull rain that comes after battle; and still the confusion, the distress, the thirst and hunger continued undiminished. A swarm of civilians, many of whom had seized the opportunity offered by General Pope's request for nurses, merely to gratify their longing to look upon a battle-field where they fancied that we were victorious, came hurrying out from Washington and added to the confusion. Wandering purposely about, obtruding their counsel upon the harassed surgeons, pic-nicking on the provisions which they had brought with them from Washington, these volunteers, with some noble exceptions, were a nuisance only to be conceived by those experienced in such scenes, hindering instead of helping the systematic arrangements by which alone benevolence on a large scale can be applied.

Happily, however, others came beside these. Medical Inspector Coolidge, with a staff of surgeons was early on the ground, and under him ranged themselves the best of the civilians. Scarcely had he arrived, before order began to emerge from the confusion. The Sanitary and Christian Commissions, with other minor associations, came to the hospitals with judicious assistants and necessary supplies; and faithfully and well they labored. The work was very different from that which the excitement-seekers had anticipated. It was no riding to a victorious field, looking at its spectacle, and occasionally picking up a wounded man. Washing unsavory men, dressing disgusting wounds, sweeping and purifying filthy buildings, were the first and prime necessities, and had to be gone through with in a business-like and very unheroic manner. The heroism consisted in the very absence of self-consciousness and personal exaltation among those mutilated men, and the promptness with which their comrades laid aside the musket to engage in menial duties for their benefit.

Before night on Sunday, under the judicious administration of the medical authorities, many of the hospitals were clean and well provided, hundreds of the wounded were on their way to Washington, and the rest were wrapped in the heavy slumber of exhausted nature.

Monday, the first of September, opened with active duty for the cavalry. Stuart had, during the night, swept down upon Fairfax Court House, and we knew that that heralded an attempt to cut off the army from the fortifications. All the morning Bayard's men were scouting the country to the right and rear, watching for the enemy's approach, while the long trains of the army slowly defiled upon the road to Alexandria. Early in the afternoon vigorous skirmishing began along our front, and from down the road sounded the roar of battle. In the midst of our cavalry skirmish, a tremendous thunderstorm burst above our heads, its reverberating peals drowning the report of the carbines, and its dense obscurity veiling the combatants, until every effort to continue the action seemed to be by mutual consent resigned. Through the flashes of the lightning and the fury of the rain, the deadlier conflict upon our right continued unabated. The active and eager enemy thronged down from Chantilly in an endeavor to complete the victory of the thirtieth with the destruction of the Army of the Potomac; but they were met with a firmness and resolution superior to their own. Burnside, with the men of Roanoke and Newbern, Heintzelman, with the poor five thousand remaining of his noble corps, stood like a wall of fire, protecting the retreat of that army upon whose existence depended the vitality of the nation; and as the thunder of heaven died away in the murmuring distance, and the pure drops of rain ceased to baptize anew the surface of the blood-stained earth, the rebel force drew back from the encounter, leaving its dead with their ghastly faces to the sky. But Stevens and Kearney fell. On that field we lost the man who would have been the grandest cavalry leader of the war.

The day's duty, coming as it did after the incessant watching and fighting of the preceding fortnight, had worn out the men until they could scarcely keep on their horses; but they were not yet allowed to rest. Though they had been in the saddle since the dawn, they had not a moment's respite during the night. All through the dark hours, the cavalry of Bayard moved slowly along the flank of the rear-guard, men reeling with drowsiness and horses staggering with fatigue. The day dawned on our entrance into Fairfax Court House, where the road was still thronged with troops and lined with artillery, while the baggage trains, in the front, with many a gap and halt of their columns, ascended and descended the hills that intervened between them and the fortifications. It was not until night again drew near that the exhausted troopers, closing the retreat, came to their appointed camping-ground, at Bailey's Cross Roads, where, with a deep sense of relief from continuous care and painful responsibility, they rested beneath the trees and drank the water of the crystal springs. Though the campaign had ended in disaster and defeat, the consciousness that for a little time our slumber at night would be unbroken, our hours of wakefulness unabridged by the sabre or the ball, that our food would be nourishing and our clothing free from dust and vermin, was too grateful to permit of gloom and dissatisfaction. To be at rest was for the time a sufficient ground of happiness.

Into the hall of Willard's walked Lieutenant Yorke, to greet the first arrivals. Given up by us as a prisoner in Richmond, he had not so easily resigned himself to such a fate. By a remarkable combination of prudence, good luck and daring, he had brought all his men and horses safely out of a three days' travel among the forces of the enemy.

On the evening of the twenty-eighth he had gone, as directed, in the direction of Hopewell Gap, watching the wood-cutters' roads that in all directions traversed the mountains. Shortly afterward, a squadron of the Second New York was sent by Bayard to a position in his neighborhood, though still too distant to be much of a support. Yorke sent a man to acquaint the captain with his position in order that they might be enabled to work effectively together; but just as the man turned the angle of a spur of wood descending from the hills, a body of rebel cavalry emerged from it, and formed in front of the New Yorkers. Yorke was thus cut off, but he was also fortunately unobserved, and he began to take measures to turn the interposing body so as to rejoin the brigade. Stealing along, under cover of the woods, he endeavored, after retiring half-a-mile, to strike the road leading toward the force of King; but as he approached it, he found it filled with rebel cavalry, moving carelessly along with an absence of discipline and steadiness which sank them considerably in his opinion. They were, however, much too formidable to be attacked by eight men, and a great deal too well mounted to be fled from by his over-ridden horses, so he had to remain in hiding while he watched them coolly cutting off his only chance of escaping into our lines.

As soon as the road was once more clear, he led his troopers rapidly across it, instead of upon it, and soon had them hidden deep in an adjacent wood. Then directing them to take off and roll up their blue cavalry jackets, he displayed them clothed in the grey woolen shirts which the government had last issued, looking to a casual observer sufficiently like the Confederate uniform. His own jacket had been purchased at a ready-made clothing store in Washington, and had by exposure to sun and rain assumed a neutral tint that might represent anything. Taking forcible possession of the name of an old class-mate at the Naval School, he announced himself to his men as no longer Lieutenant Yorke, of the First New Jersey Cavalry, but as Captain Duncan Moore, of the North Carolina Partisan Rangers; and desired them to take temporarily the oath of allegiance to the Southern Confederacy, that all over-scrupulous consciences might feel at ease in answering questions as to their character and identity. Having settled all these preliminaries, he, as dusk was coming on, boldly ventured out upon the road, taking a direction away from our forces. Though he met many stragglers, yet they were not of a character to cause him any especial apprehensions, and even of small bodies of infantry he was not afraid, for he knew that he could calculate upon their ignorance of the details of the cavalry organization. His great fear was lest he might encounter cavalry, and let drop something in the ensuing conversation which might lead to his detection. It was with a sensation of relief, therefore, that he at last struck off into a country road which took him away from the general line of route of the rebel forces. The night was dark and rainy, and there was no danger of discovery except by persons on the very road itself. While he was congratulating himself upon his escape, he was startled by seeing at a turn of the road, a fire burning brightly, surrounded by moving figures. Should it be an outlying picket of the rebels he feared he was lost; for he must be entangled in the chain of videttes already, and any movement might bring him into collision with them. He doubted whether he even could withdraw with safety, and therefore resolved to push boldly on. As he rode forward to the fire, expecting each moment to receive a challenge, he was delighted to hear the rude sound of boisterous negro laughter; and the supposed picket post transformed itself into a group of belated negroes making themselves comfortable for the night. In answer to a few passing inquiries he learned that many of the rebel trains, instead of pushing down toward Manassas, had continued journeying in the direction of the Upper Potomac; a matter partly perhaps of prudence, partly significant of ultimate designs in the mind of the rebel general. Keeping along the road toward the Little River turnpike, until day began to dawn, Yorke sought a place where he could rest his men and horses in concealment. On the side of the road, near the border of a wood, stood one or two large stacks of hay, at which the hungry horses began to elevate their noses. It was impossible to go to them in the open field, and it was equally impossible to keep the horses quiet anywhere in their neighborhood unless they had a share of the hay; for the starving creatures refused to pass the place, and already their whinneying became dangerously loud. Leading them through the fences into the woods, he and his men, therefore, cautiously crept up to the hay-stacks, and began to draw bundles of the forage from the least exposed parts of them. Thus, in a short time they had provided sufficient to satisfy the appetites of the horses, and could feel at ease with respect to any betrayal by their means.

Late in the afternoon they were once more in the saddle, anxiety having kept most of them from obtaining any sleep. They were now endeavoring to reach Fairfax and the rear of our army by the Chantilly road; but the confusion of the two armies interfered with their design. Jackson, in his forward march had spread out widely the cavalry that accompanied him; and from the battle field almost to the fortifications, parties of them were on all the roads.

Thus, though Yorke was enabled to pass himself off on the inhabitants as the commander of such a squad, he soon was made aware that his doom was sealed if he persisted in that direction; and his heart beat to the tune of "Libby Prison! Libby! Libby! Libby!" as he began to despair of ultimate escape. If it had not been for the treatment inflicted upon the officers of General Pope, he might even have given up his efforts; but he was too hungry at the time to relish the idea of a permanent diet of bread and water.

As he turned back upon his track and diverged in another direction, he began to meet the evidences of the sanguinary contest in which Jackson was engaged. Not a cottage but was filled with wounded men, and every spring and well was guarded for their use. It was only by demanding it in their names that he obtained permission for his men to fill their canteens. Everywhere he was questioned as to how the day was going, and he always gave the same encouraging answer as to the success of the Confederate arms. At length, away up in the neighborhood of the mountains, beyond the line of the Loudoun and Hampshire Railroad, he was forced again to come to a halt.

All day, as they lay upon the ground, they heard the reverberation of the distant cannonade; and in the midst of the roar of the fatal flank attack, they once more resumed their march. They now directed their course toward Drainesville, hoping by that route to make their way into the city. As they passed by a pleasant looking farm-house, whose denizens came to the door to watch them, Yorke, who had fasted from tobacco longer than ever before in his experience, began to feel a mighty longing for a pipe, and he determined to beg a light from these retired country people. Perhaps the fact of one of them being a very pretty girl, strengthened the desire, though he always affirmed that tobacco was the attraction; but, at any rate, he marched boldly up, and, with his most insinuating smile, preferred his request. Obeying a cordial invitation to enter, he passed into the kitchen, where an appetizing meal displayed its fascinations before him. But, unfortunately, he saw in the chimney corner something which took off the edge of his hunger more effectually than chickens, corn-bread, eggs and bacon. There sat, comfortably, a full-fledged Confederate cavalryman, in whose honor, evidently, the repast had been provided.

The meeting was startling, but there was no chance of evasion. Coolly walking up to the fire, and applying a brand to the bowl of his pipe, Yorke put a series of questions to the soldier, letting out incidentally all that he chose to reveal concerning himself, and thus forestalling any inconvenient inquiries. It was very hard to resist the invitation to supper, but it was harder to risk detention and discovery; so, with the feeling of a martyr renouncing the flesh, Yorke turned his back upon the supper, and bade farewell to the young lady. Then, rejoining his men, and feeling that the crisis must come, sooner or later, he boldly rode into the village of Drainesville. In front of every house stood one or two horses, and within, the men of White's cavalry were regaling themselves. If there had not been such certainty of being captured themselves, afterward, this little squad of our men could have bagged fifty of the rebels. As it was, Yorke considered himself fortunate at having got through the town without stoppage or inquisition. The poor horses could make but short journeys, and long before the party got near to safety, their steeds refused to answer to the spur. Besides, they knew that between them and the National pickets, parties of irregular Southern cavalry were watching along the road, when perhaps to speed alone could they trust for escape. Making, therefore, a virtue of necessity, Yorke turned from the road into the adjoining wood.

Near the place of their halt stood a farm-house with something in its look different from the slip-shod Virginia dwellings. The men were almost starving, and were rendered reckless by their hunger, so that Yorke determined to apply for food to the owner of that place.

The door was opened to him by a pleasant-faced, old woman, who seemed the only resident.

"I am a Union officer," said Yorke; "I have some men outside. We have been three days in the Confederate lines, and we are almost starved. Cannot you give us something to eat?"

Blessings on the old woman, she opened her heart to him at once, owning her own attachment to the Union. All that her poor store-house could afford was spread upon the table, and she herself engaged with enthusiasm in baking cakes for the hungry soldiers. Warning them that the enemy was all through the country, she counselled them to lie very quiet during the night, and to try to escape by day; for that the wandering parties of the enemy were much more restless in the hours of darkness. Early the next morning therefore, after having partaken of a breakfast which she rose before dawn to prepare, the party was once more on its way. Fortunately encountering the husband of their entertainer, who himself was hovering around in the wood, they trusted themselves to his guidance, and by secret ways and circuitous roads, at last came in sight of the Union pickets above the Chain Bridge. It was on Sunday noon that they got within the lines, having left the army of Virginia at nearly the same hour on Thursday, thus having spent three days and three nights in their dangerous environment.

When Yorke went to headquarters to report, he was shown into a little room, where sat a quiet-looking officer, smoking his cigar. Yorke told his experience, making his comments very frankly as he proceeded. When he had finished, the officer took his cigar from his mouth and said to him:

"You have shown the true spirit of a cavalry officer, sir, in not giving up under your difficulties and disappointments. I am glad to know that there are men who can run risks without rashness, and conduct themselves at the same time with prudence."

Something in the tone and manner of the speech made the lieutenant think that this must be some one of position, and as he went out he asked an orderly:

"Who is that short officer smoking a cigar?"

"That?" answered the soldier, with surprise, "why, that, sir, is General McClellan."

CHAPTER VII.

FROM ALDIE GAP TO FREDERICKSBURG.

Though the brigade of General Bayard did not accompany the Army of the Potomac upon the Maryland campaign of eighteen hundred and sixty-two, it was given even a more arduous duty in the region around the Capital. Before the two armies had met together at South Mountain, the First New Jersey Cavalry had reconnoitred the whole country about the late battle-fields, and while Northern newspapers were speculating upon the numbers of the hostile force still at Manassas, that position was in the hands of our regiment. Many were the stragglers who fell into our hands, and fearful the number of wounded from whom we took a parole. The flank attack which had proved successful had purchased the victory at the cost of a terrible number of lives; and the hastily dug graves were already sinking in and exposing the heaped up corpses that they had enclosed. Obscene birds stalked slowly from trench to trench, or, with the sluggishness of satiety, rose heavily upon the wing; and the mongrel dog, or gaunt and half-savage hog, prowled around their horrible repast.

Soon the excursions of the regiment extended over a wider space. Lieutenant-Colonel Kargé, who, in response to General Bayard's special and urgent request, had returned to duty before his wound was fairly healed, took command of a force composed of detachments from several regiments, and swept the country near Leesburg to the base of the Blue Ridge; and Wyndham, in command of the cavalry of Sigel, dashed through Thoroughfare

Gap and harassed the communications of Lee. On one occasion, in the face of infantry, cavalry and artillery, he fought his way through the gap, with a number of prisoners and wagons previously taken, and while the rebels continued thundering away at the position which they supposed him to occupy, he had coolly moved off by echelons, and was five miles on his homeward road.

In the early part of October, Kargé received an order to go into Warrenton. So well was the movement executed, that our troops were dashing into the town by three roads before the rebels had an intimation of our approach. Those who could, leaped upon their horses and fled toward Sulphur Springs, leaving their colonel and many of their comrades in our hands. A lot of stores and sixteen hundred prisoners was the recompense for the journey.

It was nearly the end of October when the brigade started from the fortifications of Washington, fully prepared to take the field. Wyndham was still detached from the regiment, and in command of the cavalry of the defences of Washington, thus leaving Kargé as the senior officer. It was late in the day when the troops got fairly started; and as it was inexpedient to make the first day's march, after a period of comparative rest, a long one, the brigade was halted before it entered Fairfax. Thus, inside the regular line of pickets, and consequently relieved from vigilance on the part of our own force, all bivouacked comfortably in the woods, and before many hours, none but recumbent figures surrounded the various fires.

In the very dead of night, a shot in the direction of the picket-line struck the quick ear of the lieutenant-colonel; and rising on his arm, he listened for any repetition of the discharge. In a moment afterwards the reports of a half-a-dozen muskets sounded distinctly upon his ear in dangerous proximity to the bivouac. "Bugler!" cried the colonel, "To arms! sound To arms!" and from the lungs which had just emitted a snore, issued the wailing notes of that startling call. As the sleepy soldiers turned out from their warm blankets into the chill night air, they looked in vain for any further sign of the enemy; and the carbineers, who spread themselves dismounted through the woods, could not imagine what had become of the men who had discharged the weapons. At length they lighted on an infantry corporal, who trembling and out of breath, begged to see the commanding officer. He was led before Kargé, and delivered to him an explanation of the firing. He belonged to a regiment of nine months' troops, who had just entered upon active service, and who were all, from the colonel to the corporal, equally ignorant of all military duties. When this man, therefore, was placed on picket he had no idea of the significance of a shot from his post to men accustomed to regard such a sound as an indication of the enemy; and his regiment would probably have allowed the guards to expend all their ammunition without any excitement or inquiry. When, therefore, a restless litter of young pigs had passed in the neighborhood of his station, the corporal, thinking of the pleasant addition they would make to the next day's rations, had directed his men to shoot them; and he was only awakened to the impropriety of the action when he heard the bugles sound, and observed the excitement about our bivouac. The feelings of the troopers may be imagined at having their rest broken for the gratification of the appetites of half-a-dozen New York militia-men; but no fancy can approach the reality of the lieutenant-colonel's wrath. All the rich stores of a vocabulary acquired in the Prussian Life Guards were exhausted without apparent relief to his feelings; and then, almost suffocated with indignation, he took refuge in a fearful silence, accompanied by a tremulous motion of the right boot. The unhappy corporal fled in time to avoid the threatened danger, and as his coat-tails were shrouded by the night, the roar of the surrounding officers relaxed the visage of the infuriate commander. A gentle melancholy took its place, and he was heard to murmur, "the scoundrel did not even bring the pigs as an atonement." The arms were laid aside, and slumber once more resumed dominion over the regiment.

Though a regular camp was pitched at Chantilly, the brigade was not allowed to occupy it in quiet; for in the early morning of the thirtieth, all the effective men were on the road to Aldie. With a brief halt among the straggling houses which transform that gap into a village, the troops continued on through the rich fields of Loudoun county. Passing through Middleburg, with its crowded hospital full of paroled rebel wounded, and occasionally picking up and paroling other invalids scattered through the entire region, the brigade paused in the vicinity of Upperville, sending a squadron of the Second New York to make a further reconnoissance. While they drove in the rebel pickets and pursued them pell-mell into the town, parties of the Jersey gathered up the wandering squads who were to be found in almost every field or farm house, and then having discovered the situation of the enemy and gained some knowledge of his designs, the whole force retired through the mountain pass by which they had come.

They did not, however, return to camp, but bivouacking in a retired quarter, marched back with the approach of day, and quietly re-occupied the pass which during the night had seemed deserted. The road to the right was guarded by the advance pickets of the Army of the Potomac; that on the left was patrolled by Captain Lucas, and thus, covering the movements of the infantry in our rear, the line of mountains was guarded as far as the great pass of Thoroughfare. There thus seemed little danger of an attack, and none whatever of a surprise; so while awaiting the occasion for further movement, the forges of the brigade were ordered up, and the shoes loosened by travel on the macadamized pavement were tightened or replaced.

While this work was quietly proceeding, a rush of galloping horses was heard coming down the road, passing our pickets, and hurrying to the rear; and presently a number of frightened horsemen, with and without saddles, blankets, equipments and arms, came racing with one another by the halting-place of the brigade.

"They are coming! They are coming! Run! Run! Don't wait to saddle, or anything!" shouted the men, in a paroxysm of fear, without pausing for an instant in their headlong course." "It is Stuart, with all his cavalry! You will be cut off! You will all be taken prisoners! Run! Run!"

They were a portion of Stoneman's picket, on the Snickersville road, whose officers had accepted the pressing invitation to dinner of some cunning inhabitants, and had thus left their post to be ridden into and over by the sharp-eyed Southerners. A burst of savage laughter from our men followed the fugitives, and before the sound of their horses' hoofs had died away in the distance, the First Jersey was galloping to meet the enemy.

But the enemy had been already met. With the first intimation of attack, Captain Kester had gathered his men together, and, forming in the village street, awaited the onset of the rebels. Down the hill they came with a headlong dash, expecting to carry everything before them, and wheeling into the village, rode at our little squadron. But the little band never wavered at their approach, and instinctively the leading files of the Virginians began to lessen their speed. At the moment when their ranks were thus thickened and confused, Captain Kester poured into them a volley from his carbines; and then, with sabres drawn, and a ringing cheer, our troopers charged the startled enemy. Back rushed the rebels to escape the shock, and after them went the captain, while close upon his heels followed the rest of the First New Jersey, eager to press the advantage. As the regiment rose the hill, Kester made his squadron swing off to the left, and led them on as skirmishers, the regiment keeping to the turnpike, and, in close column of fours, seeking to ride the rebels down before there should be a necessity for deployment. Only a quarter of a mile beyond, the ground dipped with a rapid descent to the level of the valley, and if the rebels could be driven over the brow of the hill, they would be exposed helplessly to a plunging fire of artillery.

Already the advanced party which we pursued had scattered wildly over the fields, and but a single turn of the road intervened between the head of the column and the desired position, when around that bend came a column like our own, charging to meet our charge. Even our blown and exhausted horses had sufficient vigor to meet this assault, and as the columns approached, the head of the rebel regiment broke and turned before us. But then, as the chase commenced, a squadron in single rank crossed the summit of the hill, and opened a flanking fire upon the close column of the Jersey. Men and horses went down beneath the volley, to which could be made but a feeble and scattering return. The rush for the position had failed, and now in turn our men had to run for shelter that would allow of due deployment and a regular engagement. As the column wheeled by fours, Sawyer, who was last in the retreat, was struck by a bullet in the loins; and though he retained his seat on horseback, he was disabled for further present duty. The horses of two or three men sank under them, and they became prisoners of the quickly pursuing enemy.

By this time, Kargé had brought up the Second New York as a support to the force engaged, and their appearance, with the steady fire of our skirmishers, relieved the flanks of the First Jersey from the annoyance of pursuit; so that it was easy to form in line under cover of the undulating ground. And now each side had taken its position, from which the other was to seek to drive it. The whole force engaged of the National troops consisted of the First Jersey, Second New York, and a section of a horse battery, all under command of Colonel Kargé, General Bayard holding the remainder of the brigade in reserve, ready to meet the contingency of a flank attack. The rebels had two or more of their most distinguished cavalry regiments, and a battery of four guns, all under the immediate command of General Stuart; so there was a fair opportunity of testing the ability of the famous rebel under circumstances very favorable to him. Several times the rebels formed to charge, and came forward from the wood against the skirmish-line, but each time they were driven back by the rapid fire of the skirmishers alone; and while they were vigorously striving to break through that apparently slight obstruction, Lucas, returning from a scout to Middleburg, swept from behind their line, and formed threateningly upon their right flank. Kargé also had sent a squadron of the Second New York to proceed by a blind road about a mile and a half around the rebel left, and then turn in and attack them; and while waiting for this operation, nothing was attempted on our part but resistance.

Unfortunately the officer commanding the flanking party failed fully to comprehend his orders; and after going the distance ordered, instead of pressing the enemy, he halted and made no further movement. Thus the afternoon passed away with no perceptible advantage to either side; and after a continuous artillery combat, which seemed to damage nobody, the first signs of approaching night were gladly welcomed by both parties as an excuse for a dignified retirement.

Scarcely had the two forces separated, when the sound of troops approaching was heard on the road behind us, and followed by a long column of quickly moving cavalry, Wyndham came riding toward the gap. He had heard the guns from his quarters at Chantilly, and his instinct led him to our support. As our brigade retired to prepare for the serious operations which were approaching, he pushed on after the retreating enemy; and picking up stragglers and sweeping over the country, he harassed their flanks and rear during the night.

Stuart had designed to make a reconnoissance in force of the whole Piedmont region, and to interfere with any advance on the part of Sigel's troops. Could he destroy the bridges and interrupt railway communication, a fatal obstacle might be opposed to the advance of the Army of the Potomac, while at the same time the line of Lee's retreat might be covered and kept secure. By the skirmish at

6*

Aldie, not only was this prevented, but his own retreat was delayed until it was endangered. Caught in the vicinity of Union by Pleasanton, all day on Sunday Stuart fought at a disadvantage, and it was only by the sacrifice of two guns and many men that he was enabled to make his way by Ashby's Gap to the shelter of the rebel infantry. Thus, though not twenty men were lost by both sides in the action, its results were such as to entitle it to mention in the regimental history.

On Monday, the third of November, Bayard's Brigade united finally with the Army of the Potomac, joining it in the vicinity of Upperville, as it pressed down toward Warrenton, turning the flank of General Lee. With the operations which threatened the destruction of General Hill at Culpeper, while Lee was at Gordonsville, and Jackson had not left the Valley, the First New Jersey Cavalry had nothing to do; for it was entrusted with the delicate and arduous duty of protecting the long line of army wagons, which moved in its rear along the different roads and passes of the country. Under Major Beaumont the regiment was kept incessantly in motion, picking up guerillas, watching dangerous defiles, scouting across the country, forever on the alert against attack or surprise. It is not to be wondered at that such harassing duty quickly began to tell upon the horses, and that every available animal in the country was needed and sought for to remount the men. The seizure of such horses, therefore, was entered upon with energy, and in most cases accomplished with success. But in one instance the proceeding was resisted with a power which overcame the resolution of the major and the eagerness of the men.

At a secluded farm-house on a by-road near Hillsboro', the *regimental quartermaster* discovered a very handsome sorrel mare, and brought her to the road-side in waiting for the column. As the major rode up, a battered-looking old man came forward and petitioned for the mare's restoration; but the complaints of battered old men have been so numerous during the war, that they have ceased to excite sympathy or rouse attention. Then a tall, shambling young fellow, lounging over the fence, ventured to say a word; but he looked so much as if he had occasionally been at night on the back of the mare to take a shot at our outposts, that he was threatened with arrest on suspicion if he presumed further to interfere. But then a shrill, rasping, female voice proceeded from the doorway of the house, and a tall, thin, bony, wrinkled, yellow, very middle-aged and remarkably uncrinolined spinster crossed its threshold, ejaculating pathetically:

"O! Don't take my mar'! Don't take my mar'!"

As the major looked with wonder at this extraordinary apparition, another spinster, taller, thinner, bonier, yellower, more middle-aged and less crinolined, displayed the angles of her visage and lifted up her voice:

"Don't take my mar'! Don't take my mar'!"

While the major yet staggered under this unexpected reënforcement, a third female, tallest, thinnest, boniest, yellowest, oldest and most scant-skirted of all, followed the other two, and joined in the dismal chorus:

"Don't take my mar'! Don't take my mar'!"

The combined attack was too strong for ordinary humanity. "Let the mare go!" exclaimed the major, mournfully; "If we try to keep her, we will have all the old women of Virginia shrieking after us in ten minutes." And, completely routed, the First Jersey hurried from the spot.

As the regiment started on its return from Berlin to rejoin the army, a squad of ten men from Company D happened to get separated from the main body, and, ignorant of the direction which it had taken, took by chance the road to Snicker's Gap. A couple of pieces of artillery which had been sent forward to supply the place of disabled guns, had also wandered off in the same direction; and with a sutler's wagon or two were about to fall a prey to the swarm of guerillas who swept over the country in our rear. Just as the rebels were rushing out upon the vehicles, our men appeared in sight, accompanied by a few infantry stragglers. In a moment the infantry sprang behind the stone walls, and opened a steady fire upon the crowd of thieves, while the Jerseymen with a yell rode in upon them pistol in hand. Down went two or three of the rebels, and over went several of their horses. Into the woods darted the rest pursued by our few troopers. In ten minutes there was not an enemy to be discovered, except the few left dying on the ground. Extricating the guns from their awkward situation, and partaking of the sutler's gratitude, the Jerseymen turned about for Leesburg, and in an hour or two were within the lines of Wyndham, who had again come into the Valley from Chantilly.

The rebel cavalry, hearing of the unprotected condition of the guns and wagons, were not long in following their trail; and seeing the advanced guard of Wyndham, rushed upon it, mistaking it for the few troopers who had before rescued their desired booty. Never were men more sadly mistaken. Wyndham let them through his advance, and then, wheeling his flankers inward, enveloped the Southern cavalry with six hundred men. Hopelessly surrounded they yielded to his force, and the partisan troops of Loudoun county were at nightfall a hundred and fifty weaker than in the morning.

While the army was preparing to move upon Fredericksburg, Bayard was already in the Northern Neck, sweeping the country of rebel scouting parties, and confiscating the goods of innumerable smugglers. Enough calico was seized to have *redressed* a good many Southern grievances; and the prevalence of mourning patterns offered a melancholy testimony to the ravages of the war among the people. The only other remarkable characteristic in the selection of the goods was the apparently extensive demand for all varieties of fine tooth combs.

For three weeks after this the regiment lay encamped at Brook's Station, on the Acquia Railroad, picketing from Stafford Court House to the river; and here, for the only time in its history, did its pickets suffer a really humiliating surprise. The lieutenant commanding the post so far forgot his duty as to take supper in the house of a lady living near his station, and while enjoying her society was caught by the enterprising enemy. The officer lost his commitsion, but the regiment felt deeply the disgrace of having its name appear in such connection in the General Orders.

The December cold was bitter, and the spirits of the troops by no means high, when the army left its camps to commence the movement upon Fredericksburg. There was a wide-spread conviction that we had already lost the fruits of the successful march of McClellan; and though General Burnside was universally beloved, he did not possess the general confidence reposed in his predecessor. But as the sound of the heavy guns echoed from the river banks and the fringes of forest upon the ears of the marching columns, the incessant thunderous roar roused the combative element in the men; and with the spirit which always precedes a fight, the soldiers stepped gaily forward to take their places for the coming fray.

Attached to Franklin's grand division, Bayard's cavalry crossed the Rappahannock on the left; and the First Pennsylvania and First Jersey were thrown forward to find the enemy. Riding through the line of infantry skirmishers, Kester's squadron rapidly deployed, and pushed into the thick white fog that still hung over the low ground occupied by the National line of battle. On their right the First Pennsylvania quickly came upon the enemy, and after a brisk skirmish retired on the infantry supports; but Kester, separated from the others by a wide ravine, still advanced, feeling for the rebels. As his carbineers began a sharp interchange of shots with those whom he met in front, he looked across the ravine into the fog beyond. A momentary rift in its veil revealed to his view a brigade in line of battle actually nearer to our forces than he was himself, advancing where they would cut off his retreat. Cleverly manœuvering his men, he gradually withdrew from his exposed position; and falling back toward our front took part in the support of a battery that had been left uncovered. Here he remained until the whole line advanced, and then rejoined the rest of the cavalry in the rear.

That advance of the whole line of battle was a spectacle of such extended grandeur as almost to be called sublime. As the shrouding mist cleared away, and the bright rays of the sun glanced back from their glittering muskets, over half a mile of disciplined men moved forward with one accord, without a waver in their alignment. In their appointed intervals the batteries of artillery rumbled across the plain, while before all the lightly equipped skirmishers darted onward from cover to cover toward the enemy. Immediately from high up among the hills, a rebel battery of heavy guns began to throw shell over our position, the formidable missiles in many cases passing over the river, and exploding in the neighborhood of the trains that were packed there for security. As there was no occasion for cavalry to continue exposed to these long range pieces, Colonel Kargé withdrew the regiment under cover of the bank, upon a small flat that had been formed there by the river; in which position with comparative safety we listened to the progress of the action.

Presently the fire of small-arms began to grow heavy on the left, and wounded men straggling to the rear announced the splendid behavior and brilliant success of Meade's small division of Pennsylvania Reserves. Then we heard of the capture of several hundred prisoners, and then came to us with a shock the intelligence of the mortal wound received by our beloved brigade commander. Rarely has there been a man who conciliated so perfectly affection for the man and respect for the officer. Every officer and man in the brigade felt that he had lost a personal friend, and the mourning of the troopers was sincere and enduring. He met death calmly as he had met every accident of life; and the day that was to have united him to the woman of his love closed upon him in his coffin.

As the wounded passed along the bank to the bridge, the rays of a cloudless Southern sun, exhausting even at that season of the year, aggravated the fever of their wounds. Unable to aid them otherwise, Captain Kester at once arranged to remove this element of suffering. Ordering camp-kettles to be filled with water, he took them up the slippery hill, and there, as the wounded passed, he dealt out to them the cooling beverage. All that day, and half the next, he and some brother officers stood there engaged in this charitable work.

At noon the next day came a command to cross the river. The order did not surprise us, for we knew that in any event we could be more useful scouting the Northern Neck than awaiting the progress of the battle on the shore.

Under the command of Colonel Gregg, of the Eighth Pennsylvania Cavalry, who received the brigade of General Bayard, we moved down to the old quarters at Major Seddon's, and there established our camp. From this position there could be obtained a view of the left portion of the field of battle. Back among the hills were visible the ambulances and ammunition wagons of the enemy. Nearer to the river rose the smoke of their batteries, whose thunder came sullenly upon the ear; and upon the plain beneath was seen the dark line of the troops of Franklin, half-concealed by many a fringe of wood. All that day we watched the varying smoke, speculating upon the movements that it indicated, and the next morning early parties were again at the post of observation. To their surprise all was silent, and no sign of a military strength was seen where we had discerned our line of battle in the evening. By noon we had learned that, after a sanguinary battle, our army had, under cover of the night, re-crossed the Rappahannock.

Over the whole land resounded a cry of lamentation. With no reconnoissance of the enemy's weak points, with no adaptation of design to the conditions of the situation, a mass of troops that might have carried any other position, were hurled against the very stronghold of the enemy; and while one-third of the army wasted the hours in countermarching, the weakest division of all was forced to abandon the position which it had carried, for the want of any support to retain it.

The brave and honest commander confirmed his hold upon the hearts of the nation by his magnanimous dispatch after the battle, but he at the same time irretrievably lost the confidence of his soldiers in his tactical ability; and amid the recriminations of the leading generals, aggravated by Congressional inquisition, the demoralization of the army proceeded with rapid strides. It was perhaps providential that the advance of the twentieth of January proved abortive; for, in the condition of the army, disaster might have superinduced utter rout and ruin, and disaster was no improbable contingency.

Burnside was relieved, and Hooker assumed command. Whatever may be the capacity of this officer for grand combinations on the field of battle, there can be but one opinion as to his management of an army in winter quarters. Finding the Army of the Potomac a disorderly, dissatisfied, ill-provided, uncomfortable crowd of men, in a few weeks, by the ability of Butterfield, chief of staff, he transformed it into a well-disciplined, contented, enthusiastic body of soldiers. Reforms, which before him were much needed, were now introduced; comforts which were lacking were systematically provided; duties hitherto neglected were now strictly performed. One of his regulations alone did more for the restoration of a healthy tone to the army than anything else in the history of the war. He introduced a system of furloughs to deserving men, which, by gratifying the longing of the best soldiers to see once more their homes, revived their spirits and stimulated their zeal. The Army of the Potomac still enjoys the benefits of the arrangements which he inaugurated, and though he is associated with the memory of a defeat, he is the object of many a grateful recollection.

Troops soon learn to appreciate this kind of administrative ability, which is daily felt relieving them of a portion of the constant toil which makes up the routine of their military life; and during the winter of 'sixty-two–'sixty-three, "Joe Hooker" held a place in their esteem only second to the man who first organized them into an army. After the first bitterness of the disaster at Chancellorsville passed away, many of them felt the same sentiment return; and it would not be difficult for "Fighting Joe" to find men in the Army of the Potomac to follow him once more to battle.

As the cavalry corps was not engaged in the contest at Chancellorsville, the history of that action has no rightful place in these pages, and but a few passing comments can be permitted in relation to it.

Up to the commencement of the fighting, as is generally conceded, the design was grandly conceived and in a masterly manner executed. The first part of the engagement corresponded with the most sanguine expectations. Lee being forced to weaken the troops stationed on Marye's Heights, the strong entrenchments were stormed, and the Confederate Army threatened both in front and on the flank. As far as could be anticipated, there was no weak point in the Union line of battle, and the rebels were cut off by it from all hope of victory, and even of successful retreat. But at the very time when General Sickles in the excitement of the action, pushed his corps further forward than was consistent with perfect connection with the Eleventh Corps upon his right, the advanced brigades of that body, confident that he shielded them from attack, without the ordinary precaution of cavalry videttes upon their flank, stacked their muskets and devoted themselves to making coffee. It was upon men thus engaged that

Stonewall Jackson made his famous attack, and (as months afterwards one of the attacking column assured the writer of these lines) actually drove in one whole brigade before they had time to take a musket from its stack. The troops whose carelessness thus lost the day, aggravated the disaster by their panic-stricken rout, sweeping away before them those of their comrades who struggled to resist the victorious rebel advance. The weakness of Sickles' position was by the same attack laid bare; for, instead of being checked by his right wing, the enemy, passing in its rear, cut it off from the main body of the army. The salvation of the whole army can be attributed to General Pleasanton, who, with his cavalry and horse-artillery, was in reserve behind the corps of Sickles; and General Pleasanton gives the chief honor to the Sixth Independent Battery of New York Artillery. Though a flying German battery, deserted by its drivers, ran right over his position, knocking one section into ruin, and though the enemy came bursting out of an adjacent wood, driving before them a tumultuous rout of fugitives, Martin and his remaining cannoniers stood firm, pouring at pistol range case-shot and canister into the advancing column. With a fearful shriek the enemy recoiled; the other batteries came up and added their fire; the flank attack was checked, the National line saved from being taken in reverse, and an utter rout averted.

CHAPTER VIII.

STONEMAN'S RAID AND BRANDY STATION.

On the thirteenth of April, eighteen hundred and sixty-three, the cavalry division of General Gregg left its camp near Belle Plaine Landing, and uniting with the rest of the cavalry corps, moved toward Bealton Station, on the Orange and Alexandria Railroad.

The whole command was in fine condition, quite strong in numbers, and eager in its desire for action. Though there was constant movement, however, there was for some days no corresponding result apparent; and the various evolutions grew so wearisome to the restless spirits of the men, that they found vent for their impatience in some half-bitter jests. Rising among the woods which spread in every direction from the railroad, a large white house, upon a little eminence, forms a conspicuous object in the landscape. Day after day, as the men marched along, hoping that at length they had really commenced their serious movement, some turn of the road or opening among the trees would reveal to them this edifice in close proximity, till at last, through the whole corps, it was nicknamed "Stoneman's base of operations." The name has clung to it ever since, and even in official instructions and communications officers have indicated their course by reference to "Stoneman's base," as a point of departure.

After five days of this roundabout manœuvering, the First New Jersey Cavalry was sent upon a scout to the neighborhood of the Sulphur Springs, examining whether there were any signs of an enemy in that direction, and to pounce upon any unsuspicious partisans who might be visiting among their friends. This was only the diversion of a day, however, and the next morning the regiment returned to the old routine, taking as its central point the camp at Warrenton Junction, and waiting until the state of the roads should permit the Army of the Potomac to enter upon active operations.

It was not until the twenty-ninth of April that the weather gave any promise of settling, and on that day the cavalry moved down to Kelly's Ford, on the Rappahannock. The next morning the First New Jersey led the way across the river, whose depth so hindered the passage of the column that it was not ready to advance until the evening. Then the regiment, brushing from its front the few rebel skirmishers who offered opposition, moved onward to Mountain Run, where, in a hard rain, without fires, they passed the dreariest of bivouacs. While Averill made a strong diversion in the direction of Culpeper the main force moved to Raccoon Ford, on the Rapidan, and with little obstruction, except the height of the stream itself, crossed the swelling current of the river. Here, again, fires were prohibited to all except General Stoneman, before whose headquarters a noble pile of logs and fence-rails sent up their brilliant and tempting blaze. The men, whose longing for some hot coffee, to comfort them in the chilly air, was aggravated by the wet garments with which they had emerged from the river, gazed enviously at the flames, as they diffused around their genial warmth, and the most discontented spirits amused themselves for a while by letting off a constant succession of matches for the pleasure of seeing the staff officers forced to rush down and order their suppression. At length some bold spirits of the First Jersey ventured to bring their camp kettles to the headquarter fire, and receiving permission to make their coffee there, were subdued by the indulgence, and lay down to sleep contentedly.

The next morning, the Jersey regiment still leading the division, on the road to Orange Springs, Major Beaumont surprised and charged a small party of the enemy, capturing their major and several other prisoners. In the village itself a stock of boots and shoes was discovered, part of whieh was distributed among the men and the remainder destroyed, to preserve them from the rebel quartermaster, by whom they had been left in store for the army.

Halting to feed the horses and allow the men to obtain refreshment, the march was resumed again at nightfall, continuing steadily until the break of day, when the command arrived at Louisa Court House and railroad station. The forenoon was occupied in tearing up the track and burning the sleepers of the railroad for several miles on either side of the village, which employment was only intermitted on an alarm that the enemy was approaching. In the fatiguing position of preparation for attack, the whole command standing in line of battle, waited vainly for the rebels until half-past four o'clock. Then it advanced upon its journey. At Thompson's Cross Roads, where it caught sixteen six-mule army wagons *en route* for Gordonsville, the command sent out its various detachments, each charged with its especial duty. Colonel Wyndham, with his own regiment and some auxiliary forces, was ordered to proceed farthest south of all, to Columbia, on the James River, and in that direction they now marched with all convenient expedition.

From the commencement of the movement it had been one of the objects of the command to collect and carry off all the serviceable horses of the country; and as the troops penetrated farther in their captures became more and more numerous. The advanced guard was constantly employed in withdrawing valuable animals from stable or pasture and delivering them over to the main body for safe keeping, the colored grooms and attendants generally accompanying the horses into our ranks and declining to go out again. As Major Beaumont rode up to a very large and tolerably handsome residence the lady of the house rose up from the breakfast table to plead for her favorite horses. She was, she said, a niece of General Scott, and for his sake she thought that her stable might be spared the general visitation. Major Beaumont listened politely to her remonstrances and assured her that a favorable reply was not in his power, but if she waited till the commanding officer made his appearance she would find a man with the necessary authority.

"Who is the commanding officer?" she asked.

"Colonel Wyndham," answered the major.

"What! Sir Percy Wyndham?" cried the lady, whose ideas of that officer were all derived from the Richmond newspapers and play bills.

"Yes," said the major.

"Then there is no hope," was her melancholy ejaculation, and she sadly turned into the house.

Alas! its threshold had been desecrated by the Yankee marauders, who did not even respect the sanctity of the breakfast table. While she had been engaged with the major, his mischievous little orderly, Wilson, of Company B, had quietly transferred to his haversack the dainty white rolls, the fresh butter, the fragrant ham, the delicate chicken, which had been destined for her palate, and miles away they served to appease the hunger of the major and his brother officers.

As the column moved along, striking terror into the hearts of the rebellious whites, those whom they were fond of styling their faithful slaves, displayed, in a new and unexpected manner, their devotion to their master's property. From every quarter negroes flocked toward us, riding their masters' favorite horses, and arrayed in their masters' best and handsomest clothes. They found out very quickly that as long as they brought a horse to ride, there was no obstacle to their accompanying the column on its march; and had our cavalry remained forty-eight hours longer in that region, we would have undoubtedly brought back with us hundreds more than our own number of able bodied negroes. As it was, the column of blacks was nearly as long as that of whites, and the horses afforded a very necessary remount for the troopers.

Into Columbia rode the Yankees, Robbins and Bristol in advance, chasing a small party of rebels two or three miles down the river, while the rest of the detachment engaged in their appointed work of destruction. The canal bridges, the boats loaded with commissary stores, a medical store-house, and a ware-house of government tobacco, were all quickly reduced to ashes, or in some other way utterly destroyed, and a large addition made to our train from a number of mules and horses collected in the neighborhood. Unfortunately, the officer sent to inspect the aqueduct over the James River, reported its destruction to be impossible, and the command started on its return without impairing its effectiveness. When the troops were already three miles on their return, Major Beaumont happened to hear some reference to the omission. He at once offered to take fifty men and a bag of cartridges, and to return to blow it up.

With a squadron of the First Maryland he regained the place and began to work a hole in the stonework of a buttress of the aqueduct; but before he had made much progress the discovery of several barrels of gunpowder and a thousand feet of waterproof fuse suggested a change of plan. While, however, he was preparing to sink the powder to the bottom of the canal that he might thus blow out the sides of the structure, a peremptory order reached him to leave everything and return to the main body. His first barrel by careless handling had been saturated with water, and he had no time to arrange another before the order was more urgently repeated; and he was forced reluctantly to abandon the attempt.

Fitzhugh Lee had collected all his available cavalry and was pushing down to intercept our return; so that Colonel Wyndham's order was not only prudent but imperatively necessary. So close were the pursuers that they passed the still burning fires which had boiled our coffee; and a collision would have endangered all the valuable train which we had gathered during our advance. As it was, by a forced march the detachment arrived in safety the next day at Thompson's Cross Roads, rejoining there the force of the commanding general.

The day after, having collected all the parties not finally detached, General Stoneman began his retreat, reaching Raccoon Ford at day-break the next morning. All that day and well into the night the First Jersey was under arms, covering the passage of the other troops, and then with great difficulty it succeeded in getting safely through the swollen stream. By that time General Stoneman was already at Kelly's Ford, on the Rappahannock, which he wished to cross before morning. He therefore requested one of his subordinate commanders to order some of his soldiers to try the ford. The officer looked at the stream, which by the incessant rains had been swollen into a perfect torrent, and then replied, that if the general insisted, he would make an inquiry for volunteers, but that he could not take the responsibility of *ordering* any man to what seemed almost certain death. The passage was then postponed until the next morning, when the flood had somewhat subsided and there was daylight to assist the men. Though the water was still fifteen feet deep, the command succeeded in swimming across it with the loss of three men and several horses drowned, and the whole of the artillery ammunition abandoned. It appeared wonderful to all that the loss was so slight in contending with such a danger, perils like this forming a much more appaling portion of a trooper's life than the mere ordinary risk of death or wounds in action.

The cavalry then returned to the neighborhood of its starting place, where, with occasional changes of encampment it remained until the time of the formidable encounter which next brought it to the notice of the public.

Though this *raid*, as the people in obedience to the newspapers have named the expedition, called general attention to the cavalry, and was indeed the first grand appearance in its distinctive character of that corps, it will probably strike the reader of these pages that the cavalry of General Bayard had frequently dared greater risks, done severer duty, and in its degree accomplished greater results, than anything recorded of this operation. In fact, among the cavalry themselves there was not the same feeling of satisfaction as was expressed over the country; and that these sensations were experienced by others is evidenced by the appearance soon after of General Pleasanton in command of the corps of cavalry. But that a great moral effect was produced by this independent manœuvre of the mounted troops is undeniable, and they owe a debt of gratitude on that account to the then commander of the

Army of the Potomac. For the first time the cavalry found themselves made useful by their general, and treated as something better than military watchmen for the army. They saw that the long desired time had come when they would be permitted to gain honor and reputation, and when they would cease to be tied to the slow moving divisions of infantry without liberty to strike a blow for the cause of the nation and the credit of their commanders. It gave our troopers self-respect, and obliged the enemy to respect them; and was thus a fitting inauguration of that campaign which included in it the cavalry combats of Brandy Station, Upperville, Gettysburg, Shepherdstown, and Sulphur Springs.

It was on the eighth of June that Gregg's Division broke camp at Warrenton Junction, to march to Kelly's Ford. Arriving there after nightfall, the men, formed in column of battalions, holding their horses during the night, bivouacked without fires or sound of bugles. In consequence of these and other precautions, Duffie's Division was well on the road to Stevensburg, and Gregg moving towards Brandy Station, before the rebels had taken the alarm. Capturing or cutting off the videttes, Captain Yorke led the advance around the position of the rebel cavalry, and debouched through the woods beyond Brandy Station, while the enemy was still between that place and the Rappahannock River. As Jones' Brigade hastily formed to receive us, the First New Jersey Cavalry dashed out of the woods, charging down among them. Without even an attempt to charge, the rebel line broke in confusion; and driving them back, pell-mell, the regiment pressed upon their rear. With a hundred and fifty prisoners, taken by a body of only two hundred and fifty-nine enlisted men, the regiment then rallied and re-formed for the greater work before them.

Nearly half a mile apart, on two eminences of a continuous line of hill, stood a couple of country-houses, surrounded by their customary farm-buildings and enclosures, though both had been dilapidated by the frequent presence of the soldiery of both armies. At the one facing the right of the line General Stuart had established his headquarters, and each of them was protected by a battery of horse artillery. Leaving the First Pennsylvania Regiment to support his battery, Wyndham formed the First Jersey for a charge. Lieutenant-Colonel Brodrick was at its head, and in column of battalions it advanced, with a steady trot, its line more accurate than ever in parade. As it passed over the difficult ground in the vicinity of the railroad, there was danger of its front being compressed by the narrowness of the defile. Without a pause, Hobensack led the left squadron of the first line down the steep bank of the cutting, and up the other side—a steep descent and rise of nine feet each way, taken by the whole body without a waver or hesitation. While the right squadrons of the other battalions followed Brodrick against Stuart's headquarters, the left wings, under Lucas and Malsbury, accompanied Hobensack and dashed at the hill on which stood the other battery. So rapid was the advance of both columns that the batteries of the enemy endeavored in vain to get range upon them; while our own guns, admirably directed by Martin and his officers, played with terrible effect upon the stationary rebel line. With a ringing cheer Brodrick rode up the gentle ascent that led to Stuart's headquarters, the men gripping hard their sabres, and the horses taking ravines and ditches in their stride. As the rebels poured in a random and ineffectual volley, the troopers of the First Jersey were among them, riding over one gun, breaking to pieces the brigade in front of them, and forcing the enemy in confusion down the opposite slope of the hill. Stuart's headquarters were in our hands, and his favorite regiments in flight before us. At the same time, far away at Beverly Ford, were heard the guns of Buford, as Pleasanton hurled his division, in column of regiments, against the shaken enemy. By the same orderly who carried off Stuart's official papers, Wyndham ordered up a section of his battery and the regiment of Pennsylvanians. Leaving the artillery to the support of the First Maryland, the noble Pennsylvanians came to the attack. It was time that they did so; for a fresh brigade of rebels was charging the hundred men of Brodrick. Gallantly did the Lieutenant-Colonel meet the charge. As the enemy advanced, down against them rode our men: Brodrick and his adjutant in front, Hart, Wynkoop, Cox, Jemison, Harper, Sawyer, Brooks and Hughes, all in their places, leading their respective men. With a crash, in went the little band of Jerseymen into the leading rebel regiment, the impetus of the attack scattering the faltering enemy in confusion right and left. Through the proud Twelfth Virginia they then rode, with no check to their headlong onset; and with dripping sabres and panting steeds emerged into the field beyond. No longer in line of battle, fighting hand to hand with small parties of the enemy, and with many a wounded horse sinking to the earth, they met a third regiment of the rebels, no longer faltering before an unbroken enemy, but rushing eagerly upon the scattered groups of combatants. Even in this emergency the confidence of the men was not shaken in their leaders. Against that swarm of opposers each individual officer opposed himself, with such men as collected round him; and slowly fighting, breaking the enemy with themselves into bands of independent combatants, the Jersey fell back up the bloody hillside. Not a man but had his own story of the fight to tell. Kitchen, left alone for a moment, was ridden at by two of the rebels. As one was disabled by his sabre, he spurred his horse against the other. As the animal bounded beneath the goad, a bullet penetrated his brain; and, throwing his rider twenty feet beyond him, the steed, all four feet in the air, plunged headlong to the earth. As the adjutant, trembling from the fall, slowly recovered his senses, he saw another rebel riding at him. Creeping behind the body of his dead horse, he rested his revolver on the carcass to give steadiness to the aim; and frightening off his enemy, managed to escape to the neighborhood of the guns, and catch a riderless horse to carry him from the field.

In the middle of the fight, Brodrick's horse fell dead beneath him. Instantly his young orderly bugler, James Wood, sprang to the earth and remounted him. While the bugler himself sought for another horse, a rebel trooper rode at him with an order to surrender. As Wood was taken to the rear, he came upon a carbine lying upon the ground. Seizing it and leveling it at his captor, he forced the man to change places with him; and thus, with an empty weapon, repossessed himself of arms and horse, together with a prisoner. Jemison, on foot and alone, was chased around the house upon the hill, when he saw Brodrick again unhorsed in the midst of a crowd of enemies, and Sawyer riding to his rescue. At the moment when Jemison was giving himself up for lost, he saw his pursuers stop, wheel and hurry away; and running himself around the corner, he beheld Taylor, sword in hand, leading the charge of the Pennsylvanians. Around the base of the hill the sturdy regiment swept along, driving the enemy before it; and making a complete circuit of the position, returned again toward Brandy Station.

In the meantime, the left wing of the regiment had directed its efforts upon the other battery of the rebels. Keeping to the trot, their unbroken ranks moved steadily against the hill, on whose top stood the cannoniers and a few horsemen observing their approach. As they came nearer, all these men disappeared except one, who maintained his position; and as they came within two hundred yards of the summit, this man lifted his hat, beckoning with it to those in his rear. In one moment the whole hill-side was black with rebel cavalry, charging down as foragers, pistol and carbine in hand. Hobensack glanced along his squadron. Not a man was out of place, and every horse was taking the gallop without a blunder or over-rush of speed. At the sight of this united band of enemies, the confused rebel crowd hesitated and shook. With an ill-directed, futile volley, they began to break away, and the next moment, a shrieking mass of fugitives, they were flying before the sabres of our men. The rebel battery of four guns was left with but two men near it, and with their eyes fixed upon it our officers pressed upon the fugitives. When within a hundred yards of the guns, and when looking over the hill, Lucas could see yet another brigade coming in the distance to reënforce the broken enemy, an ejaculation from Hobensack caused him to turn his eyes to his own rear. There was the main body of the force that had broken the right wing, coming in line of battle full upon their rear.

"Fours, left-about, wheel!" was the instant order. "Boys, there's a good many of them, but we must cut through. Charge!" and obliquely against their line rushed down the Jersey troopers.

Enthusiasm and desperation supplied the place of numbers, and cutting their way out, the little band opened a path toward the section of our battery. Three times was the guidon of Company E taken by the enemy. Twice it was retaken by our men; and the third time, when all seemed desperate, a little troop of the First Pennsylvania cut through the enemy and brought off the flag in safety. Once the rebels who hung upon the rear attempted to charge our retiring men; but the wheel of the rear division sufficed to check their assault, and the left wing of the Jersey reached Clark's two guns, annoyed only by the revolvers of the rebels.

Under cover of the fire of the artillery, and assisted by the charge of the Pennsylvania, Hart had succeeded in bringing off the remnant of the right wing. He was the senior officer of that half of the regiment. Brodrick was dying in the enemy's hands; Shelmire lay dead across the body of a rebel; Sawyer and Hyde Crocker were prisoners; Lieutenant Brooks was disabled by a sabre stroke on his right arm; Wyndham himself had just received a bullet in his leg. Men and horses had been fighting for over three hours, and were now utterly exhausted. Duffie was in line of battle two miles and a half to the rear; but there was no support upon the field. Kilpatrick's brigade, which had charged on our right and rear, had beaten the rebels opposed to it, the First Maine bearing off a battle-flag; but it was now formed on our flank, some distance from the field, to cover us from being entirely cut off. The enemy were indeed terribly demoralized, and the charge of a dozen of our men again and again routed a hundred of the rebels; but now there were not a dozen horses that could charge—not a man who could shout above a whisper. The guns were across a ditch, which rendered their removal very difficult; and it was their fire which kept the rebels from crossing the hills to charge against us. So, with a desperate hope that Duffie might come up after all, our worn out troopers stood by the gallant cannoniers of the Sixth New York Independent Battery—New Yorkers by commission, but Jerseymen of Rahway in their origin.

Presently the apprehended moment came, and the last reserves of the rebels, fresh and strong, poured down on three sides upon the exhausted little knot of Jersey troopers. While the cavalry fought band to hand across the guns, the artillerymen continued steadily serving their pieces and delivering their fire at the enemy upon the hill. Time after time, as a rebel trooper would strike at a cannonier, he would dodge beneath a horse or a gun-carriage, and coming up on the other side, discharge his revolver at his assailant, and spring once more to his work. At length, from mere exhaustion, Hart, Hobensack and Beekman, with their comrades were forced back a little way from the guns; and while they were forming the men afresh, the rebels rode again upon the cannoniers.

As one of the gunners was ramming home a charge, a rebel officer cut him down, with three successive sabre-strokes. Then, springing from his horse, he wheeled the piece toward our troopers, not fifty yards away. Hobensack turned to Hart, stretched out his hand, and said: "We must shut our eyes and take it. Good-bye!" and clasping each other's hands, they waited for their death. The roar of the piece thundered out, and the smoke wrapped them in its folds; but the charge flew harmlessly over their heads. The piece had been elevated against the hill, and the rebels had not thought of changing its angle. They were so savage at the harmlessness of the discharge, that they actually advanced half-way towards our men; but beyond that they dared not come; and the

Jersey regiment marched calmly off the field without an effort being made to pursue them.

No other comment can be needed to tell the impression made by them upon the rebels. If there had been five hundred fresh men upon the field, they might have swept the whole rebel cavalry force into the Rappahannock River.

It would be mere repetition of the same thing, with respect to every officer and man, to speak of their instances of gallantry. There was scarcely an officer present with the regiment who did not acquire distinction, and the enlisted men who have been mentioned were not exceptions to the average behavior, but happened to be connected with particular crises of the combat. Thus, when it is recorded that Sergeant Craig killed four of the enemy in single fight, it is not pretended that others did not do as much; but his action happened to come under the observation of comrades, who reported it; and when it is stated that Captains Lucas and Malsbury, with Lieutenants Beekman and Hobensack, charged once with eleven men into a crowd of the enemy, from which they emerged with only three, the historian does not desire to insinuate that they were more closely engaged than others of the officers. When memory cannot do justice to all, it is no reason why some names should not be mentioned with the credit that they deserve; and the unmentioned private soldier will not grudge the sentence that praises Sergeant-Major Canse. It is enough to say, in illustration of the severity of the engagement, that the second squadron, out of thirty-nine horses left twenty-seven on the field; and that, of two hundred and eighty officers and men in the regiment, six officers and over fifty men were killed, wounded or missing.

Of the three senior officers on the field, Wyndham received a ball in his leg, which unfitted him for months for active service, and Brodrick and Shelmire never came off the field alive. As is frequently the case in cavalry combats, but little quarter was asked or given. Men fought as long as they could, and then fell beneath the sabre or the pistol, the loss of the enemy almost trebling that of the National troopers.

The name and character of Colonel Wyndham are known throughout the country; Brodrick and Shelmire were known to few beyond their own immediate sphere of duty. Within that sphere they were valued, and their loss was severely felt.

Lieutenant-Colonel Virgil Brodrick was in the prime of health, strength, intelligence and ambition when, at the age of thirty-five, he fell at Brandy Station. A plain, practical education had developed his naturally vigorous intellect, and, without elaborate refinement of mental culture, had trained him in habits of thought and observation. Lacking somewhat in rigidity of discipline and tactical knowledge, he supplied their place in time of action by a contagious enthusiasm and a quick perception of advantages; and thus, though frequently lacking as a camp commander, he was never found wanting on the field. When he regarded a man as worthy of his confidence and affection he bestowed on him a fullness of reliance corresponding to his own steadfastness of character; but when he had found any one false or weak he was apt to withdraw too entirely his esteem and charity. This was his own judgment upon himself, and a fault which he often desired to correct, his own efforts at self-improvement thus sometimes puzzling others as to his consistency.

Very different was the other field officer who fell upon that day. A plain, Pennsylvania farmer, with daughters married and full-grown sons, Major Shelmire had marched to war at the head of a company of his neighbors. The fact that he was accepted as a leader by men who had associated with him for years is in itself a testimony that he had deserved and obtained their respect and confidénce. From the very first, his standing in the regiment corresponded to his position at home. The sturdiness and integrity of his character, the sterling worth of the man, had supplied the place of that military bearing and knowledge which come slowly to middle age. What he learned became part of himself, and whatever he had to do was done well and thoroughly, though his regard for the substance made him often too regardless of the form. The weight of his personal character made him, in his company and in the regiment, the centre and support of those who preferred the faithful and quiet performance of duty to the restless ambition after distinction.

His religion was of a character akin to his other traits. It was a part of his daily life, rather than something outside of or above it. Faithful to his God as to his country, it is by his deeds, not by any remembered words, that his fidelity is assured. His death was as unostentatious as his life. No one beyond his immediate command marked him in the action, and no one saw him when he fell. Heading his battalion bravely, he penetrated the ranks of the enemy. When the rebels closed around him he took no backward step. That he did his duty to the end is only proved by the position of his corpse, lying surrounded by the dead, across the body of a foe.

A detail of the splendid achievements of the cavalry of the Army of the Potomac, during the later days of June, belongs to a chronicle of wider scope than this, for the First New Jersey Cavalry was called to take but a very subordinate share in the fighting, and was only under fire while covering the rear, when the corps was commanded to retire. An imperfect, and, it may be, erroneous, sketch of the operations is therefore all that the experience of the regiment can furnish to the reader.

It was on Wednesday, the seventeenth of June, while Duffie and his brave Rhode Islanders were struggling with skill and gallantry to extricate themselves from the fatal trap sprung upon them at Middleburg, that Kilpatrick and Stuart met on the hills beyond Aldie Gap. Though when Stuart came in force upon him, Kilpatrick had but part of his brigade upon the field, he wisely took the most daring course, and charged his small force as vigorously as he could. It was but a few minutes that his few men, consisting chiefly of the Second New York, could maintain their front against the numbers of the enemy; but those few minutes were the saving of the position. As they galloped back to find a rallying point, the First Maine came on the field led by their noble Colonel Doughty. The rebels were thronging the fields and road, and had lined every fence and haystack with dismounted sharpshooters; but those stern descendants of the Ironsides were not to be checked by numbers or by scattering fire. Gallantly supported by the Harris Light Cavalry, the First Maine rode upon the enemy. So tremendous was the charge that the rebels could not even avoid it, their own defensive preparations turning into obstructions in their flight. A battalion of the dismounted men, ridden through by the Maine, fell a prey to the New York Cavalry before they could reach their horses; and the mounted rebels, vainly endeavoring to fight, went reeling down the hill. Colonel Doughty was the first man in the charge and in the pursuit, and in the shifting current of the flight became isolated from his men in the centre of a crowd of enemies. To their demand for his surrender, he replied with the sabre, over whose management he had a perfect mastery. Had he been riding his own powerful charger, his men assert that he would have cut himself out; but the troop-horse which he had been riding on the march was unable to break through the dense masses of the enemy. In the sight of his men, who were struggling frantically to force a passage to him, the gallant and heroic soldier, overwhelmed by numbers, was driven to the ground a corpse. The fierce spirit of vengeance among his troopers then broke through all restraint. Like the passage of the destroying angel was the fury of their pursuit, and not till night hid the enemy from their sight did they withdraw from the bloody work.

For four succeeding days, while the columns of our infantry were moving toward the Potomac, Pleasanton and Stuart continued this cavalry contest, fraught with momentous consequences. The consequence of Pleasanton's defeat would be the exposure of the flank of the Army of the Potomac to the annoyance of the rebel cavalry, the destruction of essential stores, and the loss of vitally important time. His victory would save the fields of Maryland and Pennsylvania from the marauding of rebel cavalry around the whole region commanded by their army, and ensure the safety, rapidity and secrecy of the change of Hooker's position. The game was played for a mighty stake—larger than was then imagined; for the Union cavalry, defeated then, could not have saved the flank of the Army of the Potomac at Gettysburg; the rebel cavalry, victorious then, would not have been checked at the all-important moment by nothing but the skirmishers of the First New Jersey Cavalry. The great game was fairly won by Pleasanton. While Stuart was still hovering around the gaps of the Shenandoah Mountains, the Army of the Potomac had already gained two days' march in Maryland; and before Lee had again discovered their position, he found them face to face with him at Gettysburg.

The grandest cavalry combat of the war took place at Upperville, on Sunday, twenty-first of June. While Gregg engaged the enemy in front, Buford, by a masterly manœuvre, swept entirely around their flank, and threw his whole line of battle full upon their weakest position. Every field was the scene of a sanguinary contest, and every stone wall was made a fresh line of defence. On one occasion, a regiment of rebels, pouring into a field, commenced forming line behind a wall, as the Eighth Illinois were forming on the other side of it. The race for first formation was one for life and death; and the eager horses came bounding into their places with a speed that partook of desperation. At length the Illinois regiment opened a deadly fire from their carbines, The rebels gallantly attempted a reply, but the effort was too much for their failing endurance. Breaking in disorder, they were chased by Buford's exulting men, leaving twenty men stone dead in that short minute of fire. From that moment there was no longer a pretence at a resistance. At full gallop the enemy hurried into and through Ashby's Gap, leaving nearly all their wounded, a crowd of prisoners, two guns, and several colors in our hands as trophies of the victory. The Confederate cavalry had lost its prestige forever.

It was now time for Pleasanton to retire and prepare to join the rest of the army in its march against the invading enemy; and the next day, therefore, the retrograde commenced. The First New Jersey was now ordered to participate in the duty of covering the rear, a duty not very arduous or dangerous against an enemy so demoralized as ours. It was almost impossible to coax the rebel skirmishers within range of our Burnside carbines; and only when a few of our men would linger behind the rest, could they make an effective shot. Spitefully but harmlessly they sent their shell into our skirmish line, a proceeding too little damaging to pay for the expensive cartridges. All day long, under such a fire, our men moved back at their leisure, calculating so correctly the rebel gunnery that Dan Everman, of Company M, declined to follow his file-leader, because, as he correctly stated, the enemy had range on him.

Just at the close of day, when we had retired nearly as far as was intended, Louis Vandegrift of Company D, who had been displaying remarkable daring as a skirmisher. was struck in the side by a shell, which inflicted an instantly fatal wound. As the order to fall back had just been given, his comrades were only able to place his body safely in a corner of the fence before they had to yield the ground to the advancing enemy. They could not consent, however, to have so gallant a fellow unburied, or in the hands of the rebels, without a further effort to remove him; so immediately on the halt, Craven, of Company A, Allen, of F, one of the Pennsylvanians, and two other volunteers, rode back to the place where he had been secreted. Close upon it was the rebel skirmish line, but undeterred by this, the little party rode out to the fence corner. While the other four faced the enemy, Craven dismounted and took the body on the horse. Then, carrying the corpse in his arms across the saddle, he was guarded by the others back to the regiment. This was the only casualty in the course of the retreat.

CHAPTER IX.

GETTYSBURG.

On Saturday, the twenty-seventh of June, the cavalry of the Army of the Potomac commenced that series of rapid, continuous and exhausting marches which culminated in the junction with the other corps upon the field of Gettysburg, and continued, with scarcely an intermission, until the opposing armies were once again confronting each other across the Rappahannock.

Having marched through the whole preceding night, on Sunday morning the First New Jersey, the last regiment of the army, crossed the Potomac at Edwards' Ferry, and took the road to Frederick. Halting for a few hours' rest during the extreme heat of the day, at four o'clock in the afternoon they were once more in the saddle and marching along the turnpike road to Baltimore; their duty being to guard the right flank of the army from any dash of Stuart's Cavalry, whether for the purpose of reconnoissance or the ordinary desire of plunder. A division of rebel horse had indeed crossed after our army had left the river, and was now between us and Washington; but while their movements were too rapid to permit them to be cut off, we, on our side, were too vigilant and too active to allow them either to acquire any information or to inflict any serious damage upon the country. Pressing upon their rear, picking up their stragglers, though we did not overtake their main force, we followed on their heels, knowing that they must lead us to the desired presence of the enemy, or else fall ultimately into our hands.

The transition from Virginia to Maryland, from a region inhabited by active or secret enemies, to one where every village poured out a throng of enthusiastic friends, was one that delighted and inspired the war-worn veterans of the army. No longer scowled at as invaders, or repaid by hate when they sought to supply their necessities, the march of the cavalry through the fertile country was one long series of ovations, a succession of grateful greetings. All along the road, the inhabitants came thronging out to gaze upon the hardy figures and weather-beaten visages of the troops who had defeated the famed cavalry of the South, and with shouts and joyful tears they cheered us forward in the pursuit. From doorways, windows, balconies, handkerchiefs and scarfs were waved in welcome; young girls saluted us with patriotic songs; matrons brought out abundant provision for our refreshment; men opened barns, and granaries, and store-rooms, with one impulse of zeal for the glorious standard of the nation, displayed upon every house. Not a village in that noble little State of Maryland, whose sympathies the rebels claim to be with them, allowed the soldiers of the Union to pass without a tribute of hearty sympathy and unrestrained applause; though of the rich northern inhabitants of Pennsylvania, many gazed stolidly upon their defenders, and with a sordid spirit of extortion drained from them their few hard-earned dollars for the supply of their simplest wants.

All the next day and night the march continued, the column entering Westminster at noon, and capturing stragglers from Stuart's rear-guard. Though the welcome was even warmer than before, of those who were looked upon as rescuers from a present enemy as well as defenders against a future invasion, the troops were not able to pause to enjoy it. But the people were not thus to be balked. From the cellars where they had been secreted from the marauding Southern horsemen, casks of beer and ale were rolled into the street; and as the men marched past, the owners offered to each trooper a brimming glass of the strengthening and refreshing beverage. At Manchester, near the Pennsylvania line, wreaths of flowers were thrown down upon the dusty and haggard soldiers, while the hands that had woven these graceful tokens of welcome were quickly busied in providing a more substantial tribute. In those few hours of halt, feelings of gratitude and affection were aroused in the hearts of men hardened to cold looks and bitter words, which have survived the hardships and privations of all the succeeding campaigns, to endure long after the war shall be a thing of the past—when the fierce struggles of the battle-field shall have softened into subjects of pleasant recollection. Every man who could leave the ranks was certain of a warm reception; and in the presence of kindly faces and cheering smiles, the weariness of the long march sweetened the delicious moments of repose. Brief, however, was the period of rest; for on the next morning early the march was resumed across the line into Pennsylvania, and continued without a pause until three o'clock in the morning of the second of July. Then, again, came a few hours' rest, and then, with quickened pace, the troops hurried on, until they debouched upon the field of Gettysburg.

The army was still assembling, corps after corps hurrying to the field, and as they arrived taking their places in the battle. The day, that at first had gone against us, had turned toward evening, and prisoners by the thousand were sadly marching to the rear. On the extreme right where there had been the first contest, the struggle had dwindled into a skirmish; and the infantry posted there being removed to strengthen other threatened points, McIntosh's brigade of cavalry, in which was the First New Jersey regiment, was ordered to supply their place. Coming to the front on the gallop, the troopers leaped to the ground, and soon, covered by the fences, lay in wait for any advancing enemy.

They had not long been in position before under a vigorous fire from their skirmishers, a considerable body of the enemy made a resolute advance upon them. From behind the stone walls, taking advantage of every ditch and little inequality in the surface of the ground, the dismounted cavalry poured forth the contents of their carbines. This had the effect of checking the advancing columns, and, in fact, of driving back the assailing force.

Sent forward as a forlorn hope, to give time for the rest of the division to come up with unblown horses, this little band of one hundred and fifty men, by their undaunted bearing and their steady fire, staggered the troops that by a single charge could have ridden over them. Refusing to dismount in spite of the storm of bullets constantly whistling over our men, Janeway rode from end to end of his line of skirmishers, encouraging, warning and directing its every portion—showing here as on many another field a coolness and bravery that made him a marked man among men. Advancing from point to point, heralding each charge by a cheer which shook the enemy worse than the bullets of their carbines, for more than a hundred yards the First Jersey pushed their little line; and at last, with ammunition exhausted, they still held their ground, facing the rebels with their revolvers. Then Janeway rode back to the reserve, and reported to Major Beaumont the condition of his men, requesting ammunition and reënforcement. At Major Beaumont's request, Colonel McIntosh ordered another regiment to take the place of the First Jersey. That regiment halted a hundred yards to the rear of the line where the Jerseymen were stationed, and would not advance any further, while the latter resisted every effort to move them back. Presently, Colonel McIntosh rode up to Major Beaumont, saying, "Major, where is your regiment?" "On the skirmish line, sir." "But I ordered them to be relieved." "The other regiment cannot be got to relieve them." "I will see about that," said the colonel; "recall your men." "I have recalled them," replied the major, "and they won't come." Even Colonel McIntosh failed to get the relieving regiment up through the tremendous fire to the position of the First Jersey; old soldiers as they were, they could not calmly face it. At length, however, the Third Pennsylvania came upon the line, and the First Jersey was at liberty to retire from the action. But no! They sought every method to avoid falling back. Borrowing ammunition from the Pennsylvanians, they kept their boldly-won position, and cheering like mad, defied the efforts of the enemy—only a handful retiring, casting reluctant looks behind as they went. And now the rebels essayed to charge and turn the position which they could not take in front, but each assault was repulsed, the fine old First Michigan Cavalry charging straight into their ranks and putting them ingloriously to flight. By this time, the grand attack of Longstreet had been made and repulsed, and all that remained was for the cavalry to sweep away the rebel horse from our flank. With charge after charge they were beaten from the ground—the Third Pennsylvania making one magnificent dash upon a greatly outnumbering body of the enemy. Newhall, the adjutant-general of the brigade, and five officers of a single squadron, fell beneath the sabre and the pistol, but the enemy was cut to pieces; and with cheers of triumph the cavalry of Gregg saw Stuart's battalions gallop in rout to the protection of their artillery.

But the First New Jersey had work still to do. Guarding the line and picketing far to the front, they watched through the night upon the bloody ground, until the welcome light of the birthday of the nation permitted them to seek a brief season of repose.

At five o'clock on the afternoon of that day the cavalry was again in motion, following up the retreating columns of the enemy. And now each day brought its skirmish, each march its batch of prisoners. On the fifth, in the mountain passes above Emmettsburg, the First New Jersey was sharply and successfully engaged; and again on the sixth it had another contest. Though again successful, it lost the services of an officer—Lieutenant Cox receiving an ugly wound. Captain Boyd had been disabled at Gettysburg, and small as it was, the regiment had scarcely enough officers left to perform the duty required.

For three delightful days the regiment enjoyed the hospitality of the little town of Waynesboro', in the vicinity of the boundary line between Maryland and Pennsylvania. Then, on the tenth, it dashed at the rebel pickets, and swept the country to within four miles of Hagerstown. On the twelfth the whole army was in motion, and we moved with it to the neighborhood of Boonsboro'. The evening of the fourteenth saw us once more on the Potomac, opposite to Harper's Ferry.

Crossing the river, we found the rebel Twelfth Virginia Cavalry in possession of the country beyond, and soon began to make advances to a closer acquaintance; attacking them so suddenly that their colonel, who was accidentally dismounted, was cut off and enveloped by our line. A few minutes afterward, as Major Janeway advanced his skirmishers, a little knot of rebel officers, bearing a flag of truce, appeared in front of the enemy, requesting an interview with our commanding officer. The object of the flag proved to be to satisfy the anxiety of their adjutant as to the welfare of his uncle, the colonel; though perhaps some other purposes were concealed beneath that pretext. Up to that time the colonel, favored by the twilight and the high grass of the meadows, had escaped the notice of our men, and if attention had not been aroused by the inquiries of his nephew, he might possibly have remained concealed until darkness would cover his escape. Now, however, the active search which was commenced quickly revealed his hiding-place; and, lifted out of the grass by the burly, bearded orderly sergeant of Company M, he was presented to the rebel officers, that they might be assured of his physical well-being. It is an evidence of the selfishness of human nature, that the colonel did not seem to feel any gratitude for the solicitude of his nephew, or express any thanks for their exposing themselves on his account to association with the northern invaders. Indeed, it must be confessed that he yielded to the impulses of anger, and used what was considered by the hearers as very forcible language to his afflicted relative and subordinates.

While his condition was being investigated, the officers of the Twelfth Virginia treated the First Jersey with a graceful condescension, which cannot be too highly appreciated. They were good enough to acknowledge that we fought very well at Brandy Station, and had indeed a little the best of the day; but they benevolently warned us that in them we would meet a very different style of antagonism, and that we might prepare ourselves for a decided reverse of fortune. They especially admired the black stallion ridden by Major Janeway, and delicately expressed their hope soon to have it in their possession, intimating, moreover, that it would make a capital mark upon the skirmish line. Having thus overwhelmed us with their affability, and awed us by their chivalrous gallantry, they retired to their own lines; whereupon Major Janeway moved forward, drove them a mile and a half without stopping, and then went to supper, without being hit, and still maintaining his title to the black steed, Rappahannock.

The next morning, for the purpose of securing forage, Gregg's Division advanced to Shepherdstown, a position unsupported by any other troops, but still tenable for the brief period for which the general designed to occupy it. All through the night rebel scouts and partisans prowled around the pickets, whose vigilance was indicated by an incessant firing at the suspicious objects; so that, as a precaution against danger, the division, in the middle of the night, rose up, saddled, cleared away the fences, and then lay down once more to rest.

When nearly all the forage had been secured the next day, and two ambulances and several prisoners had been picked up in the vicinity, the division prepared to retire from the place. Suddenly, with a vigorous and unexpected charge, the enemy drove in a portion of the picket line of the Second Brigade. It happened that the First Maine was at that moment moving in that direction to complete their stock of forage. To throw down their grain sacks, draw sabres and dash at the rebels was the work of a moment, and a charge from the First Maine of course occasioned the repulse of the rebel cavalry.

Line of battle was quickly formed, the First Jersey being thrown out as skirmishers upon the left of the division; but the fighting, for once, did not fall to our share, the First Pennsylvania monopolizing almost all that came in the way of the First Brigade. Upon the Second Brigade, however, the enemy came with all their weight, pouring down regiment after regiment with fiery impetuosity. Here General Gregg showed the same high qualifications for command which saved the flank of the army at Gettysburg. In spite of the advantage of the rebels, in being the attacking party, and being able to choose the point against which to launch their squadrons, and notwithstanding the fact that Stuart had massed his cavalry against our one division, still, without losing ground, without exposing a weak point of which the enemy could take advantage, he held his position through the day, and until after night had put an end to the engagement. Then, before daybreak revealed his movements, or enabled the enemy to interfere with his line of march, he proceeded with the retreat which he had commenced before they had assaulted him, and before noon he was again at Harper's Ferry, having suffered severely in the fight, but inflicted much more damage than he received. It is curious and significant that, with equal caution and celerity, the enemy evacuated their position; and some stragglers, who had slept too soundly to notice the departure of the division, found, in the morning, our barricade faced by a similar one of the rebels, within a hundred yards, deserted, like our own. These missing men, who had been reported as prisoners, not only made their way safely to Harper's Ferry, but also brought in as their prisoners a party of the enemy, who had also overslept themselves.

As the army moved forward again to the Rappahannock the division of General Gregg guarded the train of wagons, a duty the most wearying that cavalry has to perform, requiring, as it does, constant vigilance and readiness for action, while the rate of progress is slow and the halts numerous and harassing. When relieved of this task General Gregg's men were employed in alternate scouting and picket duty, on both sides of the Rappahannock, in the neighborhood of Warrenton, thus acquiring a perfect, practical knowledge of the roads and the character of the country, which has since then been turned to good account.

Before quite concluding the story of the Maryland campaign it may be as well to mention a little incident illustrative of the very vague conceptions formed by the peaceful inhabitants as to the extent of the privileges of a military commander. During the march toward Harper's Ferry the First New Jersey halted, before daybreak, near a nice little farm-house, somewhat removed from the public road. As the officers were both tired and hungry, Major Janeway, who was in command, roused up the tidy old German woman who lived in the house and requested her to provide them something to eat. Hearing the sound of a younger feminine voice, he also suggested that perhaps her daughter would favor him with her society. Both propositions were acceded to with exemplary promptness; and, while the old lady plunged into the operations of the kitchen, a nice, plump, fair-haired girl descended to the parlor and sat herself down by the major's side.

The gratification of the appetite of a dozen hungry officers took up some time, and all the while the young German girl sat by Janeway's side, answering docilely the questions which he asked her, and receiving meekly and blushingly his gallant speeches. He began to feel that he must be making an impression, and, perhaps, to wonder how he should get out of the scrape, when his vanity received a terrible shock from the mother. She came up timidly, and humbly inquired if *he would not let her daughter off* for the rest of the morning, as she had now been attending to him since before sunrise. The two had actually imagined that the major had ordered the girl to come and be flirted with, and had fancied that obedience was obligatory upon both of them. The discomfitted commander, of course, at once gave his consent to the request and retired, enlightened as to the extent of military jurisdiction in the region of German Maryland.

On the second of September the regiment enjoyed the diversion of a visit to Washington, as escort to the train of sutlers' wagons. To spend three days in the society of the capital was really delightful to men who had been roughing it for months; and, though the duty was fatiguing, it was cheerfully undertaken. To govern a train of army wagons is no light duty, and a train of sutlers, with no controlling organization, is far more difficult to manage; but, though there were more wagons than the regiment numbered men, all were conveyed safely, with their full loads, to the army, and Major Moseby was cheated of his expected plunder.

With that suddenness which characterised the movements of the army during the last campaigns, the whole force at an hour's notice was in motion upon Culpeper, the First Jersey, after three days' unsupported picket duty following the rest of the brigade. Kept constantly moving from one part of the line to the other while it remained at the front, on the twenty-fourth of August, in company with the rest of the division, the regiment marched to the rear to guard the railroad, left uncovered by the departure of the Eleventh and Twelfth Corps to the West, and on the twenty-fifth it was placed on post at Bristow Station.

From the twenty-fifth of September to the fourth of October, the First Jersey revelled in the lap of luxury. From every part of the surrounding country negroes flocked into camp, bringing milk, eggs, poultry, sheep and vegetables for sale; and the paymaster having made his welcome visit, every one was able abundantly to supply his mess. Even from the markets of Alexandria hampers of peaches found their way to camp; and never before had the cavalry been so delightfully situated.

Of course, this state of things was too pleasant to last, and no one was surprised when the Sixth Corps sent down a brigade to take possession of this land flowing with milk and fragrant with onions and other delicacies. Transferred to Hartwood Church near Falmouth, we remained for a week on picket, when we were again called to share in a fresh series of operations.

CHAPTER X.

SULPHUR SPRINGS AND BRISTOW STATION.

On the morning of the tenth of October a large portion of the regiment started from the picket line at Falmouth on an expedition into the Northern Neck of Virginia. Scarcely had it disappeared from sight when an order arrived directing the brigade to be moved at once toward Kelly's Ford, and couriers were sent after the regiment to summon it to return. Unfortunately the messengers mistook the road taken by the regiment; and it was only at the end of a march of twenty-five miles that Major Janeway received the orders which they carried. It was necessary to start forthwith upon his return; and after a very brief period of rest the tired men and horses commenced to retrace their steps. Twilight was fading away when they reached again the camp, where the work of packing the camp equipage, distributing rations and securing forage had still to be performed; so that the night had completely darkened before they were able finally to depart. The brigade had been obliged to wait for the movement of the regiment, and therefore, in spite of the fifty miles already traveled, not a moment's rest could be allowed; so, combating fatigue and drowsiness, the regiment followed in the rear of the little train of wagons allotted to the regimental property of a cavalry brigade. Through the long hours of the dark and starless night, over roads in many places deep with mud, and ploughed up by passing trains, the tired column marched on, until at three o'clock in the morning the appointed spot was reached, and the men received permission to throw themselves by the side of their tired horses.

At five o'clock, having obtained but two hours' rest after seventy miles of marching, the men were once more in the saddle, and crossing the ford on the road to Brandy Station. Here to the surprise of all but the commanders we met the trains and marching columns of the army rapidly retreating from Culpeper toward the Rappahannock. Kilpatrick in a reconnoissance which had cost him many men, had unmasked a formidable flank movement of General Lee, the whole rebel army stealing along the base of the mountains to cut us off from Washington ; and General Meade did not feel himself strong enough to risk a battle where a reverse would leave the Capital entirely unprotected. While Buford, therefore, held the rear, inflicting a severe chastisement on the rebel cavalry, which, as soon as they detected our movement, the rebels sent after the army, Gregg was ordered to take the ground around Warrenton White Sulphur Springs with which his troops had become familiar, to guard the flank especially threatened by the enemy. The Second Brigade remaining in the neighborhood of Jefferson, on the south side of the river, the First occupied the vicinity of the Springs; each force establishing a line of pickets for its own defence and the protection of the army.

The next morning, as it was necessary to guard the country further to the rear, the Second Brigade, after sending the First Maine to scout toward Sperryville, divided its forces so as to occupy our position, as well as its own, and the First Brigade picketed and scouted around the town of Warrenton itself. The First New Jersey, whose late expedition had reduced its numbers again to three hundred and sixty effective men, was allowed to remain in reserve, at rest, with the exception of one squadron as its own especial picket, while nearly the whole of the remaining force was employed in watching for the enemy.

Early in the afternoon the cavalry, which had been driven off by Buford and Kilpatrick at Brandy Station, made its appearance in front of the Second Brigade, and Colonel Gregg, with the portion of his force beyond the river, was soon hotly engaged with a much superior force. While, with a large proportion of his men dismounted, he was holding his ground nobly against this enemy, the advance of Ewell's corps, in full force of infantry and artillery, marched around his left flank, cutting him off from the river. In this situation, he had to sacrifice most of his dismounted men or lose the whole of his force. Promptly choosing the first alternative, he charged the enemy with his mounted troops, cutting his way straight through them, and, under the fire of twenty pieces of artillery, dashed across the bridge and gained the north bank of the river. In this condition of affairs another danger began to threaten. Not only was the First Maine completely isolated and nearly one hundred and fifty of his other men taken prisoners, but the enemy commenced to evince an intention of crossing at Freeman's Ford, below, thus getting between the division and the flank of the army which it was bound to cover. Under these circumstances, the general was obliged to take all of Colonel Gregg's brigade from Sulphur Springs to guard the lower fords, and to send to Colonel Taylor to supply their place as rapidly as he could hurry his men forward.

To Lieutenant-Colonel Kester, at that time acting on his staff, the general entrusted the execution of the first duty. Though struck by a piece of shell, which almost knocked him from his horse, the colonel transmitted the order promptly, and assisted ably in its fulfillment When all the rest of the brigade had departed, however, he discovered a piece of artillery exposed to a tremendous fire, which had not been removed with the rest of the battery. Beside it was the sergeant of the piece with his men, staunchly steadfast to their duty. The fire was so terrible that the colonel was actually unable either to ride or to walk to the position of the gun. Throwing himself upon his face, he crawled near enough for the gunners to hear his voice, and directed them to remove their piece from its dangerous exposure. Their first attempt to touch it brought on such a storm of canister that they were obliged to crouch behind a little rising ground. Then, keeping close to the earth, they managed, by little and little, to draw the carriage into the hollow where they stood, and then, with greater ease, to move it to the locality of the limber. It was then attached and carried to the battery, after running the gauntlet of the fire of the enemy. In the meantime, Colonel Taylor was exerting himself in obedience to the order sent to him. The First New Jersey was all that was available of the troops under his command, and they were instantly mounted and sent toward the scene of action. At that moment it was discovered that almost all the ammunition in their cartridge-boxes had become so unserviceable from rain and damp that the regiment could not average more than three effective rounds for every carbine. From the stock of other regiments there was hastily procured enough to provide the greater part of the regiment with ten rounds apiece; and with this scant supply the little body of three hundred and sixty men advanced against a force of cavalry and Ewell's corps of infantry,

So sudden had been the whole transaction, that we did not even know that the passage of the river was now open to the enemy; and it was supposed that we were to relieve a force of the Second Brigade still employed to hold it. Notwithstanding this impression, however, Major Janeway fortunately took the precaution of sending Captain Hart's squadron forward as an advanced-guard, directing that officer to bear to the right on approaching the river, in order to be ready at once to hold that flank of our line. As this squadron passed out of sight beyond the woods, and while the rest of the regiment followed with more deliberation, Captain Harper, who was on the brigade staff, galloped past us to examine the condition of things in front. Almost at the same time, the major sent the adjutant to see whether Captain Hart clearly understood and was fully carrying out the instructions which had been given him.

These officers, emerging almost together from the last belt of woods, saw, as they commenced the descent to the river, what they supposed to be a portion of the Second Brigade coming towards them from the enclosure of the ruined Hotel at the Springs. Lieutenant McKinstry, the adjutant, apprehensive that Captain Hart had passed beyond the hotel, instead of turning to the right, spurred his horse to inquire of these comers. As he closed with them, he heard a call to him to halt, and found himself under the pistols of the Twelfth Virginia Cavalry.

"Surrender!" cried their lieutenant-colonel, Massey.

"Not exactly!" replied McKinstry, wheeling his horse around at full speed, and dashing up the road once more.

Harper dodged around the remains of the old summer camps of the Third Corps, and so evaded his pursuers; but the adjutant was forced to rush up the open road under the fire of the rebels' pistols and the sharp pursuit of the whole party.

Captain Hart had done exactly what had been ordered. Turning to the right, under cover of the woods, he had struck the river above the Springs, where the trees nearly shadow its waters; and rescuing a portion of the Second Brigade, which was trying to escape in that direction from the enemy, he, with the able assistance of his lieutenants, Wynkoop and Hamilton, checked every attempt of the enemy to cross upon that flank. He trusted confidently to the ability of Major Janeway and the courage of the main body to cover him in his exposed position, and without a moment's faltering, carried his men to the position ordered him, in defiance of the troops advancing to cut him off upon the road. This promptness of action and steadiness of obedience was the first of the many circumstances which concurred to render the ground tenable against so apparently overpowering an enemy.

As Captain Harper at full speed emerged from the wood, Major Janeway directed Major Lucas to take the fourth squadron, Companies D and F, and deploy a skirmish line in advance of the other squadrons, now forming for action. As Lucas led them at a trot around the bend of the road which turned the corner of the timber, they came full upon the adjutant, chased by a column of the enemy reaching from the Springs, a furlong distant, nearly to their own position. There was no time to deploy: there was barely time to get in line, before the enemy were entering the wood. With a withering volley from the carbines, the major, followed by Jemison and his men, dashed forward at a charge, the adjutant wheeling his horse and taking a foremost place in the attack. Taken by surprise, reeling from the fire, and staggered by our ringing cheer, the rebels broke, wheeled and raced for the cover of their infantry, who could be seen running behind the walls and into the houses to prepare to repel our charge. With difficulty could Lucas restrain his eager men from pursuit of the enemy into the enclosure; but, chasing the Twelfth Virginia just far enough to drive them through the infantry columns below the springs, he succeeded in halting his own men before they were absolutely periled by the fire from the buildings. Then, taking advantage of the confusion, Lucas ordered Jemison and Inglin to deploy their men, and deliberately began to fall back within supporting distance of the regiment.

Emboldened by this movement, the rebels again charged forth from their cover, to be met boldly as before by our men; and again, at the critical moment, Janeway launched another squadron, H and K, under Kinsley, Craig and Hughes, against the enemy, who were charging in column against our little skirmish-line. Again came the volley, the cheer, and the charge; and the rebels broke as before at the enthusiastic onset of the Jerseymen and the destructive fire of the carbines. Driving them pell-mell, our troopers closed upon their rear, the officers leading on the men, and the men striving to get even with the officers; until Lucas once more re-formed his line, Inglin halting far in the front, that his pistol might do equal execution with their carbines.

In the meantime Janeway, as Lucas advanced, had formed his squadrons under cover of the wood, and sent Captain Gray, with Companies C and I, to extend the line formed by Captain Hart upon our right. Scarcely had the squadron gone, when Lieutenant Jemison made his appearance on the road, coolly walking along with his saddle on his back, as a workman carries his tools upon his shoulder returning from the labor of the day. His horse had fallen dead upon the skirmish-line, and he, determined to deprive the enemy of the equipments, had waited under fire until he could strip them off, and now began, more at leisure, to destroy them. As the major provided him with another horse, the firing grew again sharper and louder, and the balls with greater rapidity struck up the dust from the ground about us; and Janeway, rightly interpreting the indications, at once sent in that supporting squadron which had arrived so opportunely. But now he had left as a reserve only the squadron of Captain Robbins; and with anxious eyes he looked back over the hills for the approach of the squadron left on picket under Captain Malsbury.

At this time Colonel Taylor, knowing the force of the enemy opposed to us, and hesitating to compel a single small regiment to continue such an unequal fight, sent a message to Major Janeway, directing him to begin slowly to fall back. The major replied that to fall back would inevitably bring pursuit, which must occasion loss and might possibly cause a rout; that he thought that he could hold the ground until dark, and that, with the colonel's permission he would try; and, assured of his superior's approval, he addressed himself once more to the arduous duties of the field.

It was indeed a very anxious time. Major Lucas sent him word that the enemy was deploying against him a formidable line of infantry, and that their cavalry force was strengthening every minute; that many of his men had exhausted their ammunition, and that the next attack would certainly force him back; and yet Janeway had only a single squadron left, the advance of which would leave him bare of all support. Just at this moment, on the crest of the hill behind, Captain Malsbury appeared, forming his squadron as he came, and advancing at a trot to the assistance of his comrades. As he arrived upon the ground, dismounted men and stragglers with empty cartridge-boxes already began to emerge more and more numerously through the wood; the bullets from the long line of rebel infantry came thicker and thicker across the hill, wounding men and horses, even in the reserve; and another message was brought from Major Lucas that the enemy was charging, and that he had not the men to hold them. Then Janeway, with Robbins' squadron, went through the wood and met the rebel charge, while Lucas, under cover of their advance, withdrew those of his men who had expended their ammunition, and began to form them upon the flank of Malsbury.

Now, as the day drew towards its close, the fighting became fiercer than before. Scarcely had Malsbury taken the place of Robbins, when Hick, the junior captain of the squadron, received a ball in his leg which forced him to leave the field; and the missiles of the enemy penetrating the thin wood which screened the reserve, fell around them even more thickly than they did in the front.

In the early twilight, the enemy succeeded at last in getting a force around upon the flank; and, turning the right of Captain Gray, drove him and his men, fighting as they went, across a ravine, back to the point where Lucas was rallying his men. Through the trees upon this flank, a cross-fire was thus whistling above our heads.

Lucas, though conspicuous upon the skirmish line, on account of his cream-colored horse, had returned unscathed from that exposure. Often as he had been in action, and gallantly as he had always ridden to the front, he had passed without a scar through each fiery ordeal, and it seemed incredible that he, whose noble manhood so impressed itself upon all who knew him, should fall at last by the random bullet of an unseen enemy. Yet so it was. Retired from the scene of immediate conflict, out of sight of the enemy, and surrounded on every side by his men, a ball, whizzing through the wood, crushed into his brain, and without a word he fell to the ground a corpse.

He died as he lived, calm, heroic, silent. None but his comrades, can estimate the loss to them, for it was only to those brought very near him that the excellence of his nature could be known. They, in the midst of the contest against enormous odds, bore his body from the field, to be mourned over by the mother to whom he had been more than a son, and to her who had grown still nearer to his heart, though not yet a sharer in his life.

But, though the day was over, the work of death went on. Gray, taking the duty of Lucas, his lieutenants, Corneil and Rodgers, with such men as had been rallied and supplied with a round or two of ball, dashed into the wood to the assistance of the little force still struggling there. Though Rodgers was soon wounded, and McKinstry, Lame, Craig, Canse, Dye and Hughes had their horses shot beneath them, still they all staunchly stood their ground with Janeway, Robbins and the rest. Until the last gleam of light had faded from the sky, the stubborn Jerseymen kept the wood from the possession of the enemy; and even then, after every cartridge for carbine and for revolver had been expended, and when the rebels had slowly crept up upon the flank until they were firing on them from the rear, Robbins and Lieutenant Canse could only by reiterated orders persuade the second squadron to abandon the position which they so long had held.

As the little band steadily retired, Lieutenant Kinsley happened to diverge slightly from the track of those who had preceded him, and was thus alone upon the field. Just at that moment a bullet struck him in the shoulder and drove him from his saddle. In the noise of the fight he could not make himself heard; and though we held the ground for twenty minutes afterwards, his absence was not noticed. Thus, by an accident, we left him to be picked up by the enemy.

The rebels made an effort to occupy the wood and to debouch through it into the road to pursue our men; but the reserve which Janeway had persisted in retaining unbroken in spite of every apparent crisis, now justified the wisdom of his action. Galled for hours by a fire which it had been unable to return, it now opened upon the advancing enemy with such vindictive energy as to cow them back behind the cover, incapable of another movement to the front. The voice of their commanding officer was heard announcing that "The whole line will advance at a trot;" but no part of the line appeared inclined to obey the direction. Falling back to the height beyond, Malsbury again drew up his men prepared to resist any attempt of the rebels; but the column moved off the field without any molestation from the enemy, and he fell into his place in the rear without firing another shot. Lieutenant Kinsley, whom we recovered when we afterward re-occupied the ground, informed us that for half-an-hour after our retreat, the field was left unoccupied by the enemy; and that then, with skirmishers deployed and a long line of battle formed, the rebel infantry marched against the deserted position. In an hour from that time the whole of Ewell's Corps was camped upon the field of battle, having been detained by the First New Jersey Cavalry until it was too late to close upon the flank of the National Army.

The First New Jersey came out of this remarkable contest with the loss, wonderfully small under the circumstances, of four officers and thirty men; but seven officers and one hundred and thirty men had their horses killed or wounded; so that the casualties amounted to nearly one-half of the force engaged. The only prisoner lost was Lieutenant Kinsley, who was missing by accident, and not fairly taken from us by the enemy.

The First Maine, which had been cut off, succeeded in safely rejoining the army. Picking up a hundred men of the First Maryland, who had likewise been isolated from the division, the regiment attempted to pass through the neighborhood of Warrenton. At one time they were actually in the camp of a Virginia brigade, and were only saved by the presence of mind of Major Thaxter, who, favored by the darkness which had occasioned the error, deluded the rebel commander into the notion that they were a force sent to picket the roads beyond his line. Sweeping around to the North, and quietly reconnoitering the rebel force by the light of their own camp-fires, the Maine regiment, by a wide circuit succeeded in passing around them; and on their arrival at Bristow Station were able to communicate to General Meade the very information which he most required—a knowledge of the exact position of the enemy's advance.

Falling back along the road to Fayetteville, the First Brigade halted in a wood, near that village of a single house, the Sixth Ohio doing the needful picket duty. And here, with a strong protest against its veracity, must be introduced an account of a little incident of the bivouac, as related by the lieutenant-colonel of the Sixth Ohio. He declares that, as he remained wakeful, in the discharge of his duty, and the First Jersey rested, after its fatigue and fighting, in the woods behind him, suddenly, in the direction of the enemy, he heard the faint sound of the far-off crowing of a cock. After a brief pause chanticleer again essayed to sound his clarion note. He got out the first syllable of the crow, then there was a struggling sound, as of strangulation, and then all was silence. The lieutenant-colonel of the Ohio, moreover, solemnly avers that the *First Jersey had chicken for breakfast the next morning.*

In the midst of such conflicts it often happens that trifles occur, producing mirth from their contrast with the surrounding circumstances. It is vain to think to reproduce the effect of such incidents by their relation afterwards in cold blood; but, as the representation of the fight would be but partially correct without some mention of them, the insertion of one or two particulars may perhaps be admissible.

Captain Malsbury's squadron was composed, to a great extent, of recruits—men who had received, on enlisting, the large bounties offered at that time. Many of them had never been under fire; none of them had any idea of cavalry service, and all were intensely anxious not to disgrace themselves in the eyes of the older troopers. In the very heat of the action, while the bullets were falling thickly around them, a jolly voice would now and then be heard exhorting them to do three hundred dollars' worth of fighting, and announcing that now was the time for them to earn their money. One of them had scarcely got upon the field when he was hit by a rebel bullet. With all the vivacity of his French disposition he tossed his hand savagely above his head, and, boiling over with rage, answered, when ordered to the rear, "I won't; I want to shoot! I will shoot somebody for zis!" He staid until he had an opportunity to let off his carbine once or twice, and then went contentedly to the surgeon.

Another, who had probably been used to the close order and file firing of infantry, was heard solemnly exhorting his rear rank man to take care and fire *over his head,* though he did not explain what damage he expected the Southern Confederacy to receive from an aim at the planet Jupiter.

Another of them, relating his sensations under fire, admitted that he felt very much disposed to run. Once, he confessed that he actually began to draw his horse back from the ranks. As he did so he heard the captain cry, "Steady!" and glancing at that officer, saw that he was looking straight at *him*; whereupon he postponed his retreat until a better opportunity. Presently the bullets came still thicker, and he determined to try again. He looked, and there was the captain's eye still upon him. In short, whenever he wanted to run away he found the captain looking at him; so he gave the matter up, and fought for the rest of the time with distinguished gallantry.

The captain himself was not the least amusing man in the squadron. Every one who observed his behavior was struck with the ability displayed by him in making men, who had never been drilled or under fire before together, stand and fight in the midst of the confusion. Feeling that the safe retreat of the regiment had been secured by him, the first impulse of the officers was to go to him with congratulations. Scarcely, however, had they begun to refer to his share in the combat, when he interrupted, with a melancholy tone of indignant remonstrance: "I declare that I did the best that I knew how, and the men themselves are good enough; but what *can* an officer do when *his men do not know how to wheel by fours?*" The confusion that had naturally occurred when he attempted to change his ground so occupied his own thoughts that he fancied it must be prominent in the mind of everybody else, and not an opportunity could any one get to praise him or his men, so full was he of his grievance and his resolution to take the first chance to drill his men until they knew how to wheel back and forth in line.

During the whole of the next day, the thirteenth, the regiment was permitted to march as escort to the train, obtaining thereby a half ration of forage, the first since Saturday, and the last until the next Saturday, the poor horses having to do exhausting duty, even for full-fed animals. Rations, also, were given out, and a full allowance of ammunition, so that, at daybreak on Wednesday, we started to rejoin the brigade, at Auburn, in better condition for fighting than when we left it. On the road from Cattell's Station, we passed the headquarters of Generals Meade and Pleasanton, with the joint escort of the Sixth Regular and Sixth Pennsylvania Cavalry drawn up in line beside the staff; and, advancing half a mile, had our advanced guard fired upon and one of its horses killed. Captain Hart charged instantly the audacious outpost which had attacked him, forcing them to leave their cards and the confederate notes which they had staked lying on the ground, and in a few minutes had picked up a prisoner or two, belonging to Rosser's Brigade of rebel cavalry. The major, thinking it important to inform General Meade at once of the presence of an enemy so close to his headquarters, sent off, at the first shot, an officer of the regimental staff to carry the intelligence. The officer did not find General Meade's equanimity in the slightest degree discomposed by the announcement. He simply returned his advice to Janeway to drive the enemy at once, adding, to General Pleasanton, that the Second Corps ought to be on that road at that moment. In truth, before our advance could overtake any more of the rebels, Warren's line of skirmishers made its appearance, into whose clutches the gentlemen who ran away from us had fled, without possibility of evasion.

After the Second Corps had passed by the regiment rejoined the brigade, and soon was in its place participating in those clock-work-like alternations of retreat, halt, wheel, formation, deployment, which constitute the operations of the rear guard of an army.

A very beautiful display for the mere spectator is the steady, deliberate retrograde of a large force, in the face of the enemy. Nearest the main body march the infantry reserves, moving back from one commanding point to another, and facing to the rear at every halt. With equable movement, behind them is the long double or triple line of infantry skirmishers stepping along, with their wide intervals between man and man, yet preserving as perfect an alignment as if in close order on parade. Still further to the rear come the regiments of the cavalry rear guard, preserving carefully the distance between the infantry and themselves, and all moving simultaneously in obedience to the guidance of their general commander. Behind them, again, come the numerous reserves of the skirmishers, regulating their motions, in their turn, by those of the several regiments, while last of all the skirmishers themselves, chequered along the whole rear, alternately retire and wheel, as the reserves indicate to them the occasion so to act. To see the whole force, stretching over miles of country, thus passing steadily along, or wheeling into position, with one accord, like a wondrous piece of mechanism, moved by some mighty unseen power, is one of those magnificent military panoramas which are elevated to a grandeur almost sublime by their association with ever impending violence. When the sharp crack of the rifle and the sudden roar of the gun form the music of a march, beneath a canopy of thick white wreaths of smoke, the last touch of terror is added to a picture whose beauty is that of the angel of destruction.

As the rear guard passed over the crest of an eminence which commanded for more than a mile the line of the retreat, Colonel Taylor directed Major Janeway to retain his regiment in support of the line of skirmishers, and, taking command of the whole, to hold that position until the rest of the force had got out of range of artillery fire from that hill. Even while the squadrons formed beneath the cover of the rising ground the report of a gun reverberated against the distant woods, as the rebels threw shell after shell at our skirmishers to drive them from their ground. Keeping out of carbine range, the enemy used nothing but artillery, producing, of course, no effect upon our seasoned soldiers, though the approach of a shell through the air and the explosion which succeeds it are among the most horrible sounds invented by the art of man. All the while the left of the enemy could be discerned marching steadily around our right flank, until the danger of being cut off from retreat became painfully imminent.

At length the order came, and, breaking by fours, the regiment moved rapidly to the rear, followed at a sufficient interval by the skirmishers, and protected by them, we hastened to rejoin the column of retreat. Suddenly, miles in our front, sounded out the heavy boom of artillery, and smoke-wreaths rising directly in our way announced that the enemy had gotten before us. When we came within sight of the cavalry they were at a halt; but before we reached them they took the trot and dashed over the hills in front of us. Just then, coming to a point where the woods were more open, we saw, in fearful proximity to our flank, the line of the rebel skirmishers, and the cannon in our front sounded out more and more clearly. As we descended the hill toward Kettle Run the air above us rang with the whistle of minie bullets, and athwart the creek appeared the advancing enemy pressing to cut us off. Without a moment's hesitation, Captain Gray, commanding the regiment, with the officers of the leading squadron, dashed at the ford, commanded by the rifles of the enemy; but the passage of the regiment would evidently be attended by fearful loss. Beneath the arch of the railroad bridge stood an orderly, making earnest gestures, and an officer at once concluded that there was a practicable passage where he was standing. Calling to the regiment to follow, he changed his course toward the opening between the buttresses, and, though bullets flattened against the stones on either side, the whole body passing through, emerged in safety upon the other side, to be joined beneath the cover of the railroad embankment by those who had miraculously passed unharmed through the terrible fire at the ford. It was now but an easy passage to the main body, and in five minutes the regiment had again united with the brigade.

It was some hours before we heard from the troops detached with Major Janeway. Before he had come up the rebels were thronging across the road and over the line of railroad. Forming his skirmishers in column, he was preparing to charge right through, when an order came from Colonel Gregg to follow him across the railroad; and he therefore wheeled to the right, and formed a supplemental skirmish line on the right of the Second

Brigade. Here he held the enemy at bay till after night, losing several horses, and receiving himself a slight wound as a warning not to set himself up as a target for ball practice by Georgia riflemen.

Though the major was restrained from charging, an officer of the Sixth Ohio, sent with a squadron to communicate with him, performed the feat with remarkable success. Dashing under the railroad bridge which had saved the Jersey, he came upon a column of the rebels on the fair open ground, preparing to cross into the woods beyond the railroad. He was on them before they could prepare for resistance, and the whole party, four times as numerous as his own, threw down their arms and surrendered. If he could have paused he might have brought them all in; but having to go on with his message he was only able to select two and send them back to be questioned by the general. The rest he had to leave at liberty to take up once more their arms. The act, however, increased the nervousness of the rebels, and no doubt aided us in the maintenance of our ground upon the left.

The plan of the enemy had evidently been to push in between the rear guard and the main body, cutting off the former at the same moment when an attack should be made upon its rear; the whole force of the rebel army thus overlapping it, and pouring down upon the immense wagon train which it covered. By taking circuitous roads, Hill succeeded in striking the Second Corps at Bristow Station, and charged impetuously upon Webb's Division marching by the left flank along the hills above. Fortunately there was not a foot of the ground with which Webb had not made himself familiar, and he instantly remembered the admirable breastwork formed at that point by the line of the railroad. With a command not discoverable in any authorized tactics except those of emergency, he ordered his division, "By the left flank, double-quick to the railroad-cut, March!" and his men gained the cover just as the rebels began to rise the hill. Advancing their colors, they commenced to bob their caps above the ridge as if their heads would appear the next second, expecting to draw an ineffectual fire from our men; but Webb had seen that game played at Gettysburg and was prepared to meet it. By strenuous exertions he prevented all but about one-sixth of his men from firing; and thus, when the rebels hoped to spring upon a line of empty muskets, they were met by a point-blank discharge, which caused one of the most awful slaughters of the war. With an appaling shriek, this fine division of General Heath, the most dashing in their service, reeled back before the fire, and the whole plain was covered by a thronging mass of fugitives. Along the whole line of the Second Corps the same reception awaited them; and hurled back in confusion, these veterans ran for shelter, leaving five guns, five hundred prisoners, and all their wounded to be gathered in by the skirmishers alone of the Second Corps. If Warren had had a brigade of cavalry on hand he could have taken prisoners by the thousand instead of the hundred; but our cavalry was fully employed keeping back the advancing force of Ewell. Even when we arrived on the field our whole force had to be deployed at right angles with the line of the Second Corps to cover the space between them and Buford's train escort, so that the enemy could not annoy the train. Till late in the night our artillery kept up a duel with that of the enemy, each side firing at the flash of the other's guns, until our batteries succeeded in silencing the enemy's without themselves incurring any loss. Then nothing was heard through the darkness but the agonizing groans of some of the rebel wounded.

Without an opportunity of rest, the cavalry of General Gregg moved across to Brentsville, to assist General Buford in the protection of the wagon train; and after standing to horse almost all the night was again in motion hours before daybreak. Struggling along the narrow roads, up and down precipitous hill-sides, over which the tired mules were laboring painfully to drag the heavy wagons, the way blocked up at times by the stalling of a team in some muddy hollow or at some slippery bank, the troops filed slowly past in a column extending from Brentsville nearly to Bull Run. Even when, late in the afternoon, the division had halted in the fields beyond the Run, the First Brigade was not permitted to rest, for the enemy recklessly rode at the train in defiance of Buford, who sent for support as an advisable precaution. It was already sunset, and the gathering clouds rapidly brought on the darkness. The trains still filled the roadway to the ford, and along the steep banks of the stream the cavalry had to seek a crossing. Time after time the horses who attempted to ascend the precipitous hill-side, whose clayey soil was rendered slippery by the falling rain, slid back and tumbled headlong into the water; and it was not until the whole brigade had got drenched with splashing through the stream that a portion of them managed to effect a crossing. Up and down the sides of thickly wooded ravines, in an obscurity so deep that the ear alone could be the guide, the troops sought to pick their way into the road; and then such as succeeded had to exert all their horsemanship to escape collision with the line of wagons which hurried towards the ford. Happily Buford was able by himself to accomplish the repulse of the enemy: for the supporting troops of Gregg got so completely confused and astray that they could barely have defended themselves. At length, after the trains had all passed by, we returned again toward Fairfax Station, and at midnight were inducted into the smallest piece of woods ever occupied as a cavalry bivouac. Every step taken by the men was certain to bring them in collision, for in trying to avoid a horse they were sure to tread upon a sleeping man; and in such a situation, wet and too weary even to satisfy the cravings of hunger, the over-tasked troopers sank upon the ground to sleep. The next morning, sent to picket the Wolf Run Shoals on the Occoquon, the regiment enjoyed a period of comparative repose; and being joined by Major Janeway with his skirmishers, and some remounted men from the depot at Washington, the First Jersey was enabled to present a somewhat more formidable appearance. The night before it had dwindled down to *sixty* men present for duty,

Friday, Saturday and Sunday having been passed in quiet, on the evening of the last the regiment was once more in motion, going into bivouac at Fairfax Station a little after midnight. The nineteenth was spent in hard marching along the left flank of the advancing army, from Fairfax Station to Union Mills, at the Bull Run railroad bridge. Then, while the brigade moved toward Centreville, the First New Jersey diverged to the left, to examine the country in the direction of Brentsville, and below Manassas. In some small portions of the route we were able to follow country roads and distinguishable by-paths; but for most of the distance we were entangled in the low thickets of unreclaimed swamp lands, or lost amid the dark alleys of the untraveled forest. In the obscurity of the night, and in such a deserted region, it was only by toilsome reconnoissance and continued vigilance that we were enabled to ascertain with certainty the absence of outlying parties of the enemy; and it was not until midnight had passed, and horses and men were weary, that we struck into the old military road of the rebel cantonments of eighteen sixty-one, on our return to our point of departure. It had a strange, weird effect, while struggling along the broken and disused track, through the thickly-growing, solitary woods, to emerge every now and then upon the deserted huts which had lodged the brigades of the enemy during that first winter of the rebellion. They still stood by hundreds, so sequestered from the central point of the fortifications that our garrisons for two years had not found them convenient either for fire-wood or lodging; and there they will probably remain until they moulder into the soil, years after the rebellion itself shall have crumbled into nothingness.

The feelings of our weary men may be imagined when, on arriving at Centreville, they were told that the brigade had departed on the Gainesville road. The thought of a night march of fourteen additional miles was a terrible blow to men who were already almost dropping from their saddles; yet with scarcely a murmur the troopers prepared to continue on their journey. Scarcely, however, had we passed beyond the town, before we saw a line of fires on the border of Bull Run, and to our delight we marched into the camp of the brigade, when we had feared that they were twelve miles distant. Scrambling into our appointed position, amid tangled brush and fallen trees, we slept soundly and delightfully until the sound of réveille aroused us at sunrise to resume our march.

For two days Gregg's Division attended the slow marching trains along the turnpike road to Warrenton, surveying, as we passed, the ravages of the artillery among the trees and dwellings of Groveton, and the well-remembered localities of the Manassas fight, and at length, on the twenty-first, re-occupied the camp which we had left ten days before to fight the enemy at Sulphur Springs.

Lieutenant-Colonel Kester was here relieved from duty on the staff of General Gregg, and for the first time assumed command of the regiment which had long been expecting him.

With the usual alternations of picket duty, alarms, change of camping-ground, and ordinary routine of duty, affairs went smoothly on, until on the seventh of November there came a slight innovation upon the monotony of our life.

During the day, a vigorous cannonade in the direction of Rappahannock Station had indicated that hot work was there going on; and, on the arrival of the brigade, in compliance with orders, at Bealton Station, we learned of the brilliant success of Sedgewick and French at Rappahannock Station and Kelly's Ford. The next morning the First New Jersey was directed to escort the two thousand prisoners taken the day before, from Bealton to the cars at Warrenton Junction, whence they were to go by rail to Washington.

Among Sedgewick's prisoners were all the officers of a rebel brigade, from the colonel commanding to the lowest subaltern. Some of them were sulky and dignified, a few inclined to be abusive, but the majority behaved themselves like gentlemen in their adversity. Their astonishment was extreme at beholding the railroad, which they had, a fortnight before, utterly destroyed, already in running order to the Junction, with the track going down at the rate of miles a day toward the Rappahannock River. They assured us that they had calculated so certainly on its requiring three months to repair it, that they had built their winter quarters around Culpeper, secure in their own opinion that an advance on our part would be impossible before spring.

All the prisoners were warmly clothed, some wearing overcoats of English frieze, whose materials had run the blockade, and others in the common, homespun negro-cloth, dyed with the juice of the butternut or other vegetable tincture. Though these garments were not old, they already looked weather-beaten and shabby, the coloring matter rapidly fading into a dingy, dirty hue, which took away from the wearer all that military pride in his appearance which is so desirable in a soldier, and so conducive to cleanliness and good health. The majority were without overcoats, some even without blankets, a few carrying pieces of rag-carpeting as covering at night from the weather. The whole party was well shod, a new issue having evidently been made since their last movement. Though, man for man, they might not be considered equal to the troops that guarded them, they were generally effective-looking soldiers, and many of them very handsome men; and the two bodies were so nearly matched that accident would give either party the superiority. As is always the case, a strong spirit of kindliness was displayed by our men, awaking responsive feelings in the prisoners, and the march went on without any untoward incident or unpleasant collision.

After the prisoners had been delivered over to the provost marshal at Warrenton Junction, and a night's rest had refreshed the horses, the regiment returned to the brigade, which was ordered to picket, from Fayetteville as a centre, the whole country around Warrenton and Sulphur Springs. In this duty, guarding the communications of the army, which was again across the river, the time passed away, winter drawing nearer and nearer, yet no evidence being presented that the army was to take up winter quarters.

CHAPTER XI.

ACROSS THE RAPIDAN.

Nothing had been asserted by our friends the rebel prisoners with more frequency and confidence than their conviction that it would require two hundred thousand men to force the passage of the Rapidan. General Meade soon gave us an opportunity of testing the truth of their predictions.

With remarkable celerity and secrecy the different corps of his army were moved to the positions from which they were to advance upon the fords, without the enemy detecting in which direction the movement was to be made. Gregg's division of cavalry, on the extreme left, on Thanksgiving Day, the twenty-sixth of November, surprised the rebel pickets at Ely's Ford, and threw itself across the Rapidan; while, simultaneously, Sykes passed the stream on pontoons at Culpeper Ford, and other corps at points further to the right. Thus, before nightfall, the whole army was across the river, and, pivoting upon Raccoon Ford, was wheeling round against the right flank of Lee's position.

Gregg's Cavalry, still guarding the extreme left, halted for the night on a narrow by-road through the wilderness, leading across from Culpeper turnpike to the main road from Fredericksburg to Richmond; and the First Jersey, which had been left to cover the rear, was placed on picket to connect with Sykes' infantry. The night, though still, was intensely cold, and in the low-lying, open fields which formed the place of bivouac, the frost penetrated through all the blankets which the men could venture to remove from their horses; and around blazing fires of fence rails, without any Thanksgiving dinner, and but a poor pretence of supper, officers and men lay down to catch what sleep they could. The especial annoyance was that one side of the body roasted while the other froze, equilibrium only being restored when wandering parties of rebel cavalry ran by accident against our pickets, forcing us to expose the whole of our persons to the frost, in order to be prepared for the possibility of more serious attack.

The next morning orders came for the regiment to rejoin the brigade, which was in its turn in the advance of the division. Turning off into a still narrower cross-road, we made a strenuous effort to comply with the command; but it was soon made evident that the attempt was almost impossible of success. The by-road which the division was traveling was barely wide enough for an army wagon or for a column, two abreast; and on either side rose steeply-slanting hills, thick-set with scrubby saplings, briery bushes, and trees connected by hanging vines and creepers. Out of the road itself there was scarcely a spot of level ground; and wherever there was an opening among the trees there was sure to be a precipitous ravine or a stagnating swamp. Through this tangled maze of worthless timber the regiment had to force its way, endeavoring to pass a column which had the advantage of the open road, in order to gain our proper station.

The adjutant, a short man, led the way on his very small horse, through places which were almost impassable for larger bodies; and consequently, after three or four miles of travel, the lieutenant-colonel and half the regiment showed faces so severely scratched as to resemble Indian warriors in their war paint, rather than soldiers of a civilized community. Human energy could not hope to penetrate the increasing difficulties in front of us, and the colonel gave up the effort in despair. At that moment there was a gap in the column of the Second Brigade, half of which we had succeeded in outstripping; and the colonel, seizing the opportunity, led the regiment out into the road, waiting for more open ground before he should attempt to pass the remainder.

After a short march we emerged upon the plank road from Fredericksburg to Orange Court House, passing the head of the Fifth Corps, which was to follow our column. The greatest difficulty in the whole movement was occasioned by the character of the country, intersected by but very few roads, and entirely impracticable except in the roads themselves, thus forcing the troops to move in narrow columns, and delaying the promptness of necessary evolutions. An illustration of the evil was exhibited at once in our front. A small body of rebel cavalry, with two field pieces, held a position which commanded the plank road on which we marched. In a more open country the division would have swept over these men with scarcely a moment's halt or the trouble of formation; here it had to dismount a body of skirmishers and fight the rebels upon equal terms. At length the Third Pennsylvania and First Massachusetts dislodged the enemy, and the column advancing, gave us an opportunity to gain the rear of the First Brigade.

Though the rebels had been forced from their first position and the troops had succeeded in obtaining possession of ground sufficiently open to allow the regiments to form, yet beyond the few cleared fields around a little meeting-house and a couple of dwellings, the wilderness of woods once more covered the country. As our battery got into position to shell the woods beyond our skirmishers, the fire of small arms in our front increased in volume, and presently, from among the densest low-growing pines was heard a Southern yell, answered by a hearty Yankee cheer. Rebel infantry had come up and charged our dismounted men with the bayonet, only to be checked by the fire of the short but quickly-loaded carbines.

The firing grew sharper and sharper within the cover, extending off upon the flanks, and gradually approaching closer and closer to our position. Soon an aide-de-camp rode up with an order to Kester to send a squadron in dismounted to reënforce the skirmishers. Before the men had fairly left the saddle, another came ordering the addition of a battalion. Immediately afterward, Colonel Taylor himself rode up to Kester, saying, "Colonel, dismount your whole regiment and send them in as quickly as possible."

The First Pennsylvania on the left, the First Jersey on the right, into the thick-growing pines plunged the old troops of Bayard. As Janeway led in the Jerseymen he passed by the spot where Captain Crowninshield, of the Massachusetts, with his gallant little band of skirmishers, was clinging to the edge of the cover in defiance of the outnumbering infantry of the enemy. "Glad to see you," he exclaimed. "As soon as you get your men placed start a yell; we will take it up, and we will soon drive those fellows back again." Janeway nodded and hurried his men into line on the right. Then, with a volley that sounded more like that of an infantry line of battle than the scattering shots of carbineer skirmishers, the cheer was taken up from right to left, and forward dashed our fellows against the enemy. It took more than Southern steadiness to stand against New Jersey, Massachusetts and Pennsylvania, all emulous of distinction, and with a hasty fire the close line of rebel skirmishers fell back upon their support, leaving in the hands of our men more than forty prisoners, with their bayonets, and two or three officers in addition, the majority of whom fell into the hands of the fresher Jersey carbineers.

Lieutenant-Colonel Kester had, in accordance with the ordinary custom, remained behind when the skirmishers were ordered in; but his anxiety for his men soon got the better of his reticence. Edging closer and closer to the firing, he advanced as far as his horse could penetrate, and then, with a half apology to his adjutant, that he "must look in for a minute to see how things were going on," he sprang to the ground and plunged into the undergrowth. Just as he reached the skirmishers he thought there was a good opportunity for a charge. His sudden appearance caused a cheer to be raised by those who saw him, which was taken up along the line, and while the rebels were still startled by the sound he gave the word, "forward!" and the line pushed further on. Hart, in the centre of the line, refused to dismount from his horse, insisting that his legs were too short for bushwhacking. Keeping his seat by some mystical power, and making his horse break through the opposing branches, he cheered his squadron forward, maintaining a position well up with the foot men; and though the fire of the enemy was like a hail storm whistling among the bushes, and falling thickly even in the open ground to the rear, he and his horse came out of the action without a scratch on either.

With successive rushes the line advanced for full three-quarters of a mile, the bullets flying so fiercely that between the charges the men had to lie close to the ground, seeking every little shelter that was afforded by the saplings, stumps or casual mounds of earth. Some officer or man would start a shout; the others would catch it up; the rebels would falter, and on dashed the skirmishers, now reduced to only the Jersey and the First Pennsylvania, by the exhaustion of the ammunition of the rest. At last came a period of desperate struggle. Though every man hugged the earth as closely as he could, in the short period which the contest lasted twenty-seven officers and men were either killed or so wounded as to disable them. The loss of the enemy was greater than on our side, for their line of skirmishers had been crowded back upon their brigade line of battle until our bullets were aimed at either, indiscriminately. Jemison was shot through the heart; Gray had his hand shattered; Lame was almost stunned, and Hobensack was struck so violently by a piece of shell that he acted and spoke, for some minutes afterwards, like a man under the influence of liquor. All the while the artillery was in full play, the rebels firing at our guns, our missiles plunging into their line of battle. At last, after a vigorous rally on the part of the enemy, our men raised a cheer that rung far away over the field, and with one tremendous rush swept skirmish line, battle line and all before them for a quarter of a mile.

As the Fifth Corps had now come up and deployed its line of skirmishers, General Gregg permitted the cavalry to be withdrawn, after having displayed to General Sykes an exhibition of cavalry fighting entirely new to that officer's experience. In the confusion caused by our last charge, the desired opportunity was afforded to withdraw in comparative safety, though this operation must always be one of a very delicate nature. The only real risk incurred, however, was by Captain Penn Gaskell, of

Company F. Being among the last to fall back, he happened, in passing over a little clearing, to stumble against a root or hidden stump, which threw him forward on his face, causing his sword to spring out of the scabbard. The rebels made a rush to seize him, before he could recover himself, and he was pressed so closely that he was forced to leave his sabre on the ground. This and two dead bodies constituted the whole sum of the rebel captures from the Jersey.

It was a proud moment for the colonel when the regiment, after such a desperate fight, emerged from the cover in front of the Fifth Corps, with the line as regular as if just deployed upon the drill ground. With a high confidence that they had done justice to their reputation and served well their country, the sturdy troopers marched through the fire of the artillery to the position where their horses were awaiting them.

Even the men who had been kept out of the fight to hold the horses of the skirmishers found an opportunity to do some active service. As a regular battery of the Fifth Corps relieved Captain Martin's rifled guns, the rebel artillery succeeded in getting accurate range upon them. Before the pieces were wheeled into position, twelve horses had been shot down in the limber traces. The artillerymen, alarmed at such fearful execution, ran from the piece which had suffered most severely. The Jerseymen, who were holding the horses just behind the guns, saw the deserted twelve-pounder, and sprang to assist in serving it. Welcomed by a grim smile from the officer of the section, they quickly had it in position; and until the regiment returned from the front, they continued to aid the gunners.

The rebels did not advance against our infantry, and

General Sykes was not prepared to move his corps further forward; so that not a shot was fired except by the cavalry of General Gregg and one battery of the Fifth Corps. The hospitals showed that there had been no child's play going on, and each of the four regiments engaged had a heavy list of killed and wounded, without having lost one prisoner. The First Jersey, though last engaged, was in so hot a place that its list was heaviest of all; and in Lieutenant Jemison it lost one of the most zealous and efficient officers in the service.

Retiring to Parker's Store, the point at which the division had emerged upon the plank road that morning, the brigade picketed to cover the left flank of the army, and the First Jersey was permitted to obtain that rest which it required after the watchfulness of the night before and the exhaustion of the combat.

The next afternoon, leaving part of the brigade on duty at Parker's Store, the Jersey, with the rest, crossed by a very bad country road to the Wilderness Tavern, upon the other plank road to Culpeper, and there it was met the next morning by wagons from the rear, bringing to it a scant supply of forage, ammunition and necessary rations.

While the quartermaster and commissary sergeants were still busied with the distribution of the supplies, an officer galloped rapidly in from the brigade picket at the fork of the plank-roads; and immediately afterwards another officer, high in authority, rode up, calling to the men to get out in line to receive the enemy, who were charging in force. The poor teamsters with their wagons entangled among the trees and picket-ropes of the camp, began to struggle desperately to get out upon the road and to hasten out of danger, and several of the colored servants were in the act of rushing off in a panic stricken crowd. Whether the confusion might not have extended futther is a very doubtful question; but happily Colonel Kester did not wait for its solution. Walking coolly about on foot, he checked the teamsters and kept the men in order while hurrying their preparations to the utmost; and before a crowd would have had time to ask what was the matter, he had the regiment in line of battle, and the wagons loaded, moving in good order from the ground.

The alarm in front was occasioned by a misapprehension. A charge had indeed been made on the other road, and some of the pickets driven into the First Pennsylvania post had reported that the enemy in force was following them. Lieutenant-Colonel Gardiner had sent an officer to report *this report* to Colonel Taylor; but as transmitted the message had seemed to imply that the rebels had already charged the Pennsylvania pickets. Thus we had been hurried out by an alarm which very unnecessarily spoiled the dinner of the regiment. Unfortunately too, there was no opportunity to return to finish that meal. There was danger enough on the other road, and we had to go to meet it. The officer in command of the troops at Parker's Store had left unguarded the very path by which there was the greatest danger of surprise. The captain in charge of the other picket posts, on his own responsibility, had sent one of his men as a vidette in that direction; but just as the man drew near to his appointed station, he was driven in by the charging enemy, and three rebel brigades, under Wade Hampton, came dashing into the unprotected camps. The men of the Third Pennsylvania and First Massachusetts fought as well as men could under such a disadvantage; but with the loss of many prisoners, they were quickly driven from the road which they were stationed to cover. Lieutenant Gregg, of the division staff, had ridden down to the position but a few minutes before, and seeing the importance of warning the general, he dashed off toward the Second Brigade. Running the gauntlet of the rebel fire and outstripping their pursuit, he gave the Second Pennsylvania timely notice of the attack, and then hurried to the general. While a squadron of the Second Pennsylvania, without waiting for assault, started up the road toward the enemy, General Gregg assumed command of the Second Brigade, and quickly had them ready to receive the coming adversaries. Splendidly did the Pennsylvania squadron do their work. Without drawing rein part of them rode right through the enemy, hurling them aside from the plank road, and cutting out many of their prisoners; while the remaining portion stopped in the middle of the enemy, took a number of them prisoners, and wheeling into the cross road to the left came safely into the advancing squadrons of the Jersey.

While we pressed closer and closer toward the road at Parker's Store, the Second Brigade engaged the main body of the enemy, who had hoped to come down upon the rear of our infantry position; and before the infantry supports could come into the engagement the rebels were compelled to fall back with loss, relinquishing the attempt so auspicious in its commencement.

While this was going on, the First Jersey had formed in an admirable position to resist an attack, and had pushed Lieutenants Hughes and Craig forward to feel the enemy. Lieutenant Craig, with the advance, soon came upon some stragglers who were engaged in plundering the camps of our troops; and hovering round on every side, soon found out that the enemy were retiring. Knowing that we were too weak to make a successful attack upon them, and that the hour was already too late for an advance to the former position, he contented himself with bringing in his prisoners and making his report; and Lieutenant Hughes following his example, they retired to a proper position to picket for the regiment, leaving the road itself only watched by an occasional patrol. In the darkness which had now come on, and the intense cold of the weather, the colonel also refrained from moving forward; so, bivouacking for the night where it had formed, the regiment leisurely advanced to Parker's Store by the light of the next morning.

Provisions were now running very short, especially in the messes of the officers, and to avert the unpleasant appearance of starvation, Colonel Kester directed Captain Robbins to reconnoitre the country toward the enemy with an eye to its resources, both military and commissariat. Too much credit cannot be given to that gallant young officer for the efficient manner in which he performed the duties entrusted to him. Not finding a sufficiency of intelligence and provisions outside the lines of the enemy, he pursued the object of his expedition within the enclosure of their pickets. Driving back the enemy and capturing every turkey, chicken, goose, duck, pig and sheep about their quarters, he bore off their dinners triumphantly before their eyes, returning without the loss of a man and with the means for two days' luxurious living.

On the evening of the first of December, a long line of infantry and artillery commenced to pour along the plank road to the rear, past the position where our brigade was drawn up to guard the flank and rear. All the night, from ten o'clock till daybreak, we followed the retreating column, as it by little and little passed over the road, delayed by the frequent defiling of regiment after regiment to cross the pontoon bridges at the ford. At length it disappeared from in front of us, leaving behind a throng of sullen stragglers. These men, fagged out with sleeplessness and numb with cold, seemed utterly careless of the danger of capture by the enemy. Though they knew that two miles more of travel would bring them safely across the river, where rest and rations waited them, they seemed unable to make the exertion necessary to travel so far. Some could not even be beaten into motion, one man, especially, muttering that he might as well freeze and starve on Belle Isle as anywhere else, and throwing himself stubbornly on the ground. Leaving two or three hundred men like this soldier behind, the rear-guard saw them fall into the hands of a few rebel cavalry and gathering bushwhackers; and they probably by this time have had ample opportunity to compare the exposure and privations of a campaign with those of a rebel prison.

Desperately weary, officers and men, as soon as they had crossed the river, threw themselves upon the ground and went fast to sleep. After an hour or two of rest they went more regularly into camp, under cover of a wood, and remained there until Friday, picketing Culpeper Ford. Soon after, the whole division moved across the Rappahannock to Bealton Station, and on the twelfth the First Brigade once more reëntered the familiar old town of Warrenton, where at last it was permitted to go into winter quarters.

CHAPTER XII.

WINTER QUARTERS AT WARRENTON.

After one night of bivouacking in the rain, during which the officers found their beds transformed into pools of water whose temperature approximated towards zero, which state of things induced Captain Boyd, who was not philosophical, to remonstrate with Captain Penn Gaskell, his bed-fellow, for turning round, and so disturbing the water, which had got warm in their immediate vicinity, the regiment went actively to work to house itself for the winter. On every side sounded the ringing strokes of the axe and the thundering rush of the tall chestnut trees toppling to the earth. The timber, split into slabs, was built up at once into the walls of neat looking huts, which soon, in double and triple rows, lined the streets of the battalions. Roofed with shelter tents and with every crevice plastered with the stiff red clay which formed the soil, the buildings were rapidly made impervious to wind and rain, while scouting parties from the different companies impressed every loose board to be discovered within five miles of the cantonment. Bricks for fire-places and chimneys became the next object of inquisition, and the supply was found to fall far short of the demand. But in cases like this political economy informs us that an equilibrium is sure by some means to be attained, and the resources of a cavalryman are undoubtedly superior to those of an abstract theorist.

On the hill above the camp there stood that anomaly in a slaveholding society, a neatly built brick school house, disused at present, and offering a perpetual temptation during the frosty nights of December to the men shivering beneath their blankets in their fireless cabins. Positive orders had been issued against wanton demolition of buildings, so it is certain that the First New Jersey Cavalry *could not* have assisted the hand of time in the destruction of this edifice; yet it is undoubtedly true that it crumbled fast away, as chimneys magically uprose throughout the camp, until, as its roof fell in, every hut was provided with a sufficient means of warmth for its inhabitants.

While this work was going on huge piles of pine logs were prepared as flooring for the stables, and as soon as there was a relaxation of the frost, on ground properly smoothed and sloped, a dry and strong layer of logs was placed along the picket ropes, affording a firm standing place for the horses. No covering could be procured for them, however, and through the wind, the rain and the snow they had to remain exposed to the weather. To save the cost of a few tarpaulins the lives of many horses, worth thousands of dollars, were sacrificed during the winter.

Though the men were comfortably housed they were not left in idleness. In addition to arduous picket duty, every week saw the departure of several scouting parties to sweep the country around and to guard against any near approach of the enemy. Incessant vigilance had to be exercised against guerrillas, and squadrons kept always under saddle, ready to dash out on the slightest alarm. Whether it would not have been more economical to do the main picket work by a brigade of infantry, and retain the cavalry for other service, with an eye to their efficiency in the spring, is a subject which has not yet met with consideration by the ruling spirits of our military organization.

Still, with all this, winter quarters was a time of rest. The mere fact of having a comfortable cabin to retire to, where wet clothes could be removed and dry garments substituted; where cleanliness and decency could be preserved, and the hours free from duty could be spent in reading or social relaxation, was a great advance upon the publicity and listlessness of the bivouac. Those long, purposeless hours of idleness which make the breaks of active campaigning so wearisome and corrupting were here exchanged for lively games or pleasant studies. The facilities for intoxication were as small as they can ever be among a crowd of soldiers, and many who had been habituated to drink sought for other resources to beguile the passing time. A depot for the sale of books, periodical magazines and daily papers was established in Warrenton, at which the soldiers deposited much of that money which might otherwise have gone for drink; and sutlers, seldom seen by cavalry in the field, made their appearance with the supplies most needed by the men. Regular food and regular hours took the place of the precarious rations and sudden vicissitudes of the campaign; and good order and proper discipline pervaded every department. Gregg's cavalry can point to the town of Warrenton as a proof of the high character of the command. Not a citizen was deprived of his domestic privity or quiet enjoyment of his household rights. Disorder was kept out of the streets; no man was wronged; no woman was insulted. The people had learned by experience to submit to the needful restraints and privations attendant on military occupation, and beyond these nothing was demanded of them. As an almost unprecedented instance of good behavior, it may be stated that poultry fed around a house adjoining the Massachusetts' camp without a fowl being abstracted; and even cows went to and from pasture with no interruption beyond an occasional milking.

The embarrassment of the inhabitants was aggravated by the behavior of their avowed friends to a degree exceeding the inclinations of their enemies. But for the guerrillas, the restrictions placed upon them would have been less strict and the supply of their necessities more abundant; and the irregular attacks, which only cost us a little increase of vigilance, brought upon them many actual privations. There were few heads of families in Warrenton and its vicinity who would not have welcomed the intelligence that Moseby had disappeared from that region of the country.

There was scarcely a family in the town which was not under obligation to some officer of the brigade for something beyond the ordinary courtesy of a stranger. The natural instincts of humanity and manly generosity were allowed by National officers and soldiers to flow forth in a thousand forms to soften the inevitable hardships of people really imprisoned within the town. The Virginians, though marvellously ignorant, prejudiced, and narrow-minded, are a people of kindly impulses and quick sensibilities, prompting them to a responsive good feeling towards those who went out of their way to do them service. Yet they actually were afraid to admit the existence of such feelings, or to exhibit them without a sort of perpetual protest. The tyranny of public opinion and the system of *espionage* which had become an institution of the slave-holding society, made them dread to do anything which their friends, secure from danger, would comment on unfavorably and pronounce to be tampering with the invaders of Southern soil. Every instance of common courtesy was published in some Southern paper with coarse and brutal comments, awaking bitter feelings against the persons accused in the minds of the Southern soldiery. It speaks well for human nature and the prospects of a future union that in spite of all these opposing influences, the kindlier feelings became constantly stronger and more active.

Among the officers themselves there grew up a pleasant and wholesome social intercourse. Club-rooms and reading-rooms were established in the town as common meeting places of the officers of the various regiments; and the presence of the wives and relatives of some of them imparted that refinement which is so apt to be lost in a society composed exclusively of men. The character of the chief officers of the division and the brigades discountenanced that vulgar dissipation which is the common bane of military life; and in the First Jersey, especially, the head quarters of the regiment set a commendable example of sobriety and decency. When regular habits resumed their sway, that religion, which is, happily for the nation, so much a part of the regular habit of an American citizen, began to assert more distinctly its influence over the thoughts and feelings, which had been somewhat dulled to its power during the life for the day of the campaign. The Christian Commission established a distributing agency in the town, which formed a nucleus for the concentration and extension of the religious element throughout the division. The rector of the Episcopal Church, who alone of all the ministers had remained at his post faithfully through all the troubles of the time distributing to his people the bread of life, continued his services, which were attended by large numbers of the officers and men; and the chaplain of the First New

Jersey, in addition to frequent services in the regiment, was directed by General Gregg to hold a special service for the brigade every Sunday afternoon in the church in Warrenton. It may be hoped, therefore, that the winter quarters were not void of spiritual profit to some of the assembled souls.

The system of furloughs upon reënlistment had also an excellent influence upon the moral tone of the division. The satisfaction of that longing to revisit the home which for more than two years they had not seen, cheered and softened the spirits of the war-worn troopers; and enriched by the bounty of the government, they were able to leave their families well provided against want when they once more returned to duty. The soldiers, who had for a month felt the wholesome influences of home restraints and habits, came back to the army prepared to profit by every assistance to good works, every safeguard against temptation; and a strength to encounter those trials which had conquered home habits at their first enlistment was secured to them for their future term of service. The great fault of our military administration at the commencement of the war was the lack of a proper system of furloughs; and even the partial extension of them to the men during the last two winters saved the army the loss of thousands by desertion.

It has been stated that there was a constant preparation against surprise maintained during the whole winter; and a characteristic instance of the nature of the danger occurred in the month of January.

Lieutenant Mountjoy, a very daring partisan and favorite officer of Major Moseby, succeeded, in command of a party disguised as a patrol of the First Maine Cavalry, in seizing a picket relief of Company A upon its rounds, and hurrying off seven of the men as prisoners. Before he had galloped half a mile, Lieutenant Hobensack had Company E upon their heels. At full run, both troops raced along the road to Salem, the rebels trying to distance their pursuers, while Hobensack strained every nerve to overtake them. Discharging their carbines and revolvers to let the prisoners know that rescue was at hand, Company E pressed as hard upon the rear of the enemy as their hard-worked horses would permit, taking advantage of every little check to the enemy's speed to close a little nearer to their flying body. Presently one of the prisoners succeeded in cleverly throwing his horse as he rose at a ditch, risking his neck, but gaining his liberty. Immediately afterwards, four others pulled their horses short up, in defiance of their guards, and wheeled towards Hobensack's protection. Mountjoy, enraged at their escape, turned after them, firing his pistol, until the pursuers almost reached him; and then, by the speed of his horse, managed to regain his own troop. The other two prisoners were too timid to risk a race for liberty, and Hobensack's horses were too tired to overtake the enemy; so, with the rescued men, he returned again to camp.

On the seventeenth of February, one of the bitterest days of the year, when the Potomac River froze over firmly in a few hours, a scout was ordered from the First Brigade. A cutting wind had been blowing all day, and was still howling through the camp, when at ten o'clock Lieutenant-Colonel Kester received a command to take one hundred and fifty of his own men, one hundred of the First Pennsylvania, and fifty each of the Third Pennsylvania and Sixth Ohio, in light marching order, with one day's rations, and proceed with them to fulfill instructions given him by General Gregg.

Fortunately the violence of the wind subsided as the detachments issued from camp, for otherwise a number of the men must have been frozen to death; and as it was, the bitter cold penetrated their clothing until it numbed their limbs as they sat on horseback. To keep themselves alive, officers and men dismounted and tramped on foot over the road, many of them walking twenty miles in the course of the journey. On one occasion Sergeant Darris, of Company K, noticed a man of Company B dismount from his horse so numb as to be unable to stand or walk, who, with the natural tendency of one overpowered by cold, insisted on being permitted to lie down to sleep. Darris saw the only remedy. With sabre and hand he stood over the man, thrashing his blood into circulation, until the power to walk returned. Then, with his body tingling from the vigorous applications of the sergeant, he once more joined the column, and soon felt very thankful for the summary style of treatment which had undoubtedly saved his life. Humanity brought a reward to Darris; for this exercise had so warmed him that he considered thrashing a recruit a sovereign protection against the severest frost.

Passing through Salem, the column continued on into Manassas Gap, and turning into a mountain road, plunged into the rugged recesses of the hill-country. In that coldest time of the night, the period preceding dawn, they came to a mountain stream, on which a crust of ice had formed just too weak to bear the horses. The poor animals, slipping, and sliding, and breaking through, became frightened and restive to a degree that seriously delayed the column; and after they had once passed across, the guide, discovering that he had missed the road, compelled them again to countermarch and recross it.

The men, cold, wet, and fretted by the delay, began to grow discouraged, and gave vent to little murmurs of discomfort; but in a very few moments their spirits took a sudden turn. Colonel Kester, dividing his force, giving the First Jersey to Captain Hart, and retaining the other men with himself, pushed on into the very nest of the guerrillas.

Hart carried his detachment promptly forward along the route assigned to him. At the first house they lighted upon two of Moseby's men, quietly in bed, while another escaped in his shirt, leaving his outer garments and even his boots behind him. The farm was fully stocked with domestic fowls, which the men at once began to appropriate, their declaration having been, on leaving camp, that if they did not get guerrillas they would certainly get turkeys; but Captain Hart, having a chance at the guerrillas, checked their pursuit of the other game before the alarm had spread over the country. Dividing his men into three divisions, he kept them in constant motion, one after the other, striking different points, and reaching one place before the alarm had been communicated from those adjoining. In this way he succeeded in bagging fifteen of Moseby's men, and a much larger number of their horses, arms and equipments.

Lieutenant Lame, in the course of his perquisitions, put up a covey of game which he was not hunting. Opening a bed-room door, he found himself in the presence of six young women, in very decided *deshabille*, just, in fact, as they had sprung from bed. With combined eloquence of shrieks and blushes, they implored him to give them time to put on more seemly attire; but Lame philosophically assuring them that he was a married man, and therefore not at all embarrassed by the situation, in spite of their indignation at the idea of men being secreted in their apartment, persisted in extracting two guerrillas from the closet, to the great astonishment, of course, of the ladies.

Lieutenant Hobensack also uncarthed prizes from very curious hiding-places. One man was found beneath the bed of an old, rheumatic negro. Another was secreted within a pyramid of hoop-skirts, which was not at the time, however, as some have said, part of the actual attire of a lady. In another house, a woman shrieked at the idea of rising from her couch while a stranger was in the room; but, instructed by an acquaintance with the works of Byron, the searchers were inexorable, and a rebel was discovered beneath her mattress. Scarcely a house was visited without such scenes being repeated; and after a couple of hours' work, the two detachments again united, having secured twenty-eight prisoners, more than fifty horses, and a small arsenal of revolvers and sabres.

The colonel visited the place where Moseby was expected to be that very night, and where a party had assembled to meet him, in honor of his promotion to the rank of lieutenant-colonel; but the partisan's usual good luck attended him. The intense cold of the weather induced him to remain over night at Luray, instead of pushing on as he had intended, and this accidental change of purpose alone saved him from our hands.

As our troops started on their return, the alarm had spread through the country, and numbers of the guerrillas hovered around our rear, seeking a chance to avenge or rescue their companions; but Captain Hart, who had the rear-guard, was more likely to take them than to be himself a victim. They managed in the first dash to get a bullet through his left arm; but in return he gave them a volley which knocked over their leading men and horses, and sent the party to the right-about. Later in the day, they attempted a charge, actually galloping up as if they intended to attack. Hart wheeled his squadron to receive them, and as they came, charged to meet them. Just as our men began to think that the rebels really would fight, they broke and ran, the last seen of the party showing them half a mile away, still galloping as if an army were at their heels.

During the whole time of the running fight, our men beat the guerrillas at their own game, well-mounted marksmen dropping from the column, waiting till the rebels drew near to take them, and then firing into the enemy with sure aim and galloping back to our rear-guard. Thus the pursuit by the rebels cost them an additional loss. Hart got safely into camp, though his arm was quite painful before he could get it dressed, feeling, as did the whole detachment, that the result of the expedition compensated for all its pains and privations.

CHAPTER XIII.

THE BATTLES OF THE WILDERNESS.

Early in the month of April our pleasant winter quarters around Warrenton were broken up, and the First Brigade of Gregg's Division was transferred to Three-Mile Station, on the railroad between that town and the junction with the Orange and Alexandria road. As much of the camp equipage as could be conveniently transported was carried along, the men looking more like traveling pedlars with their packs, than like veteran troopers on the march. They felt, however, that the serious work of the campaign was not yet to commence, that there would still be cold nights and rainy days to be encountered in their new quarters; and bitter experience had taught them not to be too careless in their provisions for encountering these disagreeable incidents of military life. Thus, though their huts and fire-places were left behind, they held fast to their extra clothing and blankets, the old soldiers calculating that for six miles their horses could bear the additional weight, the new recruits loading themselves down without any speculation on the subject. Thus, even under their light shelter-tents, the men found themselves able to keep themselves comfortable, and the number of sick continued to be in the same remarkably small proportion to the well, that had been so noticeable during the winter.

In the new camp the work of preparation for active service was carried on with energy. Constant drill revived the knowledge which had been fading from the memories of officers and men through the hard service of the campaign and the repose of winter quarters; frequent and rigid inspections disclosed whatever deficiencies might exist in the clothing, armament and equipment of the men, which were at once carefully supplied. The dismounted men of the division were organized into battalions under the superintendence of Major Beaumont, whose abilities for such work had frequently been proved; and they were made to act as guards for the train, which otherwise might have required details from the mounted troopers. In a word, the whole force was in fine condition for service, when, at the end of the month, it was ordered across the Rappahannock and placed upon the left of the army.

Now, while the drills went on, all superfluous baggage was reduced in a way that proved that the real work was at hand. Nothing was retained that was not absolutely essential, officers reducing their own stock, and taking from the men everything that brought their equipment above proper marching and fighting weight. Each man was obliged to pack properly after an established pattern, into which nothing non-essential was allowed to enter; and all men, old and new, made to feel the restraints of military life during the campaign.

At two o'clock on the morning of the fourth of May, after a night of marching and open bivouac, the regiment, leading the column of the division, approached Ely's Ford on the Rapidan. The night was dark, and the air in the hollow near the river very cold and chilly, as Major Janeway, with the advance guard, cautiously drew near the bank without alarming the rebel vidette. Under the guidance of one of our most enterprising scouts, who had just returned from a reconnoissance, Lieutenant Craig, with the men of Company H., stole quietly down to an unguarded point on the river, and waded through the almost freezing water, the men carrying their arms and ammunition above their heads. Creeping up the hill-side, they plunged into the woods, aiming for the rear of the rebel reserve picket fire. In five minutes more the whole party would have been in their power, when, the head of the Second Corps of infantry having closed upon the rear of our division, General Gregg was compelled to move forward without delay. It was more important to get promptly across the river than to surprise and capture a small party of the enemy. A shot from the vidette on the river gave the alarm, which was at once succeeded by a hurried flight on the part of the enemy, who dashed back towards Fredericksburg, closely followed by Captain Brooks with Company K. Half a dozen men and horses were overtaken, but the rest escaped.

Past the old Chancellorville ground, with its low breast-works and bloody memories, the column proceeded along the plank road towards Fredericksburg, encountering nothing but a few cavalry, who, from a respectful distance, observed its motions. Then, after manœuvering to cover the advance of the Second Corps into the Wilderness, the division picketed for the night the roads leading to Fredericksburg and Todd's Tavern.

Along a narrow, rugged road we moved late on the morning of the fifth, and about noon approached Todd's Tavern, the junction with the road to Spottsylvania taken by Wilson's Cavalry and the Second Corps. When we arrived there, the Second Corps was rapidly counter-marching, to form connection with General Warren, who had been attacked furiously by Hill. The rebels anticipating our movement around their right, had hurried from their intrenchments to attack us before it was completed. The Third Cavalry Division, vigorously charged by General Rosser, had given way, and were falling back hastily upon their supports. For a short time our flank was in more danger than the enemy's. As Wilson came back along the road, General Gregg hurried his own men forward through the tangled woods, to cover them and repel the enemy.

Drawing up the First New Jersey on the first cleared ground, General Gregg ordered Colonel Kester to send a squadron up the road, and to follow himself in support. As Captain Hart, with the first squadron, trotted rapidly past the men of the Second New York, the last of Wilson's division to leave the field, he came suddenly upon the enemy, rushing down upon the fugitives, and startlingly near to our position. Without a moment's hesitation, Hart charged, trusting to the freshness of his horses and the spirit of his men to make up for any deficiency of numbers. A scattering volley from the enemy, by which Lieutenant Michener and one or two men were disabled, had no effect in checking the onset; and then, broken and disorganized, the rebels hurried back toward the main body. Through the woods and past some open ground to the right, the squadron, without support or reënforcement, drove the Seventh Virginia; and as the rebel supporting column appeared, it broke into skirmishing order and retreated, steadily fighting as it went. While yet in the wood, it was joined by Colonel Kester heading the regiment, who, deploying additional skirmishers, advanced with a cheer and a rapid fire. Again the enemy gave ground béfore the impetuosity of the attack; and the fierceness of our fire, the superiority of our weapons and the harmonious coöperation of our men giving us an advantage which the numbers of the enemy could not overcome; and with this skirmish line of two hundred and fifty men we actually bore back the effective force of the whole opposing brigade.

But when the colonel looked for his supporting squadrons, upon whom he had relied as a reserve, he found that he had nothing left under his command but the dozen men who formed the color guard. In fact the general had never expected or intended us to do more than check the enemy's advance, while he was forming his line behind us in readiness for the serious engagement; and therefore to supply a vacancy in the main line, Brigadier-General Davies had hastily stopped the three rear squadrons and formed them in the chosen position. Nevertheless, we were in for a fight, and must, of course, fight just as hard as we could; so the colonel formed the color guard upon the road to give the appearance of the support that was not in existence. By charging this small body with an especial flourish of the battle-flag, the skirmish line of the enemy was driven back, and our own rapidly advanced; for though skirmishers will often hold their own very well, or yield but slowly to an attack from a similar force, it is almost impossible to keep them unbroken and firm before a charge in solid formation. Though the rebels had got their artillery in position and were dusting the road with canister, our line kept advancing and pressing upon theirs, until we came upon a line of dismounted men behind which their mounted troopers were forming. As we felt the check of this discovery, a rebel colonel dashed forward with a cheer, followed by the whole mounted force under his command; and now we proved the truth of the doctrine above stated with respect to the stability of the skirmish line. Back through the woods we went followed at full speed by the charging enemy, until Captain Malsbury, throwing his squadron into line by the side of the road, met the charge by a close volley from his carbines. As the report rang out the color-bearer, Dalziel, wheeled his guard with a wave of the battle-flag, and, imitated by the men right and left, rode against the enemy. Once more over the same ground the contest raged, growing fiercer as the men's blood heated in the fever of battle, and their carbines gave a sharp ring as they were discharged with increased rapidity. Again the rebels charged, their skirmish line overlapping ours on both flanks, and their main body looking thick and dark upon the road. In vain the colonel held his ground to the last moment, until the colonel of the Sixth Virginia was almost upon him, and General Davies, who had come to the front, shouted to the men. The old soldiers knew that there would be no general rally until there was a support at hand; as the sense of strength which a soldier has in united effort makes him rather shrink from individual independent exertion. The officers, therefore, as a rule, devoted their attention to keeping their men sufficiently together and in line, to enable them to take advantage of any accidental opportunity for resistance; and in the meantime they yielded to the current of retreat. For several hundred yards our men were pushed back and back and back, often at a gallop, until they came in sight of Hobensack's squadron, and the Sixth Ohio Cavalry. Then Dalziel turned, and waving the colors charged towards the startled pursuers. Our skirmishers wheeled with one accord, and with a wild cheer the whole body made a simultaneous and resistless charge. Without a halt or a check, on they swept, over the dead and wounded rebels, crushing before them every attempt at a rally, and frightening into flight the dismounted carbineers who had before stayed their advance. Over the rude barricade behind which had been planted the artillery now in rapid retreat, through woods and across fields, that desperate advance continued, until the rebels hurried across Corbin's Bridge over the Po, and made the line of that river their defence. Instead of closing upon our flank and engaging our division in its defence, they were pressed back again upon their own by the enthusiasm and good fortune of that portion of our regiment.

Then when it was evident that the rebels would attack us no more, and that we were not to attempt to drive them from their position, Captain Hart inquired for the regimental surgeon. A bullet had passed through his thigh early in the engagement, but he had remained in the saddle doing his duty until the termination of the fight.

In a combat of the discursive character of this struggle there is little opportunity for the principal commander to direct the movements that take place. He can do little but make himself a central figure, giving an impulse and guidance to those immediately within his reach, occasionally riding from point to point along the line, saying a word of encouragement or counsel, and trusting to his officers to second his efforts and coöperate with his motions. On this field, therefore, much of the success and unanimity of our action was owing to the individual skill and judgment of the different officers, watching every variation in the current of the fight, helping each other at the critical times, and directing the energies of the men whenever there was occasion. Having perfect confidence in one another, each felt able to give his whole mind to his own especial work, and therefore it was thoroughly performed. In no other way could so small a body of troops have maintained their ground so long under such a heavy fire, with so severe a loss, and have finally driven back so superior an adversary. Of the first squadron alone there were three officers and sixteen men killed and wounded, and the loss of the three squadrons engaged was nearly fifty, without any prisoners.

While we were thus closely engaged, the Massachusetts regiment, a battalion of which was ready to cover us, lost several valuable men by the artillery fire of the enemy, and Martin's battery, which had seriously annoyed the enemy during the action, had one or two horses injured by the return fire. At the same time, the First Pennsylvania, which had been thrown out on another road, engaged the enemy with equal success, but with a loss much less than that suffered by the New Jersey. The Second Brigade, which was in reserve, did not come into action at all. Great and deserved credit was given to General Gregg for the brilliant conduct of the troops under his command; and General Sheridan himself came upon the field and offered him his congratulations. The hospital showed how severe had been the contest, and General Sheridan stopped there to inquire into the condition and well-being of the wounded. Then and always he showed himself to be a man whom his soldiers could love as well as trust.

It was very convenient for us that the army had entered the field with such a superabundance of clothing and blankets, for all along the road the infantry had thrown down their extra lading, thus affording us means to make the wounded comfortable. The inhabitants had gathered up a quantity, thus sparing us even the trouble of collection, and no wounded man had to lie exposed to the cold and damp, as is too often their misfortune after a battle.

Fortunately, also, we did not lose so many horses as we did men, and by drafting from the dismounted battalion we could show a diminution only of about twenty-five or thirty in our effective force. Of the officers, Hart and Michener were the only ones disabled, Wynkoop losing only a portion of his ear, and the adjutant, though struck with some fragment of canister, or a missile of similar character, being only smartly stung, not wounded. So, having done our duty well and successfully, the regiment welcomed the order to make themselves as comfortable as possible for the night. This was not very easy when the only place indicated to us in the darkness was a rather swampy field, with several almost impassable ditches running through it; but after three years of service a cavalry regiment can camp anywhere and go to sleep, horses and men, under all conceivable circumstances; and then there was the agreeable consciousness sweetening repose that in all reasonable probability somebody else would have to do the fighting on the morrow.

We thus enjoyed all the rest possible between midnight and the first glimpses of the dawn, when we were again summoned to horse. Drawn up in a cleared field in the vicinity of Todd's Tavern, we stood for hours listening to the terrible contest raging upon our right, one continuous roll of musketry, scarcely strengthened by artillery. More immediately in our neighborhood, so close indeed that many of the shells aimed at his troops crashed through the woods which shadowed us, General Custer was fighting his Michigan brigade with his accustomed vigor Captain Robbins, having been ordered to join him as a support of a section of our artillery, soon returned, giving an account how he was acting. His men, armed with the seven-shooting Spencer carbine, were pressing against the enemy, driving him back with continual charges; the artillery keeping closed up with the line, delivered canister with terrible rapidity and execution; the brigade band was there in the midst of the struggle, playing its best to stimulate the men, and General Custer himself was everywhere along the front stirring up all to do their utmost. No troops could resist an impetus thus given, and at last the rebel cavalry fell back pell-mell, far behind the shelter of their infantry line of battle. On our left the Second Brigade of Gregg was engaged in some sharp skirmishing, but evidently the enemy's whole strength was employed against our line of infantry, and there was nothing on our side of it to cause any apprehension.

Late in the afternoon the attack on Hancock was partially successful. His men, who had advanced a mile and a half beyond their line of breastworks, were fiercely charged and forced to fall back behind them. At one point even the breastworks were untenable, the fire that was sweeping through the dead leaves having kindled the logs into a scorching bon-fire. The rebels broke in, in that neighborhood, and for a moment seemed likely to obtain complete success; but Hancock, rallying his men, brought them back to the charge, and sweeping the rebels back over the ground already contested, returned as night closed in to the line which he had entrenched. While this conflict was going on, General Gregg conformed his movements to those of Hancock, falling back, when he retired, to the neighborhood of the Fredericksburg plank road, and again picketing forward in the night sufficiently to protect the flank of the advanced position of the infantry.

So far, the great struggle had resulted in a drawn battle; for though the rebels had been foiled in every effort to turn our right or to break our centre and left, we, on the other hand, had been unable to swing around their right upon the road to Spottsylvania. There had been temporary advantages, here and there, but these had in no material respect altered the relative positions of the two armies. The loss in killed and wounded, from the nature of the fighting, was probably about equal, and we had lost rather the larger number of prisoners. So now both commanders endeavored to combine manœuvering with fighting, seeking to gain by tactics the advantages which bloodshed alone had failed to secure. While Meade resolved by the transfer of his corps successively from right to left to gain ground toward Spottsylvania, Lee determined to make a vigorous effort to possess and hold the only road upon which such an advance was possible. If he could do this effectually, there would have been nothing left for the Army of the Potomac but a retreat to Fredericksburg or Culpeper to commence the operations anew. While, therefore, the Sixth Corps was quietly marching to the left behind the lines of the other two, the whole of the rebel cavalry was thrown across the Po, and took ground from Corbin's Bridge towards Fredericksburg. It was necessary for General Sheridan, who had again advanced to Todd's Tavern, to resist them and drive them away, before there was a stronger force placed there to meet the advance of Sedgewick. On the seventh of May, therefore, there occurred the largest fight between forces of dismounted cavalry that had taken place during the war.

For some distance before reaching Todd's Tavern, the road runs parallel to the line of the enemy's attack, and our pickets, thrown out to cover Hancock's left, were thus the first recipients of hostile fire. During the advance of our cavalry to the Tavern, the First Brigade of Gregg relieved the pickets which during the night had been thrown out by the Second; and as Captain Hobensack, of the First New Jersey, with the second battalion, was establishing his most advanced posts, a rapid fire was opened upon them by the advancing enemy. Lieutenant Kinsley immediately dismounted twenty men and sent them to reënforce the position that appeared to be attacked, and Captain Hobensack went with them to see what was the matter. It was at once evident to him as he approached, that this was no mere picket skirmish, but an attack in force; and he had to take measures according to the immediate pressure of the necessity. Slowly yielding the ground on his right as the rebels advanced upon him, he concentrated all his energies in an effort to hold the left of his position, covering a wooded hill, which, if once gained by the enemy, would give them an immense advantage at the outset of the engagement. In parallel lines, the enemy and our own men made for this height, loading and firing as they ran, and striving each to head off the adversary. Defeating the rebel efforts to force him back, and keeping them at bay by the steadiness of his line, Hobensack succeeded in gaining the desired cover, and, turning there, held the ground until the advancing line of the First Pennsylvania, which had been sent dismounted to his support, came up and relieved his men. But our men, unless compelled, showed no desire to leave the field upon which their comrades of the First Pennsylvania and the Sixth Ohio were doing their duty nobly; and all of the second battalion who could be spared, joined in a gallant charge of the Sixth, which swept the rebels out of a line of breastworks which they had during the night and day been elaborately constructing.

In the meantime, to the right of this point the First and Second Cavalry Divisions were meeting the massed forces of the enemy, the Third Division covering the left and preparing to coöperate if necessary. Devin's men on the right and the reserve brigade next to them were now expending the energies that had been reserved during the actions of the two preceding days. It is almost impossible to conceive of anything finer than the style in which these troopers first received the enemy's charge and then advanced against them, sweeping them back before the fierceness of their fire. The batteries on the hills above, in support of one of which our regiment was drawn up, aided our troops until they had driven the enemy entirely out of range, and then detaching sections, pressed closer to the scene of action. It was our good fortune only to receive a single shot in return. This fell directly in the ranks of Company L, at a spot where a small shrub had occasioned a gap of about a horse's width. Striking the ground between the legs of the horse in the rear rank, it buried itself in the earth; and in spite of the possible danger from the explosion of the shell and the startling effect of the coming missile, Sergeant Stout and his men sat immovable in their saddles without a waver in the line. When cavalry attain this steadiness they are thoroughly trustworthy in the heat of an engagement.

Captain Robbins' squadron, which went forward with an advancing section of the battery, had rather warmer work. At one time the enemy made a momentary rally and pressed upon them closely. Throwing himself into an isolated farm building which he used as a block-house, he and his men succeeded in driving back the rebels; and both he and Hobensack sent in a number of prisoners.

The open order movements of dismounted cavalry do not,

however, bring in the number of prisoners which result from a corresponding success in an infantry attack; and thus, except the killed and wounded left upon the field, the enemy retired comparatively intact; but this last desperate effort to gain the roads upon our left resulted in a disastrous failure. Weeks afterward, on returning from Trevillyan's Station, we bivouacked near the hospital of Rosser's Brigade after that action, and were informed by the hospital attendants that from that one brigade during the three days there had been brought in five hundred wounded. The whole loss of our two divisions for the same time did not amount to quite this number.

On Sunday, as we held the front to Corbin's Bridge, the Fifth Corps in its turn made a movement to the left; and as we were relieved by it, our regiment was sent to the right to watch the movements of the enemy. The road-side was a curious spectacle. The infantry, fresh from winter quarters, and many of them recruits, had on starting loaded themselves down with their winter comforts, and now the fatigues of marching were forcing them to reduce their burdens. Here, where they had moved undisturbed and unharassed, the ground was covered with abandoned blankets, overcoats, knapsacks, as thickly as is often the case in a hurried and disastrous retreat; and along the whole route of our columns the same appearance was presented. This aided the general effect of our manœuvres upon the enemy, who were convinced that we were retiring in confusion upon Fredericksburg, until they were startled by the appearance of our left upon the heights around Spottsylvania.

Before the enemy advanced upon our line the whole of the cavalry corps was withdrawn to the rear, and passing through the trains of the Sixth Corps, bivouacked for the night upon the Fredericksburg plank road. As much provision for the men as could be carried on their persons was issued to them here; and the forage that still remained in the trains was also given out, and then a few hours of sleep were permitted until the dawn should make its appearance.

Through the night a long train of wagons loaded with the wounded passed our resting place, escorted by the stalwart negroes of Burnside's Corps, which had just arrived from Washington. These continued on to Fredericksburg, to meet there the welcome supplies of the Sanitary Commission; while the cavalry, accompanying them for a few miles, then turned off abruptly to the right and commenced an independent expedition.

CHAPTER XIV.

SHERIDAN'S RAID TO RICHMOND.

Striking across to the old telegraph road, upon which we had before advanced with Bayard, we moved south in the direction of Richmond. As our brigade marched in the rear of the whole corps, passing occasionally a worn-out horse which had been shot where it had fallen, the First Jersey constantly came upon localities associated with the memories of the early days of their first campaign; but the aspect of the road was very different. It had been then flooded by the continued rains of that showery month of May; whereas now it was parched by the first weeks of the long drought of this famous battle-summer.

Throughout the morning's march, the column, keeping compactly together, was almost stifled in the dust which rose in clouds around it; and the brief intervals of halt for water and for rest were, even under the burning sun of noon, seasons of delightful relief from this distressing envelopement. During the afternoon, however, as the advance pressed forward to reach the Central Railroad at Beaver Dam Station, the column, with its ambulances and ammunition trains, stretched out over fully eight miles of road. So carefully were the cross roads picketed, and so well did the flankers perform their duty, that along this whole line no point was found at which the enemy ventured to break through. General Lee, imagining that this was but a couple of brigades on a marauding expedition, had detached a corresponding force to cut off the retreat; and while Stuart with a large force of cavalry tried to gain our front, this body under Wickham and Lomax attempted to strike our rear.

It was almost evening before these officers could attain their desired position, and in the meantime their skirmishers continued exchanging flying shots with our line of flankers; but every road was so well picketed along the route that it was impossible to harass or disorder our march.

An hour before sunset, an immense cloud of smoke was visible far in our front, as the rear guard halted, waiting the further advance of the column, which was watering in the North Anna River. The commander of the rearmost battalion, who should have faced his men in the direction whence we had come, had grown careless by the impunity that had attended our progress, and had closed up to the main body around an angle of the road, without leaving even a vidette to watch behind him, or taking any precautions against attack; when, with a yell, Lomax charged down upon them. Driven in upon the pack train of the brigade, they fell into complete disorder; and but for the trained presence of mind of the officers of the different regiments, there might have been a disastrous panic. With the instinct to do the right thing, which is taught by constant familiarity with danger, Taylor wheeled the Pennsylvanians into line before orders could arrive from the brigade commander; and as General Davies galloped back, he found each regiment getting into position ready to resist the attack. Following the rear guard, the rebels charged along the road, thinking that they had succeeded in causing a rout; and, blinded by the dust and their own eagerness, actually passed between the intervals of the First Pennsylvania. A volley from that regiment startled them too late into a sense of their real situation; and of the entire advance scarcely one escaped from death or capture. Some of them actually charged into the centre of the brigade; and one of them, laying a hand upon a gun of Martin's battery, exclaimed, "That gun is mine!" The chief-of-piece seemed for a moment stunned by the impudence of the speech; and then, brandishing his cowhide, with it and his fist flogged the speaker into a surrender. Another very big rebel collared a stout soldier of the Sixth Ohio, exclaiming, with several oaths, "You —— Yankee, you're my prisoner!" "You lie!" was the response, with precisely the same oaths, "you're mine!" and they tugged at one another, the men around showing fair play, until victory declared itself for the Northerner.

Captain Robbins, with his squadron, had, before the attack, been sent out to picket a cross road beyond where the rebels were now fighting, and there was reason to fear that he might be unable to extricate himself from their hands. He, however, as usual, proved equal to the emergency. As the enemy charged down along the road they left him well to their right, covering effectually that flank from an attack, unless they should sweep around him and fall upon his rear. To avoid this, Captain Beekman, with his company, quickly changed front to face the road, throwing shot among the enemy to harass their movements and delay their advance, while Captain Robbins, with the rest of the men, faced outward and met the rebel skirmishers in that direction. Slightly confused by this unexpected adversary, the enemy delayed to push forward another body of troops upon the road in support of the first attacking party, who were thus left completely at our mercy; and Robbins, thus saved from assault upon his rear, succeeded in withdrawing in safety to the main body.

Lomax had by this check lost all the advantage obtained by the suddenness of the surprise, and our whole brigade was perfectly ready to meet his further operations. His guns had been from the first throwing shot and shell very accurately at the road, which, fortunately for us, was here slightly below the general level of the ground, and thus protected from the effect of their fire; and Martin, quickly going into position, in a few moments silenced their artillery. A man or two killed, a few men wounded, an equal number of prisoners for each side, and considerable temporary confusion were all the results from an affair which threatened at first to be disastrous.

It was by this time very dark, and the main body of the corps had already reached their camping-ground. Leaving the First New Jersey and the First Massachusetts to hold the ground and barricade the road, the rest of the brigade now followed and rejoined the corps. While our skirmishers exchanged occasional shots with the enemy—enough to let them know that we were still in position—the pioneers busily plied their axes, until the road and its neighborhood was rendered impassible for artillery and impervious to a charge; and then, taking up the bridge over a little stream near by, we quietly left the field. Owing to the darkness and confusion, it was midnight before we got into camp, and even then half the regiment was forced to go on picket.

We had scarcely been roused at dawn from our feverish slumbers when a rattle of small arms was heard along the picket line, and a screaming shell passed over our heads, narrowly missing the ammunition wagons just beyond us. Timidly advancing through the obscurity, the rebels had come upon one of Lieutenant Wynkoop's pickets, and after the mutual challenges each party strove to persuade the other into an acknowledgment of its character. As soon as Captain Robbins had got his reserve in perfect readiness he directed the picket to give a decided answer; and as the words, "First New Jersey Cavalry," were uttered, a volley was given by the enemy in response. The bullets, passing over the picket line, fell among the men of the regiment in their rear without doing any damage; and the vigorous reply made by Captain Robbins convinced the rebels that it would be vain to charge a body so well prepared. Two of the picket force were wounded, and no other casualties occurred on our side.

Crossing the North Anna, whose line was for the time held by General Wilson, we passed the smoking ruins of Beaver Dam Station, which had been struck by General Merritt early in the previous afternoon. Two locomotives, with their trains, had been captured and destroyed at the same time, and some of our mechanics were still at work with axes, wrenches and sledges, to complete their ruin. They had been carrying four hundred prisoners, who had all been rescued and armed with weapons found among the rebel stores. An immense pile of crackers and other provisions, containing two million rations, was smouldering away, and for several miles the railroad was rendered useless.

While the First Division advanced toward Hanover Junction the Second moved directly to the South Anna, foraging as it went, though in a region yielding few supplies. Near the river there were some more productive farms, and after obtaining grain and fodder from them we crossed the ford and halted a short distance beyond it for the night. Having slept unmolested by the enemy, we started the next morning to perform our share in the work of destruction. General Davies, with the First Brigade, pushed across to Ashland Station and Court House; and while the First Massachusetts, after destroying the public buildings and store houses, fought hotly with the enemy, the rest of the brigade occupied themselves with the destruction of miles of railroad. Then hurrying back by narrow and tortuous woodland roads, we came out upon the mountain turnpike, along which the rest of the corps was already moving in column of platoons. Our division was again in the rear, but the Second Brigade now took its turn in protecting the march. We were now less than a dozen miles from Richmond, and from the roar of artillery in our front, knew that Merritt had met the enemy. As the column closed up and formed in a more compact order to await the result of the engagement, the enemy, with a shout, charged upon our rear. We had not, however, time to face about to support the Second Brigade, if necessary, before the struggle was over. The rebel General Gordon had attacked the rear guard, wounding Colonel Booth, of the First Maine, and losing his own life in the assault. The Second Brigade stopped the charge with their carbines. Randall's battery tore apart the advancing column with round shot and canister, and the rebels drew back from the attack. They had wasted their forces in desultory and partial attacks upon our solid, well-united corps, instead of making a determined effort to check us by a concentration on their part, and they were to reap the consequences of the blunder by a succession of partial defeats. The fight in front was of longer duration and more serious in its results, Custer finally winding it up by the capture of two guns and a hundred prisoners, and opening for us the most direct road to Richmond. There were signs of more careful cultivation of the country, and the houses were rather more numerous than we had found them heretofore; but certainly nowhere in the North could be found an important city whose environs were so inanimate as those of the capital of the Southern Confederacy.

Wilson's division having by the treachery of the guide been led astray, it was long past midnight before we crossed a high, roughly-made bridge which spanned a little stream, whose name, as we were informed, was the *Chickahominy*, and riding around several deserted earthworks, came upon the beautiful broad roads that traverse the suburbs of the city. Turning sharply to the left, we broke into a trot, up a gentle ascent, and as the daylight began to brighten, halted on the hills commanding Meadow Bridge, having turned the first line of rebel fortifications. In our front the road had been thickly planted with torpedoes, which the rebel prisoners, very reluctantly, were employed in taking up; their timid groping and shrinking being a curious and rather entertaining sight. A lady, who took pains to inform us that she was a cousin of the *Ritchies*, bewailed bitterly our barbarity in placing the torpedoes in her cellar instead of leaving them to blow us up in the road; but her expostulations had no effect upon our hardened natures. For an hour or two we lay down to rest, while General Stuart was preparing to spring the trap into which he flattered himself that we had walked. The impregnable fortifications of Richmond frowned along our right; the bridge over the Chickahominy had been destroyed in front; and the two provisional brigades of Richmond militia were thrown upon our rear to harass it. Beyond the Chickahominy, to defy us should we attempt to force a passage, was Stuart's entire disposable cavalry; and President Davis himself had been invited to come out to witness our destruction.

It depended upon the ability of Sheridan and the gallantry of his men, whether we should be caged, or inflict, instead, a severe punishment upon the enemy. There was no advantage in staying where we were, and to go back would have been still more unprofitable. To ride into Richmond would have cost half the command, and the ride out have sacrificed the rest; so that the only thing to do was to whip Stuart as rapidly and thoroughly as possible, and move around the city by Mechanicsville.

Though the roadway bridge had been partially destroyed, that which supported the railroad track had been left intact; and, covered by our artillery on the heights, the Regular Brigade and Custer's men charged across it at a run. Spreading out like a fan, they dashed upon the enemy; and while they thus covered the approach of the bridge, the pioneer force of the corps worked like beavers to make it passable for horses and artillery. There was need of rapid workmanship; for scarcely had they done, when Stuart in person led a mounted charge against our little band on foot. Lieutenant Hunt, formerly of the First New Jersey, but at that time in the First United States Cavalry, saw his first sergeant and several men cut down near him, and was just preparing to sell his life as dearly as possible, when, with a wild cheer, on came the mounted men of the division, sending Stuart back with a mortal wound, and scattering his forces through the wood. Giving them no time to rally, Merritt pressed upon their rear, until the whole country as far as Mechanicsville was open to our advance.

Gregg's work was comparatively easy, it being impossible to coax the Richmond infantry to close quarters. Tired of the amusement of a mere artillery engagement, he allowed the dismounted men to charge, whereupon the whole force opposing us took to their heels with speed. The only men who stood were a Confederate soldier on detached service, and his negro servant, who had volunteered in the defence of the city; and on coming into our hands, the negro accepted his freedom with complacency, while his master relieved his mind by very disrespectful observations on the character of the militia. The only loss to our regiment was caused by shell, one of which took off the arm of Sergeant George Wispert, of Company C, and another inflicted a wound upon Sergeant Joseph Hodapp, of Company H, which resulted fatally. They were both valuable soldiers, and were much missed in the regiment.

General Wilson had to encounter a more determined attack, the enemy at one time penetrating within musket range of the hospitals. In reply to Wilson's report of the circumstances, Sheridan said to the messenger:

"Go back to General Wilson, and tell him to hold his position. He *can* hold it, and he *must* hold it."

Gregg being relieved from apprehension as to his own line, turned a section of Martin's battery upon the advancing line, and they were soon forced to disappear. By twelve o'clock the enemy, beaten at all points, retired from the contest, leaving us to carry on our movements at our leisure.

This was extremely agreeable to us, for we were worn out from loss of sleep and the excitement of the last few days. Moreover, though the position was a good one to hold, it was a very delicate one to retire from. The hills above Meadow Bridge commanded the country on the other side for a mile and a half; and there was a small fortification there from which our rear could have been shelled with almost complete impunity to the aggressors.

As our brigade, the last of the corps, evacuated the height, and, crossing the bridges, consumed them behind us, many an anxious eye looked back to see if the enemy was making an effort to annoy us; but they seemed to have given up the whole matter, and to be glad to be rid of us as easily as possible. Without even withdrawing beyond the range of guns from the hill, the men dismounted as soon as there was a halt, and fell asleep almost before they reached the ground.

While we were thus close to Richmond, a mechanic, whose wife was already in the North, attempted to escape and join our forces. Being detected and caught, he was instantly shot by the rebels, who left the children to wander as they chose. The younger of the two, a child of eight years old, becoming separated from his brother, made his way into our lines. He did not know even his family name, and could only tell us the few facts already narrated concerning him. Surgeon Phillips, of the First New Jersey, medical director of the division, took charge of the boy, designing either to discover his connections in the North or to provide for him himself.

Without further molestation from the enemy, the corps continued its march beyond Mechanicsville; and halting near Cold Harbor, took the long night's rest so much needed by men and horses. Though there was quite a heavy rain, which made the air damp and the ground muddy, few discovered the change of weather except the pickets; and refreshed and confident, we resumed our march the next morning with perfect deliberation. Passing over the Gaines' Mills battle ground, with wonder why the opposing armies did not make effective use of their cavalry on such an admirable field, we passed by the points whose names were so familiar in the chronicle o the campaigns of McClellan, until we finally arrived at the memorable Bottom's Bridge. A few mounted home guards, who performed patrol duty through that region, had taken up the planks from the roadway of the bridge and departed, apparently convinced that they had made it impassable. They never reflected that there was a perfect magazine of timber in the form of buildings near at hand, on our side of the Chickahominy; from which our pioneers obtained material to repair the bridge rather faster than they had damaged it. Throwing the First New Jersey and the Sixth Ohio across to picket the further side, General Sheridan halted his whole command along the Chickahominy, desirous to keep the enemy perplexed as to his further intentions.

While reconnoitering the neighborhood, as the pickets were being established, an officer of the brigade staff observed two young girls on a hillside, waving their handkerchiefs to him. Though a little apprehensive of a snare, he went to see what they desired. One of them told him that it had been so long since they had seen a Yankee uniform that they wanted to look at it; and then eagerly inquired of him the news. Thinking them rebels, he answered carelessly that we had taken Richmond the night before, and wondered that they had not heard it. The girls clapped their hands for joy, one of them exclaiming, "Then father is out of prison!" It was painful to have to undeceive them, when the reason for their welcoming our approach was thus revealed, and to tell them that their father was still suffering for his loyalty to the nation.

The next morning, passing through White Oak Swamp, where the traces of battle were still visible, we came out upon Malvern Hill, and beyond the cultivated fields of corn and richly growing clover saw the James River in the distance, with the masts of Butler's transport vessels rising above the banks. Early in the afternoon we went into camp at Haxall's Landing, with the river at our feet, and rations and forage unloading at the wharf. It was the fourteenth of May. For six days we had been steadily and successfully marching and fighting on the road from the Army of the Potomac to the Army of the James.

While Butler was making his advance upon Fort Darling, and his retreat to Bermuda Hundred, we lay resting and feeding up; and then, on the eighteenth, resumed again our march. We had heard of the death of Sedgwick, of the hard fighting around Spottsylvania, and of the successful capture of Johnson's position by General Hancock; and now we were to rejoin that gallant army which was steadily fighting its way onward to the South. Crossing the Chickahominy at Jones' Bridge, and resting for twenty-four hours at Baltimore Cross Roads, our division advanced to picket around Cold Harbor, while Custer struck at the railroad near Hanover Court House. Though he was unable to do it any serious damage, he kept the rebel cavalry away from the scene of Grant's operations; and with his usual good fortune escaped from what appeared inevitable capture. The only road on which he could retreat was seized by a superior force ot the enemy; and had they held it, his fate would have been sealed. The officer commanding them, however, imagined from the reports of the inhabitants that our entire force was in front of him; and he therefore fell back to occupy a better position. Before he discovered his mistake, Custer had marched past him and rejoined General Sheridan without any serious loss. On the evening of Sunday, the twenty-second, we replenished our exhausted supplies from the transports at the White House, and then again prepared to rejoin the Potomac Army.

Passing by New Kent Court House, we halted the next night at Aylett's Factories, hearing in the distance, far south of where we expected to find the army, the tremendous cannonade of Warren's brilliant action upon the North Anna. Sheridan is reported to have said that he would give three months' pay to be then where he had been but two nights before, in the rear of the enemy near Hanover; but such chances do not often occur as they are desired, and we had now nothing for it but to re-unite ourselves with Grant.

The next night's halt was memorable for the fiercest thunder storm that we ever encountered. The lightning struck right among us, stunning several horses and melting a sabre in our regiment, killing two men and some horses in the Tenth New York.

The evening of the twenty-fifth found us encamped in the rear of our army, after seventeen days' absence, with our own supply train issuing the needed provisions, and our first mail for three weeks distributing its abundant treasures. In the expectation that we would have a little rest, we pitched our tents for the first time since the campaign opened, and slept comfortably beneath their shelter.

CHAPTER XV.

TURNING LEE'S RIGHT.

We had fancied that we were to enjoy a few days of comparative repose after so long and arduous an expedition, but we soon found that General Grant had use for every man under his command. By noon on the day after our arrival the whole corps was once more in the saddle, and while General Wilson was sent to make such a demonstration on the right as should divert the attention of the enemy, General Sheridan took the First and Second Divisions with him back again over the road which we had lately traveled. The air was tainted with the smell of our dead horses, already corrupting beneath the burning sun, as we passed their bodies, dotted thickly along our track. Soon after nightfall the First New Jersey, diverging from the main body, moved down by the first cross road to the Pamunkey, and while assuring ourselves of the destruction of the bridge, disturbed the repose of the rebel cavalry. Their bands of music were playing, the camp fires blazing, and the men apparently enjoying themselves very much, when a rapid interchange of shots between our advance and their pickets across the river caused their bugles to sound "to horse," and broke up their comfortable bivouac. For two or three hours we kept amusing them with little demonstrations, and then withdrawing noiselessly, fell back to the main road. This was now filled by the Third Division of the Sixth Corps, which, marching sixty miles in less than thirty hours, followed our cavalry in the present bold adventure.

During the early hours of the morning the two divisions of cavalry, supported by this noble body of infantry, crossed the Pamunkey River at Hanover town, and advancing upon Lee's right wing, prepared to cover the movements of the rest of the army.

It was twenty-four hours before Lee discovered the character of the movement and could take any steps to meet it, by which time its success was nearly certain. To seize his last chance, however, he hurriedly assembled his cavalry and threw them desperately against us, in hopes of either driving us back across the river, or at least of gaining time for a new disposition of his forces.

On the morning of the twenty-eighth, advanced several miles on the direct road to Richmond, Gregg's cavalry took up a position near Hawes' Shop, to cover the crossing and movements of our infantry. Very soon there was heard, on the picket line of the Tenth New York, a sharp rattle of small arms; and then, with a rushing charge, the rebels broke through and over them upon the First Brigade. It was a fierce attack, but seemingly in not very formidable force, and the First Pennsylvania, pushing forward to the relief of the pickets, regained the ground and firmly held the enemy. Gradually the firing grew heavier and heavier along that one portion of our line, and regiment after regiment was sent by General Davies to reënforce it. Neglecting every other point, Hampton massed his whole available cavalry to break through there, that gaining possession of the road he might force us back, and perhaps even disorder and check our infantry in their movement towards the left. Fortunately for our army, the division holding that ground was commanded by an officer especially remarkable for tenacity and steadiness of resistance. We have other cavalry leaders more dashing in attack, but none to equal General Gregg and his division in the ability and desperation with which ground once chosen is held to the very last. Every man goes into action assured that he will have to fight to the very uttermost of his ability, but that then he may confidently rely upon the requisite support being provided if it is in human power to afford it. Thus General Davies sent in his men, without question how large a force they were to meet, but simply that they were required to meet it, and along that narrow front of attack his single line of dismounted men stood against the thickening masses of the enemy.

His division well in hand, General Gregg soon had the Second Brigade covering the right of the men engaged and ready to support them if required; and then, except the squadrons supporting the artillery, the whole of General Davies' command was dismounted and placed upon the line. Stretching across the road, the First Pennsylvania Regiment, covered by strips of wood and by ruinous fences, displayed all the high qualities by which it has always been distinguished. The steady, business-like fire, the obstinate stand against a charge, the fierce deep shout and firm advance in unison, had been learned in the school of Bayard, and practised under Gregg. By their side now came the First New Jersey, old comrades of the battle and the bivouac. By the order of General Davies, Colonel Kester sent the first battalion under Captain Robbins, to join the Pennsylvanians on the right of the road, where they were beginning to be over-weighted by the enemy. Dividing the third squadron, which was not dismounted, the colonel dispatched one company on vidette duty to the extreme right, and another to perform a like service on the left; and then with the other three squadrons he moved across to the left of the road, reporting himself to Colonel Taylor, of the First Pennsylvania, as ready to assist him.

Robbins advanced, passing over some men of another regiment who were for the moment rather shrinking from the front, and joined the Pennsylvanians with a *Jersey cheer*, familiar and welcome to their ears.

The line which had been slowly swinging back its right for a hundred and fifty yards, now steadied itself and stopped its retrograde; and then with a redoubled force went at the enemy. Through the wood, crackling with shot and splintered by shell, Bayard's old troopers pushed onward at a run, chasing the enemy across the open ground beyond. In this there was a double ditch lined by fencing, with another of the same character facing it, about as distant as the width of an ordinary Northern road. As Captain Beekman, heading his men, sprang across the first fence at charging speed, they were met by a desperate volley from the second line of the rebels lying in the other cover. Instinctively as they saw the flash, our men had thrown themselves upon the gronnd, and now, Captain Beekman, rolling into the ditch, called his troopers there beside him. From the two covers there was kept up a tremendous fire, the breech-loading, easily handled carbines giving us the advantage over the less wieldy muskets of the enemy, so that at times some portions of their line would be almost silenced. Thereupon there would be a partial charge on our part to the ditch on this side of the enemy's line, our men firing through the fence upon the crouching rebels; but an enfilading fire from the flanks of the line would soon force them from their vantage ground to scramble back into their former quarters. As they did so, the rebels would spring up and try to follow them, meeting with such a terrible discharge from our line that they would be swept back with aggravated loss and disorder. Thus the time passed on, both parties holding their own, and neither gaining ground upon the other.

And now, Colonel Kester hearing the continuous and heavy fire along the line of Captain Robbins, and knowing that officer's reluctance to ask for help while he could possibly avoid it, sent Major Janeway with the fourth and fifth squadrons to his assistance, requesting him to assume command of that whole portion of our line.

As the main body of the Pennsylvanians on the left of the road was being driven back by the enemy, the colonel led Captain Malsbury's squadron to their support at the critical moment. The solid volley-firing, for which that command has frequently been remarked, checked the rebel advance when it had almost penetrated our centre; and at that point was some of the severest fighting during the whole day. Malsbury received a mortal wound, Dye was killed instantly, Cox was hit in the back, but remained the only officer with the squadron till towards the end of the action he received a wound which disabled him.

On the right where Major Janeway led his men, the slaughter was equally great. The ammunition of the men was giving out, and more had to be brought from the rear to be distributed on the line itself, as there were no men to relieve us while we were supplied. While this operation was going on, the officers, who were especially exposed while dealing forth the cartridges, fell very fast. Captain Beckman was shot through both hands as he stretched them forth full of ammunition. Lieutenant Bellis was almost at the same moment mortally wounded, as was also Lieutenant Stewart. Captain Robbins was wounded severely in the shoulder, Lieutenant Shaw sharply in the head, Lieutenant Wynkoop painfully in the foot. Lieutenant Bowne was the only officer of the first battalion on the field who was untouched, and he had several very narrow escapes. That of Major Janeway himself was among the most remarkable. As he was passing along the line, keeping the men up to their duty, a shell struck a tree above him, bringing down its top with a tremendous crash. As he instinctively glanced upward, a ball whistled past his forehead, just reddening the skin. Had it not been for that slight motion he would have been shot through the brain.

As Lieutenant Brooks was manœuvring the fifth squadron under fire, a ball fired close at hand struck him in the neighborhood of his belt-clasp, slightly penetrating the skin in two places, and, doubling him up, sent him rolling headlong for thirty feet across the road. As he recovered steadiness, he saw his whole squadron hurrying to pick him up, and in the excitement, losing all sensation of pain, he ordered them again forward and walked after them half-way to the front. Then he was obliged to drop upon the ground, and Major Janeway soon afterwards observing him, sent a squad to carry him from the field. Though he refused to go into the hospital, it was months before he recovered from the injury. Lieutenant Craig, also of the same squadron, was badly bruised by some missile that struck him in the breast; and though he did not go off duty, he continued suffering severely from the blow. Still the men held their own, and could have continued to do so for a much longer time, though while the right and left had even advanced, the centre had lost some ground, and was considerably pressed. The men opposed to us at this crisis, though the most desperate fighters that we had encountered among the Southern cavalry, were, nevertheless, evidently new to their business, and not handled with remarkable skill. As the colonel remarked to a staff officer, they showed their inexperience by continually half-rising to fire or to look at our line, thus giving our men an opportunity of which our marksmen took instant and fatal advantage. Their line was thus converted into a perfect slaughter house, preventing them from making any dash at our weaker front.

Now, however, Custer came up the road with his Michigan Brigade, and our men received orders to open the centre to give him room to charge. As, in performing this manœuvre, the left of our line was swung backward from the road, about eighty of the enemy, seeing the retrograde movement, and unconscious of its design, ran forward and, throwing themselves by the roadside fences, opened a heavy fire upon the portion of the command with Colonel Kester. Unseen by them, three regiments of Custer were advancing behind them, dismounted, in regimental column; and quickly some of them, springing forward and opening with their repeating carbines, killed, wounded or captured the whole body of rebels. Some of the Michigan men, seeing some troops and a mounted officer in the distance, thought they were rebels, and before they discovered their mistake, Colonel Kester's horse, which had already received a wound, was struck by two other balls, while his own coat was so torn that his escape appeared miraculous.

As the steady rattle of Custer's carbines and the rush of his advance was heard by our men, a cheer rose right and left from our line; and before he had quite gained their front, the whole body of our skirmishers sprang from their cover and dashed upon the enemy. Sweeping them away before the impulse of the charge, the combined brigades followed in hot pursuit, the quick-loading Spencer carbines keeping up an unintermitting fire, under which the rebels could neither rally nor reply. Their officers shouted and swore at them, telling them that infantry was in the wood to cover them, and that they must turn and charge; but it was impossible to check the headlong route of men so badly beaten. On their hands and knees, afraid to stand upright, they scrambled with wonderful rapidity through the grass and underbrush. As they ascended the farther side of an open field with a hollow in the centre, our men reached the near side, and had them in plain sight and range. A tremendous volley was poured in, whose smoke for a moment obscured the view. When our men had passed beyond it, no enemy was to be seen. The survivors of the discharge had dashed into the hollow to the right; and though our line advanced some distance, a cloud of dust in the distance was all that could be discovered. In front of the right of our line, a hundred and twenty-seven of the enemy were buried; opposite the left, over sixty; and between forty and fifty wounded, left on the field, were taken to our hospital. From the prisoners taken we learned that the whole rebel cavalry corps had been on the field before us, bent on regaining possession of the road to Hanover town and New Castle.

Out of the nine companies of the First New Jersey engaged, the loss of killed and wounded was sixty-three, eleven being officers. The total loss of the division was two hundred and five; the difference between the loss of the opposing parties being due to the superiority of our commander, our officers, our men, and our weapons. The troops that were finally driven from the field were Butler's new brigade of South Carolina cavalry, who had joined General Lee but the week before.

The effort to check our advance had been vain. By the time that the cavalry engagement was ended, Grant had joined Sheridan on the field, and Meade was moving upon Old Church and Shady Grove. The flank movement had proved a great success.

For twenty-four hours, Gregg's division was at rest. Then it was moved forward to picket Warren's left near Shady Grove, while Meade prepared to take the next step in Grant's scheme of advance. On the evening of the thirtieth, Torbert, with the First Cavalry Division, dashed in upon Cold Harbor, scattering the rebel cavalry and capturing a large number of prisoners from the supporting infantry force thus deserted. Holding the position, and throwing up a rude breastwork, he stood his ground until joined the next morning by Sheridan with Gregg's command; and then we waited anxiously for the infantry that was to relieve us. In the meantime, the rebels hurried forward an infantry division to drive us away and regain the vitally important ground. The deadly volleys of the carbines, combined with shell and canister from our four light batteries, were, however, too much for the enemy. Before the First Jersey, the rear regiment of the division, had fairly got engaged, the contest was over and the rebels in retreat. The last shot was fired as the advance of the Sixth Corps came upon the ground. The cavalry were then relieved and marched to the left and rear, General Sheridan expressing his satisfaction at their behavior in his jocular remark to the general who relieved him, "Wright, you will find them pretty strong in there. You will have to form three or four lines of battle, breastworks and all that. But if you have any trouble, just send for me and I'll come and help you."

On the morning of the first of June, it was the turn of

Gregg's Division to initiate the turning movement. Traveling over some of the old camp roads of General McClellan's campaign, the column struck into the road from Bottom's Bridge to Gaines' Mills, and crossing the first mill-stream, closed against the extreme rebel right. Fortified upon a hill rising above the surrounding country and commanding it, with artillery in position and its range actually ascertained, they were secure against cavalry either mounted or dismounted; while their flank and rear, covered by the swamps and stream of the Chickahominy, were perfectly protected from our attack. Feeling their position and watching it under a heavy artillery fire to which we could offer no effective return, we kept the front clear for the advance of the Second Corps, who relieved us in the afternoon. This position, the key to Lee's whole line, was the one which Hancock gained, lost, and struggled against in vain thereafter.

In a tremendous thunder storm we marched after the First Division to Bottom's Bridge, and taking up our position on the high ground above it, picketed up and down the Chickahominy at every ford and crossing. Here in a day or two our wagons joined us again, having been only near us for a few hours for the preceding month. From Savage Station the enemy could see our camps, and they soon intimated to us the fact by sending Whitworth shell with remarkable accuracy over the intervening three miles directly among our tents. Very few of them, however, exploded, and two horses killed in the Pennsylvania regiment were the only casualties. One solid shot with which they concluded the entertainment, however, almost spoiled the breakfast of a man in Company B, striking the ground at a little distance, it ricocheted towards him, and the first intimation of its proximity which his comrades received was from seeing him seize his frying-pan and dodge, as the shot struck where he had been sitting. Notwithstanding the imminence of the danger, he did not spill a particle of the gravy in his pan.

On the sixth the Third Division came to take our place, and the rest of the cavalry marched to the rear. Crossing the roads from the White House by which the army was supplied, and which were covered with fine dust from the continual passage of heavy trains not only in the roadway, but for hundreds of yards on either side, the troops marched by hidden ways to the Pamunkey at New Castle. Here were detachments from our trains, and here we fancied that we were to recruit after our severe duty. Never was there a greater delusion. The next morning saw us entering upon the heaviest undertaking that had been allotted to us in our experience up to that time.

CHAPTER XVI.

TO TREVILLYAN'S STATION AND BACK.

On the evening of the sixth of June, the brigade and regimental commanders of the First and Second Cavalry Divisions received orders to remove from the force all those men and horses who appeared unable to stand a severe ten days' march, and to provide the others with every requisite for such an expedition. The officers were recommended to lay in stores sufficient to last them for twelve days, and to relieve themselves of all unnecessary incumbrances; and all were warned that they need not expect to find themselves near any depot or resting place until the expiration of that period. Then, convoying a pontoon train and a small number of wagons containing the requisite supplies and ammunition, the two divisions started from New Castle, on the Pamunkey, for some point yet unknown.

Though the rate of marching was very moderate, even on the first day there was much suffering from the extreme heat and dryness of the weather; and the horses had to be watched carefully to save them as much as possible from the effect of over-exhaustion and of reckless riding. The early afternoon brought us to our halting place beyond Aylett's, where the passage of our trains had produced something of the usual appearance of ruin and desolation; and the First New Jersey, furnishing pickets for the brigade, remained for the night under arms. On the next day's march some horses began to give out and drop by the wayside, forcing their riders to accompany the command for the rest of the journey on foot. After accomplishing about twenty miles, we halted at Polecat Run, near the Fredericksburg Railroad, still unable to decide whither General Sheridan designed to lead us. The route which we traveled had been marched over by our infantry and army trains, so that there was no forage to be obtained in it; and our horses were therefore obliged to live on the amount carried on the saddles. Moving on the next morning towards Childsburg, and crossing the old telegraph road, along which we made our former raid, we fortunately came into an undevastated region before our forage was quite exhausted. For miles on either side of the line of march parties were sent out from the different regiments, occasionally making discoveries of horses and mules, regularly bringing in supplies of provisions and corn which were essential to the command. Though the extra distance traveled and the speed sometimes required were a severe strain on the horses, these supplies had to be secured; and at the expense of a few animals the rest were kept alive. On the evening of the tenth we were in bivouac in Louisa county, near the North Anna River, commanding several roads that led to the Court House and the Virginia Central Railroad; and General Custer, with his brigade, was sent to make a demonstration on the Court House, feeling his way toward the right. While the attention of the rebels was thus diverted, the main column, the First Division in advance, moved directly upon Trevillyan's Station, and attacked the enemy there with great energy. Though their line was good and gallantly held, it could not withstand the vigor of Torbert's advance; and when a portion of Gregg's men were dismounted and sent to reënforce our front, the retrograde of the rebels became more marked and continuous. Finally, immediately aronnd the Station they attempted to make a stand; but the Tenth New York in line of battle, charging at a run, broke their centre and swept them from the field, that regiment and the Regular Brigade taking nearly five hundred prisoners. In the charge, the impulse that can at critical times be given by a single man was noticeably instanced. There were two fences to be crossed as the troops advanced. The first one was taken without a check; but at the second, in the storm of canister and bullets, there was visible a momentary hesitation. This might have increased until the charge should be broken; but without a pause the commissary of the Tenth sprang over the barrier; and though he fell wounded and disabled as he touched the ground on the other side, his example at the instant had stimulated the men, who never again wavered as they went at and through the enemy.

In the meantime, General Custer, with his command, had struck the rebels at Louisa Court House, attacking with such impetuosity as to drive them, without a halt, completely behind the line of battle confronting our main body. Before either he or the enemy was aware of his position he had come upon Rosser's supply and ammunition train, captured it entire, and seized fifteen hundred led horses of the men who were dismounted and fighting us on foot. Turning over his captures to the Fifth Michigan, he ordered them to the rear; but, unfortunately for him, Hampton had in the interval changed front with his right, and strengthening it from his reserves, had closed the door of exit. Before the escort was aware it had marched into the arms of the enemy, and the prize was again taken, together with Custer's own headquarter wagon. Even in that emergency the Michigan men showed fight. Many of them cut their way through in squads, and it is reported that a sergeant, with forty men, making his way out in the rear of the enemy and being unable to rejoin our forces, led his men in safety the whole distance into Alexandria. Custer was now in a position which would have appalled most officers. Front, rear and both flanks were assailed by the enemy, he only having with him four small regiments and four light field pieces. Trusting to his good fortune and to the strength of desperation, he charged his whole brigade at that portion of the enemy which was between himself and Torbert's extreme left. Plunging deeply into their line, his own forces breaking into squads, but still keeping a general unity, he fought his way on. Once the rebels came on so rapidly that Pennington had to gallop off with limber alone, leaving the gun upon the ground. "They have got my gun, General," said he, as he came up to General Custer. "No, they have not," was the answer, and gathering sixty or seventy men of all regiments around him, he charged back upon the piece. "There," he cried, striking it with his sabre, "There is your gun; take it." Then shouting after the rebels, "I am General Custer; if you want this piece come and take it," he continued to force his way out of his environment.

A fortunate diversion in another direction, by distracting the rebel attention, assisted him in his escape. The First New Jersey Cavalry had not been engaged in the action, but were sent to scout and picket a road leading off to our right, around the enemy's position. When Colonel Kester had advanced his main body as far as he judged advisable, well around the left flank of General Hampton, he sent Major Janeway forward with the third battalion to examine more particularly the country in advance. The road, after winding through the woods, at length turned considerably to the left and struck the line of railroad. At this point there were a few rebel pickets, who, being struck suddenly, galloped off in all directions. Observing that the principal body kept on the railroad to the left, in the direction of the fighting, Major Janeway began to arrange his men for an advance after them. Forming Captain Hick's squadron as a support, and deploying the fifth squadron as skirmishers, he placed Lieutenant Craig, with a reserve of ten men, on the railroad, ordering the skirmish line to govern itself by his motions. As they moved forward they soon came upon a section of artillery, supported by the Fifth Georgia Cavalry, mounted, and the Ninth South Carolina, dismounted. Major Janeway then gave the order to Craig to charge; and as he rushed up, with a yell, the whole mounted force of the rebels broke and ran from the field. The guns, however, were well served, though not well aimed, firing rapidly and steadily, but without doing any damage; and the Carolinians, unable to run away, covering themselves by some houses and fences, opened with small arms upon our line. Had there been no obstructions, or had there been another battalion to follow up the charge, the guns and the dismounted men would have been taken; but as it was, the Major saw that further advance would be useless, and withdrew his men, undisturbed by any pursuit. Lieutenant Craig was wounded in the ankle; Sergeant Cook, of Company K, was killed; Michael Callaghan, of the same company, was too severely wounded to be carried off, though he was afterward recovered; private Hardy was caught beneath his dead horse and captured, and Porter, of Company L, was slightly wounded in the hand. With only these casualties, this force of a hundred men had engaged two regiments and a section of artillery, and had so surprised the rebels in our front that Custer got through with no more fighting, and the whole rebel line withdrew from their positions.

During the course of the next day, the railroad, for several miles, was torn up and utterly destroyed, while the artillery kept up a lively engagement, and there was occasionally brisk skirmishing. Near nightfall a couple of regiments made a sharp assault upon the rebel left, which was temporarily successful, but led to no permanent advantage, and it appeared throughout the whole time as if General Sheridan had done as much as he thought prudent or expedient. The lazy character of the second day's engagement was soon explained. The rebel cavalry could have with little trouble been driven from our immediate front, but in an intrenched position beyond they could rally upon a body of rebel infantry, whom Breckinridge had risked holding there rather than have our command combine with Hunter against him. It was a choice of evils for him to spare them from Lynchburg to hold this, or keep them to increase the garrison of that town. He probably chose the least. We had given all the time required to allow General Hunter's cavalry to cut the Lynchburg and Charlottesville Railroad, and had kept occupied the troops sent to oppose them. If they did not do this work properly and thoroughly, the error did not lie with us. Therefore, General Sheridan, who had to destroy quite a quantity of equipments, in order to provide for the wounded already on our hands, and whose supplies were insufficient for his own men and the prisoners already taken, did not consider it advisable to linger longer or to fight another action except for more important results than were here to be expected.

The First New Jersey Cavalry, which during the day and night had been lying inactive in a vicinity which the rebels shelled with great perseverance, received orders, after midnight, to prepare to cover the rear of the column as it retired over the ground upon which we had advanced. The movement was conducted with great quietness, but, owing to an error of direction made by the Second Brigade, was delayed some hours beyond the original intention. It was dawn before we got fairly away from the neighborhood of the station, and sunrise before we had crossed the North Anna. It was reported that the rebels had during the same time fallen back from their position to one in the rear. At any rate, they did not attempt in any way to follow up our retreat except by a squadron or two of scouts.

The line along which we retired turned out to be the most exhausted and desolate region through which we had ever passed, even in Virginia. The whole country had been eaten out by the rebel army first and the rebel hospitals afterwards, until the inhabitants were on the verge of starvation. There was scarcely any grazing, and no corn for the horses, and nothing by which the men could eke out their scanty ration of pork and hard bread. The dust and heat and glare of the midsummer sun increased in their intensity day by day; and the march became terribly wearying. The interest occasioned by passing through the rebel entrenchments at Spottsylvania Court House made some diversion and excitement. It was marvellous how our soldiery had succeeded in taking so large a number of these as was shown by the distinctly marked rifle pits of our lines, erected inside of those of the enemy in some places, and in others by the skirmishers' pits visible in the rear of the earthworks. Graves in many places lay beside such pits, or just within the fortifications.

When we passed from the region occupied by the rebels to that behind our own army, we had a little better fortune. The country itself was not so poor; and though a great deal of damage had been done, provisions had not been so utterly exhausted. Forage was obtainable to a moderate extent, and corn meal was not uncommon. After passing through Bowling Green and by Dunkirk, considerable stores of hams, bacon and poultry could be gathered together by experienced foragers; and though these did not, of course, supply the wants of the whole command, they kept them from starvation. Horses, however, were frequently giving out, increasing the number of dismounted men; and it being requisite to relieve the prisoners by allowing them occasionally to ride, four hundred more men were forced to go on foot. As the marches were long and the heat intense, these men occasionally straggled, and were picked up by the guerrillas and home guards of the neighborhood. Frequently, however, the guerrillas got the worst of it. On one occasion, Captain Todd, of the Home Guard of King and Queen County, the man who had commanded the party who shot Colonel Dahlgren, having summoned a squad of men to surrender, received in reply a volley which killed some of his followers and forced him to retire severely wounded.

From King and Queen Court House the prisoners, dismounted men and wounded were forwarded to West Point; and information having been received that the cavalry trains were still at the White House, the rest of the command countermarched to Dunkirk, where, just twelve days from the commencement of the expedition, it was met by fresh supplies.

On the morning of the nineteenth, however, a report

was received that the rebels had attacked the White House, and artillery firing in that quarter confirmed the rumor. The troops, therefore, marched with rapidity to its relief, arriving in the afternoon to hear that the gun-boats, invalids and colored soldiers had succeeded in repulsing the attack. By the next morning the cavalry was in line to cover the position, and after some little conflict, completely baffled the enemy.

It was a very serious matter for two divisions, worn down by such excessive labors to less than five thousand men, to escort nine hundred wagons across the Peninsula to the James River; but the necessity was urgent and had to be undertaken. During the night of the twentieth and day of the twenty-first, while Gregg's Division covered the flank, and the First Division guarded the advance, the wagons moved to Jones' Bridge, crossing the Chickahominy safely at that point. While it was still slowly coming into park, a vigorous attack was made by the enemy upon a small picket post from Devin's Brigade, which was guarding a cross road in advance. Two companies of colored men belonging to an Indiana regiment, though exhausted by a long night-march, hurried cheerfully forward to their support. The outpost had been pressed back to the summit of a hill near the main road by the rebel advance, while the main body was hastily protecting themselves by a barricade to assist them to hold the position just seized. Fixing bayonets as they ran, the negroes started at a charge, accompanied by an unearthly howl. The assault was so sudden and demoralizing that the rebel fire, passing above their heads, only injured the last man descending the hill; and the next moment they were darting through the barricades, using the bayonet with vigor. Outstripping their white officers, they followed on the track of the enemy, chasing them back to their artillery, and holding their ground until relieved. The cavalry received them in a very complimentary manner on their return, and decided unanimously that colored men could fight. The effect upon the enemy was so great that they could not be persuaded to make any further attack; and though they were unaware of the fact, they then lost their best chance of seizing some of our wagons.

During the following night all the cavalry was anxiously engaged guarding the approaches to the Charles City road, on which the long train of wagons was moving. It would have been possible to have taken the whole park to the landing opposite Fort Powhatan, without any further difficulty, but General Sheridan was anxious, if possible, to carry it up to our lines at Haxall's, where it could have found protection behind the infantry, and enabled us at once to rest. He therefore determined that he would, if possible, keep on up the river; and in order to do so in safety, he formed the principal part of the First Division in advance of the train, while the Second, thrown well out towards St. Mary's Church, faced the enemy in that direction. As our advance had swept the whole region of rebel scouts, the enemy was unable to tell how large a portion of our force was in line before them, and what was the position of our train. Their natural conclusion was that the main body of the corps opposed them, and that the wagons were still in our rear, covered by our line. Their commander was therefore extremely cautious in his demonstrations, sending out scouting and skirmishing parties in all directions, and feeling our line front, flank and rear. The position was a very curious one. Some wagons with the pack train of the division were in the centre of our force; a portion of the troops dismounted in temporary breastworks, the paucity of their numbers concealed by the thickness of the woods, while more than a third of the whole force formed a picket and skirmish line in a complete circle, the right and left communicating in the rear.

At half-past two in the afternoon, Sheridan had his whole train in park at Charles City Court House, and in response to an inquiry from General Gregg, sent word to that officer to fall back until he connected with the First Division. It was nearly four o'clock by the time that the order reached Gregg, and the necessary preparations had been made; and in the meantime the rebels, having captured some of our dispatches, had learned that we had only one division, and that their prey had almost escaped. Just at the moment, then, that our line of dismounted men had retired from their breastworks and partially mounted their horses, the enemy, in line of battle four deep, charged along the entire front.

Notwithstanding the disadvantage of the position, our men met them bravely, their fire being so vigorous and their line so firm that the enemy could not close with the bayonet. Owing to the formation of the ground, also, the rebels could not bring their artillery into position, while we had two splendid four-gun batteries, which opened with great effect. While the First New Jersey, withdrawn from picketing the rear, was ordered to take charge of the retiring train, and to cover it from attack, the Tenth New York and First Maine Regiments held their ground upon the right and left. The fire of the rebels was high, and more terrible in sound than in reality; while that of our men, more true, drove away the repeated charges that were made upon them. But as fast as one line fell back before the carbines of the cavalry and the terrible canister of Denison and Randall, a fresh line pressed forward to take their place; and slowly, with unbroken formation, our men began to retire across the open ground. The Sixth Ohio, through all the fire, sat firm and silent, with drawn sabres, behind the guns of Randall; and in the face of that battery, supported by such an unbroken force, the enemy did not dare to venture far from the protection of the woods. On the left, the First Massachusetts and the steady First Pennsylvania covered Denison's flank; and no enemy could live in front of those well-served guns. Thus, slowly backward moved the line, passing the guns, which still covered their retirement. Then, at the last moment, Randall hastily limbered up, and as the dismounted men, sheltered by the woods, broke at full speed for their horses, the battery was whirled away from danger, while the Ohio still threatened any advancing force. Now came the more difficult task of withdrawing Lieutenant Denison, whose right flank was thus uncovered, and against whose front the enemy was also advancing.

"Take care!" said an aid-de-camp to him as he passed, "They will get your guns."

"Take my battery?" cried the artillery officer, fiercely, "They cannot take my battery. No rebels on that field can take my battery!" and he continued his fire, his men sharing his enthusiastic confidence.

Not until he had expended his last round of ammunition, when even the First Pennsylvania were being driven past him, and the enemy was within thirty rods of his front, did he consent to leave; and then, before the smoke of the last discharge had thinned, his men had the pieces off the field.

Now, at length, the rebels could charge with greater

vigor. Happily, the narrow lanes through the thick pine woods on the flanks had been well barricaded, and the rebel cavalry were timid in attacking men who had fought with such steadiness and fallen back apparently in such good order; for, owing partly to the lateness of our dismounted men's removal from the field, partly to the narrowness of the roads, but chiefly to the obscurity and confusion created by the dust, it was almost impossible to get any of those on foot mounted and in any formation. Thus, the retreat had to be covered by those regiments who had been on picket, or whom the general had been able to retire earlier in the conflict. Thus, there were just sufficient men to make a show of resistance as a rear-guard, and a heavy cavalry charge around our flanks could have swept over the small body of Jerseymen who acted as escort to the train and cover in that direction. But the enemy, for some unaccountable reason, seemed to be afraid to trust himself in force anywhere except close upon our rear; and there, helped by the dust, our men made up in daring and steadiness for their paucity of numbers. The Eighth Pennsylvania made a noble charge, their colonel, Hewey, falling far in among the enemy. In their turn, the Fourth, the Sixteenth and the Thirteenth Regiments met the rebels with effect; and as they returned to rally, numbers of them fell in upon the skirmish line wherever it seemed too weak for resistance.

When the First New Jersey was recalled from picket to the train, Lieutenant-Colonel Kester sent the adjutant to draw in Captain Kinsley and Lieutenant Shaw, who held the posts farthest from the main body. It took some little time to gather the men together and to complete the barricade across the road; and, so close was the rebel advance, when they wheeled into the main road, that the two rearmost files, who happened to be somewhat delayed, found the rebel skirmishers interposed between them and the rest, and were forced to take a circuit through the road. As Shaw and the adjutant came out, General Davies ordered them to dismount and hold a position near the entrance of the wood. Lieutenant-Colonel Gardiner, with a small body of the First Pennsylvania, voluntarily fell in on their left, while on the right stood a detachment of the First Maine. These few men, by a determined stand and a rapid fire, held the enemy in check until their cavalry could be seen gathering in force to charge, and their guns, brought up to Denison's abandoned ground, opened down the road; and then, just in time, our men, slipping into the woods, ran alongside of the charging rebels, and, as they were checked, regained the protection of the rear guard. Captain Hick, with the sixth squadron, was placed to hold a road leading to the northeast as the wagons were convoyed past; and with good judgment he maintained his position while the confused mass of soldiers from the main action hurried from the field. The rebel left, by this time, so superior was their force, had actually swept around our right for two miles; and had they dared to close in hotly, must have cut in two our division; but they felt their way slowly and with small parties, until the opportunity was lost. Hick prepared a barricade across the road, leaving a gap that might be filled up by a single stroke of the axe. Beyond this gap he advanced Lieutenant Brower with the front rank, designing him to meet the enemy with a volley, under whose effect he could withdraw and leave the rear rank, with the completed barricade, to give a more telling check to the enemy than the combined force could have done. But when the rebels advanced upon

Brower's front and received his fire, our rear guard was already passing, and another body of the enemy was so close upon his flank that he was unable even to rejoin Captain Hick, and had to fall back by himself from the road. Hick, for the same reason, could neither deliver his fire nor complete the barricade; for the enemy on the main road had already dashed past his little party. He had to slip as quietly as possible into the wood, and to make a wide detour before he could rejoin the division. Lieutenant Canse, on another post, collected all his men except Sergeant Johnson and his command from Company G, whose position, as he drew near, was already behind the enemy. As he moved off, giving them up as lost, he saw, drawn across the road where it made an angle, a position of considerable advantage, a small squad of mounted carbineers awaiting the advance of the enemy. As he observed to a superior officer, "Those men should be supported," the enemy made their charge. As coolly as if he had a regiment, the commander of the squad gave his orders, which were as steadily obeyed. With one volley they checked the rebels; with a second, they actually cleared the road. Then General Gregg himself commanded them to withdraw; and Canse recognized with surprise and pleasure Sergeant Johnson, with every one of his men collected and in good order.

General Gregg, with his brigade commanders, their staff officers and orderlies, himself made a part of the rear guard, controlling the men as only their general can. At one time, as he dismounted beside Colonel Covode of the Fourth Pennsylvania, who lay on the ground mortally wounded, the rebels were almost upon him. His adjutant-general, Captain Wier, forced him upon his horse, and then, turning on foot, met the rebel advance with his revolver. His fire must have been unexpectedly effective, for it checked the charging column; and he was able to mount and to withdraw with impunity. At another time a friend and brother staff officer was shot in the melée beside him. "Who did that?" asked Wier, pulling up his horse and turning round. An orderly pointed out the rebel officer who had fired the shot. The next moment Wier was among the enemy, and had blown out the rebel's brains. Then, with the same suddenness, he dashed back to our line.

The dust was now so thick that it was impossible to see anything at the distance of twenty feet. The fighting was done by ear, as sometimes occurs at night. In one charge, a rebel, imagining that he was followed by his comrades, rode through the thickest dust, and suddenly came out in the presence of General Davies and a crowd of our officers. The man's pistol was raised, and he was evidently prepared to meet nothing but a flying enemy; for in the nervousness of the meeting with a brigadier standing his ground, he could only answer to the question "Who are you?" with the irrelevant response, "I surrender."

Through the intricacies of the road and the obscurity of the dust, Colonel Kester, with difficulty but with success, guided the train, the led horses and the broken column to Charles City Court House. Though the fighting had been so heavy, it had been so smothered by the woods that General Sheridan only learned of it upon the arrival of our command. While it was re-formed and rallied, and again posted to command the flank, the train was immediately put in motion toward the river at Wilson's wharf; and by the next morning, without the loss of a wagon, a gun, a wheel, or an unwounded horse, the whole train was parked in safety under cover of the gunboats.

General Gregg considered that night that his fight might be regarded as successful, if he had lost no more than a thousand men. To his surprise and astonishment, the list of killed, wounded and missing amounted only to three hundred and seventy-seven; and this number included the many men who, fainting from the dust and heat, had fallen, unable to continue their retreat. Of this comparatively small loss, about fifty who had been cut off or captured made their escape from the enemy, who were far more exhausted and demoralized than our force. Their object was the train; and losing this, they felt that they had lost all.

On the twenty-seventh of June, the mass of the wagons having already been transported across the river, the First Brigade of Gregg was transferred to the neighborhood of Fort Powhatan; and enjoyed two days' release from duty after three weeks of unintermitted and harassing service.

CHAPTER XVII.

OPERATIONS AROUND PETERSBURG.

On the evening of the twenty-ninth of June, the division moved from the neighborhood of Fort Powhatan, taking the road to Prince George's Court House. Night marches are always terribly wearisome things. There are apt to be continual little delays, occasioned by suddenly discovered obstructions in the road, where perhaps the whole division has to break by two or by file, with a period of rapid marching afterward to close up, the distance seeming greater when the column in advance cannot be discerned. The regular halts and formations for rest are also not so comfortable as they are in the day. Any accidental departure from an appointed place, for the purpose of improving the couch, is with difficulty rectified; and the sleep is broken by apprehension of some order coming which has not been observed, or the fear of some horse or man stumbling over the sleeper. There had been so much of this, however, in the course of the three years' service, that it was borne as philosophically as possible, each man fastening his horse to any convenient bush, or to his arm, if nothing better offered, and then at once pillowing his head upon his haversack. In this fashion of alternate marching and halting, regular or accidental, the whole night passed away, officers and men gradually growing snappish and quarrelsome as they grew sleepy, until the broad dawn brightened around us as we formed around the desolated court house.

In the hot, dusty night and burning sun of June, the horses suffered terribly from thirst; and it was pitiful to see the heads turn towards the little stagnant streams which we were obliged to pass because there was no possibility of watering a division there.

Further onward to the south and west we traveled, learning that General Wilson had gotten into a terrible scrape on his return from the Danville Railroad, his opponents having been the cavalry who handled us so severely at St. Mary's Church, with some of Hill's infantry, instead of Ewell's, to support them. He had apparently returned before General Grant had expected him; for the Sixth Corps, which was ordered to Ream's Station to meet him, only arrived after be had been beaten away from there; and we were sent out to afford cover to any of his men who might be straggling in through the swamps below the Blackwater River.

Our regiment, the one furthest in advance, during the first day only picked up a rebel prisoner, who had escaped from them and was lying hidden in the woods; but on the morning of the second, just as we were preparing to move off, a worn-out officer made his way into our pickets, who introduced himself as Major Pope, of the Eighth New York, one of the finest regiments in the service. He told us his experience over a welcome meal of hard biscuit.

When General Wilson determined to fall back from Ream's Station, and seek a crossing further south into our lines, Chapman's Brigade was left to cover the movement. During the whole night they lay there receiving no order to withdraw, until at last their commander determined to do so on his own responsibility. It was while this was being accomplished that the enemy, who had moved completely around the flanks of the line, struck them on all sides, seizing the road by which alone they had hopes of escaping. Major Pope led his regiment rapidly back from their rude breastwork, filing through the woods on one side of the road and fighting with the rebels, who were in it, until they came to a swampy creek, across which lay a single log. As he ran across it to examine whether the swamp was passable there, he saw the enemy come down upon his men, capturing every one, whereupon he threw himself on the ground in a small thicket, determined to make an effort to escape. While he lay there he heard hundreds of our men carried past as prisoners, and could distinguish their voices in conversation. At nightfall, the rebels having departed, he rose up, determined, if possible, to capture a prisoner and force him to pilot him through the pickets. In this he was remarkably successful, lying, with his prisoner, within ear-shot of the squad to which the man belonged until they moved away, and then being guided honorably outside of their furthest post. Then, after a long and harassing journey, he reached our position just in time to be taken in by us.

After passing a night pleasantly at Lee's Mill Dam, the division moved back to the neighborhood of the Court House, escorting a number of Wilson's men, who had come into the various posts. On the fifth of July we passed into a tolerably comfortable camp, on the road between City Point and the station of the dismounted cavalry, in which neighborhood, in the intervals of our long marches to picket the rear and left of the army, we remained until the twenty-sixth. The only action which we had was about the thirteenth, when we went out to feel the enemy's position in the direction of Ream's Station, an affair of no importance, resulting in the wounding of a few men, two or three from our regiment. It occasioned, however, some inconvenience to a large family of women, who happened to be collected in a house just upon the skirmish line. As the colonel and some of his staff were walking around the house, observing the position of affairs, one of the men informed the adjutant that there was a curious spectacle inside. On entering one of the rooms, he found the walls lined with all the feather-beds and mattresses in the house, and prone upon the floor were fifteen females, from the old woman of eighty to the girl of thirteen, all with bare feet and scanty skirts, all terribly frightened, and all drumming with their heels upon the floor in a paroxysm of fear, whenever a shot struck the house. Though it was a pitiable, it was an intensely ludicrous spectacle, not from the natural and reasonable terror, but from the remarkable and unrestrained manner in which it was displayed; and the adjutant left them there, still screaming and trembling, he knowing no way of soothing their apprehensions or diverting their emotions.

On the evening of the twenty-sixth of July, the First and Second Divisions of cavalry with the Second Corps of infantry were put in motion; and behind the lines of the Army of the James moved unperceived by the enemy across the river at Deep Bottom before morning, surprising the command of the rebel general, Pickett, and capturing four twenty-pound Parrott guns. The whole day was spent by our troops in ostentatiously taking up their positions and erecting elaborate fortifications, while wagon trains beyond the river sent up dust sufficient to indicate a movement of the main army. The next morning, the two divisions of cavalry, a portion of the infantry moving in flank and rear, advanced towards the Charles City road, above Malvern Hill. While General Torbert's division held the left towards Deep Run, Gregg moved by a country road around their left threatening their flank and rear. This soon forced them to take the offensive in anticipation of our movements. General Davies, with his two advance regiments, the Tenth New York and the Sixth Ohio, had already succeeded in turning their position, when our flankers were briskly attacked by rebel infantry skirmishers. General Gregg instantly dismounted the Pennsylvania, and threw out some mounted men of the First Jersey to assist them. These soon drove back the enemy, and formed a connected skirmish line with the First Division, while Denison's battery threw shell into the woods. In a few minutes a couple of brigades of infantry in line of battle charged over the Pennsylvanians, and with their flanks in the air moved directly upon our centre.

At the commencement of the attack, before its character had been fairly demonstrated, the First New Jersey and First Massachusetts had been dismounted and sent to the left to prevent the enemy from breaking in between us and the First Division; and beneath their solid fire from a projecting spur of woodland, the extreme right of the rebel line split off, and bearing to our left, ran directly into the arms of the Regular Brigade with three stands of colors. The main force of the enemy at the same time bore to our right, and disregarding the fire that the Jersey poured into their exposed right flank, advanced steadily and unbroken upon the guns there placed. Owing to the absence of General Davies with the advance when the attack was made, no support had been detailed for the battery; and as Denison with his accustomed gallantry continued his fire until the last moment, it happened that the wheel-horses of one gun were shot just as he limbered up. Though he and his lieutenant, Cameron, the lieutenant-colonel of the Ohio, Colonel Avery, of the Tenth New York, and a few men who were with them made desperate efforts to save the piece, they were unable to effect it; and it had to be left in the hands of the rebels. When we recovered the ground, a pile of twenty-nine rebel dead and five mortally wounded in front of the piece showed how effectually it had been served.

A charge of cavalry upon the rebel flank would have been immensely effective; but owing to the causes before stated, there was no mounted regiment of the First Brigade in the right place at the right time, and the reckless daring of the rebels proved their salvation. Though, of course, they were soon driven back with loss, they had one of our guns, and had secured their line of retreat.

The Second Division fell back in the evening to Strawberry Plains, and in the middle of the night the First Brigade, moving across the rush-strewn pontoon bridge without noise, halted under the nearest cover. In the morning, leaving their horses behind, and presenting the appearance of a fresh column of infantry, they again recrossed the bridge, and ascending the hills in sight of the enemy, began to throw up a line of breastworks. The next night the Second Corps crossed the river, and followed by the whole cavalry force marched as rapidly as possible to the left. In the morning the famous mine was exploded, the assault, so well designed and admirably masked, failed, and the whole series of manœuvres had therefore resulted in nothing but unavailing fatigue and bloodshed. The Second Division, however, was not yet allowed a rest. It was pushed on to its old ground at Lee's Mills, where the rebels during our absence, had established a picket post. The narrow bridge across the mill-dam had been destroyed by the enemy, who thus had secured a strong position. Through the swampy ground below, however, a dismounted force of the First Massachusetts, with the third battalion of the Jersey, pushed along around the rebel right flank, while the Tenth New York skirmished in their front. Under cover of the artillery the Second Pennsylvania prepared to charge across the mill-dam, while the First New Jersey mounted was ready to charge as soon as plank could be laid upon the bridge. The fire of the New York men passing over the heads of the enemy, forced our men who had gotten in their rear to be very cautious; but at length, simultaneously, the Pennsylvanians charged in front, and the Massachusetts with our third battalion on the flank of the enemy, forcing them to run at full speed into the woods, abandoning their blankets and provisions. As those of them who had reached their horses started off at full speed, the Jersey came upon them driving over the bridge and dashed after them at a charge. The movement was splendidly executed, but the rebels did not wait for its performance. As the regiment went over and through their barricades, the horses breasting the fence-rails and crashing among the trees, the enemy was seen in full gallop beyond them. After a tremendous race in which a few prisoners were captured, the regiment returned, and the ground was held by an improved line of pickets. The brigade, changing from one dusty camp to another, was able to get some sleep at night but very little rest during the day, the duty being heavy upon so small a force.

Though changing position now and then, and alternating a picket every three days, the force did not get any real repose; and when, on the ninth of August, we were directed to prepare a permanent camp, a prophetic instinct warned us to expect instead immediate marching orders. It was, therefore, no surprise when the night of the twelfth found us again on the march for the north side of the James River. The Second Corps, which had been carried down the river in transports, and whose men imagined themselves on the road to Washington, were surprised to find themselves disembarking nearer Richmond than the point where they had entered the steamers; and by noon the next day, the whole force was once again moving over the ground deserted the preceding fortnight. While the Tenth Corps advanced on the right bank of Deep Run, the Second Corps took the side away from the river; and the Second Division of cavalry moved in advance and to the right of the Second Corps. There was quite a lively skirmish over the ground of our former fight, between the First New Jersey and the rebel cavalry, in which we had one or two men killed, a few others wounded, and Lieutenant-Colonel Janeway had a finger carried off while he was using his pocket-handkerchief. The desired position was taken and held; several lines of rebel earthworks were rendered valueless; and there the operations ended for that day.

The next morning, the Second Brigade made a very gallant and successful attack upon the rebel cavalry under General Chambliss. Striking them near the junction of the Quaker road and that to Charles City Court House and breaking them almost instantly, Colonel Gregg followed up his advantage with a promptitude and energy very remarkable. When he was wounded during the pursuit, General Gregg himself headed the brigade, and with his adjutant-general, his bugler, McArdell of the First New Jersey, and two or three men of the Second Pennsylvania, came suddenly upon General Chambliss in the act of rallying his men. "Bugler, sound the charge!" shouted Wier, as if they were followed by a regiment. As the ringing notes struck their ears, accompanied by the shout of the general and his party and the sound of the charging horses, Chambliss' men began to waver; and a few shots from our party, one of which killed the rebel commander, dispersed the whole of them in flight.

Through White Oak Swamp to within a very few miles of Richmond our troopers followed the broken enemy, picking up many prisoners; and then, returning, formed line in the neighborhood of the swamp, while they prepared a barricade behind it to command the roads passing through. Being attacked here by Ewell's infantry in force, they had to make a rapid and difficult retreat, which was accomplished successfully, though Captain Wier and several men lost their horses, which mired in the swamp. The barricade and breastwork had been formed, however, and proved afterwards of very marked importance.

Though, during the fourteenth and fifteenth of August, the Tenth Corps on the left, and the Second Corps in the centre, had some severe and successful engagements, they did not come in any way within the observation of the cavalry, who were now employed in holding the line of the Charles City road, from Malvern Hill, northward, until they connected with the pickets from the Tenth Corps. Here, on the afternoon of the eighteenth, the Second Division was fiercely attacked by the cavalry of the enemy, assisted by the Richmond provisional troops, who had by this time learned tolerably well to stand fire. The extreme left and advance of the line, near the point where the road passes the swamp, was held by the Tenth New York Cavalry, a regiment which, under Colonel Avery, had rapidly advanced to a high state of efficiency. Twice already, the night before and that morning, the rebels had attempted to take the barricade, after endeavoring to demolish it with artillery; but the gallant New Yorkers had almost annihilated the charging party. On this occasion they fought under the eye of General Gregg himself, and seemed determined to especially distinguish themselves. Avery allowed the rebel line to close almost to the breastwork before his men revealed themselves. Then he poured in a fearful volley, seconded by a cheer that of itself would have shaken the opposing line. Ten minutes was enough time to settle the business; and without the loss of a man, the Tenth drove off the assaulting party. Along the right the Second Brigade was more unfortunate. The officer who succeeded Colonel Gregg had not the coolness and experience of that officer, and appeared inclined to assert his dignity by rather pooh-poohing the observations and suggestions made by Colonel Chamberlain, of the First Massachusetts, whose posts he was relieving. The consequence was that when the attack came, in the precise way in which Chamberlain had anticipated, the men of the relieving force were unprepared to meet it. The First Maine, a few of whom were still left together, and the First Massachusetts, whom their colonel had prepared to meet such an emergency, were all that could show fight; and covered by them, the rest of the troops fell rapidly back. The rebel forces would have inflicted much more damage if they had not been so undisciplined, drunk and disorderly. As it was, whenever their officers had brought them into a position from which they could have damaged us, the men, with their shrieks and shouts and excitement, made the snare so very obvious that all of the retreating force easily avoided it. Nevertheless, they had almost reached General Gregg's headquarters, and the artillery in position there was limbering up, unable to do service without support, when the

First New Jersey, which had just been relieved from picket, debouched from the woods ready to offer cover to everything. Sending part of the regiment dismounted to guard the flanks towards Malvern, Colonel Kester wheeled the rest into position to support the guns, which, unlimbering, threw such a fire into the enemy that, at once, with no more efforts to attack, they retired from the whole field.

On the afternoon of the nineteenth, the cavalry commenced re-crossing the river, over which much of the infantry had already secretly been taken. On the road we heard of the success of Grant's main design, the seizure of the Weldon road. Warren, with the Fifth Corps, had sprung upon it suddenly and unexpectedly, and though suffering severely, still retained it, and we, with such other troops as could be spared, were hurrying to his assistance. For General Grant was holding and extending that immense line with an effective force of only forty thousand men; and therefore every one of them had to be exercised to the utmost.

It was late on the morning of the twentieth that, by roads already made almost impassable with fresh mud, we came upon the hospitals of the Fifth Corps. While there, we could hear the occasional fire of skirmishers here and there, and thence get some general notion of the position of our line of battle. On our right was the fatal gap through which had come the rebel charge which had almost annihilated the brigade of Hays, and reduced to a shadow the whole of Ayres' Division; but the punishment inflicted in return gave security that the same experiment would not be tried again, when the Ninth Corps had already made connection. Beyond a broad screen of wood in our front lay the railroad, covered by intrenchments, in whose construction Warren had exerted all his engineering artifice; and to the left, with woods and swamps limiting the means of approach to a few poor roads, lay the one roadway by the side of the railroad to Ream's Station.

The rain, which heretofore during the summer had been withheld to the point of utter drought, now seemed desirous to make up all arrears in the shortest time. All the approaches were flooded with standing water; and the passage of a wagon over the light, porous ground made deep ruts of gradually thickening mud. There seemed no really solid bottom to the soil. Wagon after wagon cut in deeper; until, on a road that three days' sunshine would cover with incalculable dust, unloaded wagons sank above the axles, and had to be abandoned until the rains were over. The Fifth Corps had already been obliged, in the intervals of fighting, to call off men from intrenching to lay corduroy roads on which to transport their rations and ammunition; and now the colored division of the Ninth Corps was hard at work in adding to what they had accomplished.

Along the railroad below the breastworks a body of workmen were engaged in destroying the rails with a machine patented for that purpose; but the road was in such a bad condition that the machine could not add seriously to its worthlessness. The ties were so rotten, the rails so poorly tempered, that there was no purchase afforded for the instrument, no sufficient resistance to call forth its powers. While the engineers were experimenting along the line on the twenty-first, and the First Brigade of Gregg's was out to protect them, there came suddenly intimations of an attack upon the extreme left of Warren's line. So closely was it pushed, and so rapidly made, that the main force of our brigade had no time to gain the road on which it had advanced; but retreating across the flooded fields, reached the flank of the infantry in safety. It was amusing and provoking to hear the infantry criticising our behavior. "Look at that cavalry! Talk about cavalry fighting! There they go, running at the first shot!" Before they had finished these remarks, they saw our column suddenly halt and form; then the men, springing down from their horses, arrayed themselves with their carbines in line of battle; and then, with a cheer, past the infantry line and far in advance of them, the dismounted troopers rushed down upon the rebel flank. An involuntary shout of applause broke from the ranks of men who had just been reviling us; and, as if to emulate our daring, out galloped an artillery officer with a three-inch Parrott gun. "Clear the way, cavalry!" he shouted, as his cannoniers wheeled the piece into position; and right along the rebel line he sent a charge of canister. This terrible fire completed the work that we had begun; and the rebel force, curling away from our attack, ran directly into the arms of a reëntrant angle of Warren's fortification, where they were speedily forced to surrender. One of our officers rode up to the artillery officer who had made this gallant dash, inquiring, "Captain, what is supporting you?" "Supporting me?" replied he, looking right and left to see if he could not find some supporting body. "Supporting me!" he repeated, with a grim smile, on finding nothing in his neighborhood—"Canister!" and he illustrated his response by a final discharge of the gun.

These reëntering angles of Warren's fortifications brought terrible dismay upon the enemy. Thinking that they had turned his line, they rushed into its centre to be cooped up by a concentrated fire upon their front and both flanks, which mowed them down like wheat before a reaping-machine; and of the division that attacked, scarcely any escaped death or imprisonment.

The line of the Weldon Railroad was finally secured. There were some sad accidents that happened in our regiment during this brilliant affair. Phillips, of Company F, and one or two other gallant troopers had just completed their term of service; but they did not hesitate to join their comrades in the charge; and nearly every one of them fell dead or severely wounded in the front of the line on that last day of military duty.

Now the Second Corps, covered by our cavalry, began to move down the railroad, to complete the destruction of the track. Brigade after brigade piled the ties together and laid the rails across them, to be bent and twisted by the heat; until, on the evening of the twenty-third, the whole road almost to Stony Creek Station was a line of smoking embers and worthless iron. During that day, Gregg's Division, with the exception of the New Jersey and Sixth Ohio, who were on picket, had a brilliant engagement in front of Ream's Station. Throwing up a line of works which were masked by the surrounding wood, the general, sending out skirmishers, tempted the rebels to a fierce attack. Calling back the skirmishers at a run, he induced the enemy to follow them recklessly with a charge directly upon the face of this line of breastworks. Then his men rose upon them with a deadly fire and drove them back in confusion, leaving their killed and wounded piled upon the ground.

Though his work upon the railroad was finished, General Hancock resolved to hold the works at Ream's Station another day, to allow Warren to perfect his line of works along the rear of the new position; and on the evening of the twenty-fourth, his little corps received the attack of all the forces that General Lee could scrape together. Five desperate charges were made and repelled; and had not one of those mistakes occurred which are constantly deranging military manœuvres on both sides, the enemy would have met with an overwhelming defeat. But a division which General Parke had sent from the Ninth Corps to proceed down the railroad and turn the rebel flank, when it had nearly taken its position, was, by some misapprehension of orders or circumstance, transferred to the Jerusalem plank road, and thus kept out of action. Meantime, the enemy had seized the anticipated position, which would thus have insured their destruction, between the ground held by the pickets of the First Cavalry Brigade and the line of infantry fortifications; and the fire of twelve admirably served guns, enfilading their position, demoralized the heavy artillery regiments of Gibbon's Division, at the very moment of the sixth rebel assault. The works were entered by the enemy and captured, with seven pieces of artillery. General Gregg, with his cavalry and such of the infantry as he could gather, checked the enemy and covered the retreat of the Second Corps. The sixteen-shooters of the First District of Columbia Cavalry, whom he had withdrawn temporarily from Colonel Spear's command, poured forth such a fire as no line could withstand; and seconded by the carbines of our division, held the enemy at bay. With great daring, General Gregg himself mounted with his staff, kept his men in line, unbroken; and when darkness set in, his skirmish line was but a hundred yards from the line of captured works. If the Second Corps had been a little stronger, the guns and the position could have been retaken; but even Hancock, in the real state of affairs, did not venture to attempt it. The severe loss of the enemy accomplished nothing more. Warren had now made his line impregnable, and the position was to us of no value.

Thus, on the twenty-fourth of August, ended the last fight of the First New Jersey Cavalry during the three years of their original enlistment. On the first of September, they and their brothers of the First Pennsylvania embarked at City Point for home, leaving, however, men and officers enough behind them to worthily represent the old regiment which had seen so many campaigns.

A week after, the little band marched into the market house at Trenton, to receive the hospitality so kindly extended to them by their fellow-citizens at home; and then those who had been brothers-in-arms for three years of battle and bivouac, bade each other farewell as they separated to seek, in the quiet walks of peace, the rest and enjoyment which they had so long sacrificed for their country.

CHAPTER XVIII.

THE CONCLUDING OPERATIONS OF THE YEAR.

The writer of the foregoing pages has been able to speak from personal observation of much that he has recorded; and for the rest has relied upon the statements of eye-witnesses and actors in the adventures through which the regiment had very lately passed.

For the remainder of the book he has been at serious disadvantage, many hundreds of miles from written authorities, with no knowledge of his own (for he left the regiment at the end of the three years' term), and with only one person's unassisted memory on which to rely. For the patient way in which that one (Brev. Brig. Gen. Walter R. Robbins), has endeavored to supply the writer's lack, and to recall events fast fading away from his own memory, the writer is very grateful; and he begs it to be understood that for mis-statements of fact and errors of description he considers himself to blame and by no means his informant; but in spite of all his efforts he feels it almost impossible to attain a clear and vivid conception of events himself, and he therefore despairs of conveying it to the reader. His only aim has been to preserve the history of the First New Jersey Cavalry from being as lame and unsatisfactory as it necessarily would have been had it left out the share of the regiment in the battles that closed the lengthened combat between the Army of the Potomac and its resolute antagonist, the Army of Northern Virginia.

Colonel Kester had retired from the field; Lieutenant-Colonel Janeway was absent, waiting the healing of his wound; so the command of the regiment devolved upon Beaumont, the senior major. This officer had latterly been but little with the regiment in the field; but as at this time he was in charge of the camp of dismounted men at City Point, he was able promptly to assume command.

There were two small affairs on the north side of the James, on September fifth and September twenty-third, with regard to which the writer has no detailed information; but, Captain Robbins, having recovered from his wounds and returned to duty as acting inspector-general on the brigade staff, has been able to give some particulars respecting the succeeding actions.

Not contented with the possession of the Weldon Road, General Grant desired to extend his lines yet further to the left, and oblige Lee to cover more ground and employ a larger force to maintain possession of the Southside Railroad, his last direct line of communication with the South. When the infantry moved out for this, the cavalry was sent to sweep the country on their rear and flank, and to guard against surprise. During September twenty-ninth and thirtieth, therefore, the First New Jersey scouted and picketed the Ream's Station and Dinwiddie Court House roads, surprising and capturing a few men and horses, but encountering no further hostile force.

On the night of the thirtieth they were relieved, and rejoining the brigade, moved forward with it around the left of the Fifth Corps to the Armstrong House. This had been the picket headquarters for the Southern cavalry on vidette duty around that portion of our old position; but in consequence of the advance of our troops, it had been hastily abandoned by the enemy. Ignorant, perhaps, that it had been thus left, or else thinking that it had been reëstablished, a force of Southern cavalry was moving toward it in one direction at the very moment that the advance of Davies' Brigade ascended the hill' to it from another.

The night being intensely dark, and the ground unknown and very near the enemy, General Davies had judiciously dismounted his leading squadron, and was moving with great caution to feel his way. The captain of the Sixth Ohio, commanding the squadron, heard before him the sound of moving cavalry. Hastily forming his men along a line of fence, he challenged, "Who goes there?" "Butler's South Carolina Brigade," was the response. With great presence of mind, he coolly continued, "Advance, and give the countersign." Then, seizing the officer who approached to give it, he shouted "Fire!" to his men. The Southerners thrown completely off their guard before, and stunned by the rattling volley they received, broke and ran in all directions; and as was afterwards learned, the brigade was not brought together again for two whole days. The prisoner proved to be Captain Butler, a brother of the general.

But for the boldness of the Ohio captain, the movement might have resulted in grave disaster to our side; for it had been actually countermanded before it had been made; but the darkness had delayed the messenger conveying the order and the information that our infantry were not yet in position which it presupposed. In accordance with the order which now arrived, the brigade fell back about a mile and a half to the Vaughn road. The next morning it advanced within sight of some of the entrenchments that the infantry afterwards stormed. Major Beaumont, thinking them vulnerable, ordered Captain Hart to charge them with his battalion; but the order was fortunately revoked, as they gave some trouble to the men of the Second Corps soon afterwards.

It being found that General Hampton with his cavalry corps had appeared at the point which the brigade had just left, it was ordered to return and retake its position on the Vaughn road at the Davis House.

The road at this point takes a decided bend to the south, and enters a low cedar wood, with here and there a swamp. The Davis House, situated on a hill, commands the road for some distance; and Hampton had occupied it with a regiment and a section of artillery. These, however, were hastily withdrawn, in consequence of a demonstration by Captain Robbins on their flank; and our men, entering some partially constructed breastworks of the enemy, occupied themselves in reversing and completing them.

The Union position formed two adjacent sides of a parallelogram, meeting nearly at a right angle at the point where the road entered the wood. Picketing the road was Lieutenant Hughes with Company C of the First New Jersey. In the trenches on the right were the First Massachusetts, First New Jersey and Sixth Ohio. On the left, the Tenth New York and the First Pennsylvania. After several hours' firing, which did little damage to the Union troops behind their intrenchments, the Southerners made an attack intended to be simultaneous upon both faces of the Union position; Donovan's brigade charging the right, Young's assailing the left. Captain Weir of the division staff, who had been assisting to handle the men upon the right, had just been wounded, and Captain Robbins, of the brigade staff, took his place. As the rebels charged, Robbins ordered a charge to meet it. Leaping their breastworks, the men advanced, shouting, at a run; and the enemy hesitated, halted, opened a scattering fire, and then gave way. Captain Robbins did not pursue, but halted in his turn and opened fire, beneath which the enemy fell fast; but they displayed much individual coolness, raising and carrying off their wounded men, though many of the bearers fell and had in their turn to be carried off. As soon as they had finally retired, he recalled his men to the breastworks in time to assist in the repulse of the attack on the left.

This assault had been fortunately delayed and weakened by a happy piece of daring on the part of Captain Hughes. Hearing heavy firing in his rear, both to the right and left, and feeling himself cut off, he determined to make a vigorous effort at extrication. Forming his mounted men, therefore, he dashed in upon the flank and rear of General Young. That officer, taking the charge to be that of a mounted brigade, dispatched a note to General Hampton announcing that he was surrounded, and feared that he would be unable to make his way out; and in the meantime hesitated in his advance until our right had regained its position, after baffling the attack upon them. Hughes succeeded not only in cutting his way through, but also in bringing as a prisoner an aide of General Young.

The attack upon the left, when made, was far from being as vigorous as that upon the right. Met by a sharp fire of artillery from our horse battery on the hill by the Davis House, and by a tremendous and sustained storm of balls from the Spencer carbines of the whole force, they fell back with loss, abandoning their dead.

The loss on the Union side, though the fire was quite hot, was comparatively small, that of the First Jersey being four killed, seven wounded, and one missing. How great was the enemy's loss is unknown; though, as the attacking party, without breastworks, they probably suffered most. During the fight, not only were the sixty rounds of ammunition carried by each man expended, but forty thousand additional had been distributed along the line during the engagement. The fight had been carried on in heavy rain, and mud so deep that the Herald reporter at headquarters had thought himself quite safe in telegraphing that, owing to the weather, the cavalry had not been engaged. On the third, the brigade retired to the Jerusalem plank road. On the sixth, it had a skirmish in the vicinity of Hatcher's Run. On the twenty-seventh, the whole Army of the Potomac marched out of its entrenchments against the enemy's works in the neighborhood of the Boydton plank road, the left reaching a point within a mile of the Southside Railroad. After the infantry had crossed Hatcher's Run, the cavalry held the fords of the creek to protect their flank and rear. Here, while the infantry were heavily engaged in front, the cavalry also had formidable work to do; the honor of the day, however, belonging to the Second and Third Brigades, General Smith, of the Third, charging his famous First Maine Regiment with clubbed carbines, for want of ammunition, and driving the enemy before him. The position was extremely difficult to hold. The force in front of the Second and Third Brigades was protected by breastworks and heavy timber, while our men had nothing but the open field. Attack after attack was made by the rebels endeavoring to break through between the cavalry and the infantry, and so to turn their flank. When night fell, Smith's men, who had been fighting all day, fell back, withdrawing their picket line before the First Brigade had relieved them. The enemy, feeling their way in the dark, pushed their line forward into the gap until they were within a few yards of the road by which the left communicated with headquarters. In the meantime Captain Robbins, running his line, actually cut the rebel line in two, enclosing a considerable portion of them; but, planning too elaborately to capture the whole, he lost even this part, the rebels stealing silently away before his arrangements were perfected. At midnight, the division retired with the rest of the army, and ultimately returned to camp.

On December first, the cavalry division made an expedition to Stony Creek Station, the point on the Weldon Railroad from which the rebels wagoned their supplies around our left. The rebel pickets were found at the Nottoway River. They were swept back and followed up rapidly for a couple of miles, when the pursuers came upon a fort held by three hundred men. While the men in the fort were anticipating a regular assault from dismounted men, the Third Brigade charged it, mounted, sweeping around, entering by the gorge and capturing all the garrison. Destroying some provisions, water-tanks and steam saw-mills, the Union cavalry retired, the First New Jersey and First Pennsylvania forming the rear guard, under command of Colonel Janeway. The enemy charged repeatedly, but were always vigorously repulsed. During this retrograde movement, there was frequently a wide gap left between the rear guard and the column. Surgeon T——, of the First Pennsylvania, riding in this, *flushed* some rebel skulkers by the roadside. Drawing his revolver, he forced the nearest to surrender. Not content with this, he dashed after the others, bent on either killing or capturing the whole. He was only prevented by a slight inadvertence. As he raised his pistol, instead of shooting the rebels, he sent a bullet through the head of his own horse, and retired both prisonerless and dismounted.

On the sixth of December, the regiment took part in the Weldon Railroad expedition. The weather was cold, and rainy, and snowy, and the roads very rough and deep. Along the Jerusalem plank road, wearily familiar to the men under all circumstances of dust and mud, sun and storm, day and night, but now presenting a new but not agreeable aspect seen through half-melted snow, the cavalry pushed on toward the south, crossing the Nottaway River, passing around the late fighting ground at Stony Creek and halting for the night at Sussex Court House. The next morning, Captain Hughes, commanding the advance of the brigade, struck the enemy's pickets, but swept them rapidly before him without bringing the column to a halt until the cavalry had reached a point as far in the advance as it was practicable for them to reach, and yet keep their connection with the slower moving infantry. During the whole day, the moving column in the rear had been breaking up the railroad, and this continued through the night, the country for miles being illuminated by the piles of burning ties, across which lay the bending and twisted rails. A mile which intervened between the rear of the cavalry and the head of the infantry was destroyed by McAllister's Brigade of Jersey infantry. The next morning, the cavalry pushed still further forward, while the infantry were gradually retiring. At length, near Hicksford, where the road to Gaston and Raleigh branches off from the Weldon line, a force was found in strong works, defending the crossing of the Meherrin River. The works were covered by a thick wood extending for a mile along the road; and along the skirts of a wood, a body of cavalry was posted. Colonel Janeway sent forward Captain Brooks to charge these men and clear the way. Of course no Southern cavalry then in the field could stand against a charge in which Robbins, Brooks and Craig were all engaged. Along a narrow road, breaking off here and there to pursue a fugitive visible through the trees, the fifth squadron (poor Brodrick's pet command) swept forward at the run, until the road took a sudden twist, and lost itself in an abattis of felled trees, perfectly impassable for horses. From the rifle pits along the front of the rebel works a heavy fire was poured into the squadron as soon as it appeared. Robbins received a bullet through his hat, which grazed his head; Craig and Johnson had their horses shot, and some of the men were unhorsed in like manner; but Brooks, covering his men as well as possible, held his position until the rest of the brigade came up. Then Sargent, with the First Massachusetts, was ordered to make a charge. Nothing could be more gallantly attempted; but it was wild to hope for any success so long as the enemy were not frightened from their guns. Sargent fell dead from his horse before they took the gallop; and the regiment pulled up in confusion, with the loss of several horses and some men. Then Janeway and the rest of the New Jersey took the field. Janeway was in his element at once. There never was a quiet-mannered man who took more delight in fighting, whether mounted or on foot; and no one ever did his work more thoroughly or with more perfect management of the troops under his command. As a consequence, the regiment was always ready to do what he directed with a confidence that made them irresistible. Dismounting his whole force under cover of the woods, he charged them straight into the rifle pits, over ditches and fallen trees, under a heavy fire of musketry and artillery from the woods behind. Nothing would have been more after Janeway's heart than a charge onward into the rebel forts, a quarter of a mile beyond; and with his own men, and reasonable support, it is probable that he would have succeeded, opposing his Spencer carbines to the bayonets of the enemy; but the commanding officer, not being himself engaged in the attack, thought probably that the possible loss of men would not be compensated for by the possession of works that he did not intend to hold; so the regiment was kept in the pits under a freezing rain, with the guns of the forts firing on them at so close a range that the slightest exposure of the person was sufficient to ensure a bullet. Here they remained for three hours, when darkness enabled them to retire. The whole loss was four killed, eleven wounded, four missing. Lieutenant Reed, formerly a sergeant of Company E, was mortally wounded here, only six weeks after a promotion which his conduct had well deserved. After continuing the destruction of the railroad through the night, at four A. M. the cavalry retired, overtaking the infantry and gathering up its stragglers.

On the fifth of February, General Grant made another of those movements which kept the enemy on the alert, and extended his own lines in preparation for the grand movement in the spring.

The ground had been so fortified by the enemy that it was necessary for the troops to move to the south by Dinwiddie Court House, and then to turn to the north, turning the right flank of the rebels at the same time that another force was attacking them in front. The cavalry was at the extreme left of the army, and the First Brigade at the extreme left of the cavalry, covering as usual the flank and rear. The position which the Union troops had seized was one which demanded an attack from the enemy, to shake off, if possible, the slowly tightening grasp in which Grant was enclosing Lee's position; and they in their turn worked towards the Union left to penetrate between the infantry and cavalry. The First Brigade, all of whose men were wearied with disturbed rest and night march, and who had been fretted rather than excited by strangely languid skirmishing on the part of the rebel cavalry, began about ten A. M. to feel a marked difference in the character of the fire to which they were exposed. Infantry was coming on the ground. The line, however, was favorable to our men, who were lying behind breastworks, and so placed that the fire of one portion of the line could assist another. The First Jersey at the extreme left had not very much work to do, except a battalion on the skirmish line under Major Beaumont; but there was a rapid series of casualties among its senior officers, Major Beaumont, uninjured while at the front, was wounded by a stray shot as soon as he was recalled; Davies, commanding the brigade, was wounded; Janeway, who succeeded him, was wounded; Avery, of the Tenth New York, was taken so sick that he had to relinquish the command; Tremaine, his lieutenant-colonel, was mortally wounded while steadying his men; and Robbins, a junior major, had for a time the command of the whole brigade. Scarcely, however, had the enemy's infantry time to begin their attack, before the Fifth Corps came to meet them; and the cavalry, relieved from the brunt of the battle, were retired to the Davis House, on the Vaughn road, and posted so as to secure it to our troops. It was a weary night, the men sleeping in the mud, with no wood for fuel, no blankets, no forage for the horses, and they were intensely grateful, when on the ninth they were once more in their comfortable winter quarters. The regimental loss was eleven—seven of them officers.

For the closing campaign of the war, in the absence of further authorities and fuller details, we are forced to append the official report of the commanding officer, Lieutenant-Colonel Walter R. Robbins, which is as follows:

"On the morning of March twenty-ninth, the regiment broke camp, near Petersburg, and in connection with the brigade, moved out on the Ream's Station and Dinwiddie Court House road, crossing Rowanty Creek at Malon's Bridge. The cavalry arrived at and occupied Dinwiddie Court House that night. Colonel Janeway was ordered to move out on the Flatfoot road and hold it for the night, which he did. On the thirtieth the brigade moved up on the Five Forks road, to the support of General Merritt, but did not become engaged. On the morning of the thirty-first, Captain Craig, of Company A, commanding the first squadron, who was picketing on the Mill road leading to Chamberlain's Creek, took a portion of his reserve, cleverly passed through the rebel cavalry vidette line, surprised and captured an infantry picket reserve of the enemy and brought them into our lines, without any loss to his command. For this bold and skillful act Captain Craig is deserving of great praise. From these prisoners it was learned that the divisions of the rebel generals Pickett and Bushrod Johnson were in our front. After receiving this information Colonel Janeway directed Major Hart to strengthen and extend the picket line. He then ordered me to move out with my battalion and make a reconnoissance on the left, and ascertain if the enemy was moving around in that direction. In doing this I found the Old Scott road, leading across Chamberlain's Creek, to be entirely open, thus giving the enemy a splendid opportunity to move his troops between the brigades of Generals Davies and Smith. Feeling the importance of this road, I left Captain Hick, with Companies K, M, and L, to cover it, while I pushed further to the left with Company H, Lieutenant Killey commanding. Communicated with General Smith, and ascertained from him that the enemy was quiet on his front. I then returned to the Old Scott road, and moved my battalion down to the ford on Chamberlain's Creek, dismounted, sent my horses to the rear, caused a breastwork of rails to be made, and communicated the importance of the road and what I was doing to Colonel Janeway. The colonel came down and approved of the course I had taken, and ordered me to remain and hold the ford. About this time the enemy made a spirited attack on the lines of Generals Gregg and Smith, and vainly endeavored to drive them from their position. Meanwhile they pushed two brigades of infantry down to the ford and engaged my command, which was holding it. The firing soon became sharp and vigorous. We had a great advantage in position, being behind works and on much lower ground than the enemy, who were without any covering and within easy range. Many of the enemy fell before our withering fire, among the number was General Ransom. Seeing that we were not to be forced from our position in this manner, they moved one brigade to our right (which met Major Hart's battalion), and one to our left, thus enveloping our flanks, and charged a third brigade on our front. The battalion, I am proud to say, remained at their post and kept up the firing until the enemy were within fifteen yards of them, when hopes of longer holding the ford could not be entertained. The order was then given to fall back, which was done first in a broken and confused line, but which was quickly formed and placed in position to cover the left flank of a regiment of cavalry which had been ordered to our support some time before. That regiment, after delivering two or three volleys, went rapidly to the rear, leaving my battalion to cover their shameful retreat. The enemy were in strong force and moved rapidly against us, and my men could do nothing but keep up a running fight until we passed through Calonel Janeway's line, who with the first and second battalions and a Michigan regiment, was gallantly holding the enemy in check. Major Hart, with the first battalion, had been sent out to my support, but meeting the brigade of the enemy which had moved on my right, was unable to get to me. Hart fought his command as he always did, with signal courage, great skill, and telling effect upon the enemy. It was his last fight. He was shot dead in his saddle, the bullet entered his right cheek and passed through the spinal column. Colonel Janeway, with his own and a Michigan regiment, with detachments from other regiments slowly retired before the overwhelming force of the enemy to the road leading from Dinwiddie to Five Forks, where he connected his left with the remainder of the brigade. The enemy here changed his direction and operated wholly on the left, forcing the whole cavalry corps back to Dinwiddie Court House. Here we remained for the night, the enemy within pistol-shot distance. The casualties of this day were as follows: Major James H. Hart, killed; First Lieutenant Joseph Killey, captured; First Lieutenant and A. C. S., C. W.

Camp, captured; three enlisted men killed; six enlisted men wounded and four captured.

"Early the next morning the enemy was forced back, his forces routed, and many prisoners taken. On the first and second of April our brigade remained in camp near Dinwiddie Court House, guarding the trains of the corps. On the night of the second we moved from Dinwiddie Court House, in the rear of the train, to the Claiborne road, in the vicinity of Hatcher's Run, bivouacked for a few hours, and then (the morning of the third) pushed on, crossing the Southside Railroad at Sutherland Station to Wilson's Plantation, on the Namozine road, where we encamped for the night. The line of march was resumed early on the next morning (the fourth) on a road running parallel to the one on which Lee was retreating, and we arrived at Jettersville, on the Southside Railroad, about four o'clock, P. M. It was expected that the enemy would be found in force at this place. Nothing, however, was found, and the cavalry was ordered to bivouac for the night. Pursuant to orders from brigade headquarters, Captain Craig, with Companies A and B, reported to General Davies, who instructed him to push down the Amelia Springs road, and ascertain if any force of the enemy was there. Captain Craig obeyed his instructions to the letter, returned, and reported having captured twenty-two infantry soldiers, thirty-eight horses, and a number of mules, all of which he brought into camp. From these prisoners it was learned that Lee, with his army, was at Amelia Court House. At three o'clock on the following morning our brigade was moving toward that place. Arriving at Paine's Cross Roads, General Davies learned that the enemy's wagon train was but a short distance off. Pushing rapidly on, we soon struck the advance guard, consisting of one brigade of cavalry, one regiment of infantry and a battery of artillery. General Davies at once charged and routed this force, captured a large number of prisoners, five pieces of artillery, one hundred and eighty wagons, three hundred and forty horses and mules. The wagons were burned, and the prisoners, artillery and animals all brought off. In this charge five battle-flags were captured by the following named officers and men of this regiment: Captain Samuel Craig, Company A; First Sergeant George W. Stewart, Company E; Private Lewis Locke, Company A; Private Christian Straele, Company I.

"After the capture of the wagon train, &c., General Davies directed Colonel Janeway to move up on a road to the left and hold it until he got all captured property, prisoners, &c., well to the rear. Through some mistake, no orders were received by Colonel Janeway to retire. Ascertaining that everything had re-crossed the stream, he wisely withdrew, but upon arriving at the bridge he found it in possession of the enemy. Captain Brooks, with Companies H and K, made an elegant charge and drove the enemy from the bridge and held the road leading to it while the remainder of the regiment crossed. Captain Hick, with Companies L and M, now formed the rear guard. Arriving at Painesville, the regiment was ordered to remain there one half hour and hold the road while the captured property was being taken off. The enemy now began to show himself in large numbers in our front and on both flanks. I was directed by Colonel Janeway to take Company H, and strengthen and assume command of the rear guard. The enemy pressed us vigorously, making several charges, which were, with one exception (the last one), handsomely repulsed. The enemy routed us in their last charge and drove us back to a detachment of the regiment which had been formed for our support. This detachment made a splendid charge and checked the enemy, which enabled us to withdraw to where the remainder of the brigade was formed. In this charge the gallant Captain Brooks, of Company K, was taken prisoner and sabred by General Geary after he had surrendered. A number of the men were also wounded. The enemy here displayed a much larger force than our own. They lapped both of our flanks and engaged us sharply in our front; but the regiment, with brave, skillful Janeway in command, unflinchingly stood their ground, and used their Spencer carbine with telling effect upon the enemy. It would be useless for me to particularize the actions of any officer or man—they all performed their duty in their usual manner as soldiers; but the conduct of Surgeon Willes was so different from medical officers generally that I cannot pass it by without notice. He was in the thickest of the fight, and was of great service to Colonel Janeway in conveying orders and rallying men from different regiments, taking them to the skirmish line, remaining there himself, and encouraging them on. We were relieved by the second brigade of our division, when we retired to a point near Amelia Springs, and remained at that place until two o'clock, P. M., when we were again ordered into action. Colonel Janeway was ordered by General Davies to support two other regiments in a charge. These regiments were repulsed in the charge, and driven back to their support. Colonel Janeway immediately ordered a charge, in leading which our brave, gallant colonel was shot through the head, and died almost instantly. This cast a gloom over the whole regiment. His superior we never knew. A brave, skillful officer, a courteous gentleman, a true, earnest patriot—qualities which have endeared him to every officer and man of the regiment.

"We held the line until after dark, when we were relieved and ordered back to Jettersville. The casualties of this day were as follows: Colonel Hugh H. Janeway, killed; Captain Joseph Brooks, Company K, wounded and prisoner; Second Lieutenant James S. Mettler, Company D, prisoner; Second Lieutenant William Wilson, Company G, prisoner; First Lieutenant and Adjutant James T. Clancy, wounded; one enlisted man killed, eight enlisted men wounded, and twenty-one prisoners.

"We bivouacked at Jettersville that night, and moved at ten o'clock, A. M., the following day. Generals Merritt and Custer had captured and burned a large number of wagons near Sailor's Creek. They were heavily engaged with the enemy when we came up. The cavalry corps was formed to charge the enemy. This regiment formed the connection on the extreme right of the second division with General Custer's division (third). In front of our regiment was a plain, open field, where the enemy had a good line of rifle pits. I received orders from General Davies to charge this line of works. I expected the whole line would charge at the same time. I moved on their line of works at once. The troops on my right, instead of charging the enemy, were being pushed back. The regiment acted splendidly, but it was impossible for us to make any impression on the enemy's line. General Custer's division, on my right, and a portion of our brigade on my left was giving way. The fire from the enemy was terrible. Lieutenants Ford and Mettler, and many of the men, were wounded, and horses were dropping fast. I was forced to retire, which I did by moving the regiment to the right, in order to place them under cover of a rising piece of ground. Major General Crook and others complimented the regiment very highly for the gallant manner in which they conducted themselves. I received orders from General Davies to form the regiment in its original place in line. I understood afterwards that the order given for the regiment to charge was *rather premature.* Some two hours later, a simultaneous charge was made by the Sixth Corps and the cavalry. This was probably the grandest cavalry charge of the war. General Ewell, with nearly all his corps, was captured, besides a large number of cannon. In this charge I suffered the temporary loss of Captain Hughes, of Company C, commanding the second battalion. He fell from his horse, wounded in the head. He is a brave, capable officer, and I could illy spare him. In going to the rear he discovered two pieces of artillery, which the enemy, unable to move off, had secreted in the woods. He collected some dismounted men, and with a team of mules brought them off. First Lieutenants Johnson, commanding Company M, and Fay, commanding Company L, charged and captured two light field pieces from the enemy. Captain Craig, as usual, had his horse shot. We encamped on the battle field that night. The casualties of this day were as follows: Captain William Hughes, Company C, wounded; First Lieutenant Thomas H. Ford, Company D, wounded; Second Lieutenant James S. Mettler, wounded; with seven enlisted men wounded and two missing.

The line of march was taken up early on the morning of the 7th, and the enemy pushed rapidly to Farmville and across the Appomattox River. Here they made a stand and enticed the Second Brigade of our division (Brevet Brigadier-General J. Erwin Gregg commanding) into a beautifully laid trap, which resulted in their complete rout. The brigade came back in great confusion, and but for the timely aid of General Davies would have swept a portion of this regiment along with them. The general, seeing the state of affairs, directed me, through Captain Lebo, of his staff, to move rapidly to the left of the road, and there form and check the enemy, which order was executed to his entire satisfaction. The action of the regiment upon this occasion gave great confidence to the troops in the rear, who were following us in the line of march. The brigade was formed in line, and the enemy held by us until dark, when we were relieved by the infantry. That night we marched to and encamped at Prospect Station, on the Lynchburg Railroad. The casualties of this day were as follows: Second Lieutenant Charles Watts, Company E, wounded; Second Lieutenant Lawrence Fay, Company F, wounded; three enlisted men killed, six wounded, and four prisoners.

"On the eighth we marched to Appomattox Depot, on the Lynchburg Railroad. The regiment was not engaged that day. Four trains of cars, loaded with supplies for Lee's army, were captured at the depot.

"On the morning of the ninth our hearts were gladdened by the intelligence that the enemy were now headed off, we being in possession of the road on which Lee was retreating, and that if we could hold this road until our infantry came up, Lee and his army could not possibly escape. The bright, smiling faces which could be seen in the regiment told plainly that for their share of the work we could depend upon them. General Davies was covering a road on the right of Lee's army; the remainder of our division was fighting on our right. The General, learning that the enemy were driving them, ordered me, through his very efficient aide-de-camp, Lieutenant Robert Henry, of Company A, of this regiment, to find and engage the enemy's flank, favoring as much as possible the brigades of Gregg and Smith, who were being so vigorously pushed. Captain Craig, who had the advance in this movement, reported a rebel cavalry brigade moving toward us in an oblique direction, and apparently coming from General Davies' front, and with the intention of cutting us off. I immediately sent Captain Beekman, with the remainder of his battalion, Companies G and I, to strengthen Craig and throw out a strong skirmish line. At the same time, Captain Hick, commanding the Third Battalion, was directed to move to the left and rear, and remain there as a support. Taking Captain Brower, with his battalion, I manœuvered till I succeeded in getting between the enemy and the remainder of the brigade. Captain Beekman at the same time changed direction to the left, keeping his skirmishers between Brower and the enemy. Hick was then brought down to Brower's position. The ever-ready Henry, of General Davies' staff, coming down, I requested him to inform the General what I was doing and what was opposing me. Learning it, he sent the Twenty-Fourth New York Cavalry down to report to me, and orders to fall slowly back and connect my skirmish line with that of the infantry on my right and rear. All this was performed with the loss of one man killed, Lemuel Smith, a private in Company E.

"The infantry relieving us, we were ordered still further to the left, when we again engaged the enemy, and for the last time. Captain Beekman, with the First Battalion, was sent out on the skirmish line. An irregular and harmless firing was kept up for some time. Finally, the skirmish lines of the brigade were ordered to charge the enemy, supported by the regiments, and the enemy was quickly driven in confusion from his position. This successful charge had hardly terminated before orders were received for hostilities to cease. The order was immediately followed by a flag of truce from General Crook to the commanding general of the rebel forces in front of our lines, informing him that Generals Grant and Lee were having an interview and arranging the terms of surrender of the Army of Northern Virginia to General Grant.

"In this last engagement I cannot speak in too high terms of Captains Beekman and Canse. Beekman so manœuvred a portion of his command as to destroy the left of the enemy's skirmish line, by driving it pell mell into the road for Canse to make his last charge, and a gallant and successful one it was. Second Lieutenant Darnstadt, of Company I, we claim to be the last officer wounded in the combined armies operating against Lee's forces. Our cavalry division was the last to receive orders for a cessation of hostilities. The last flag of truce sent out was through our brigade lines. Lieutenant Darnstadt received a painful but not dangerous wound in the head after the truce had passed our own lines. Hostilities ceased and the terms of the surrender agreed upon, we bivouacked that night on the battle field, and our hearts were made glad by the appearance of Captain Brooks, who had just been released from captivity.

"On the morning of the tenth we commenced our return march to Petersburg. On the night of the tenth, while we were encamped at Prospect Station, we had the pleasure of receiving back our captured comrades—First Lieutenants Joseph Killey and C. W. Camp. These officers, before the surrender, managed to make their guard prisoners and escape with them into our lines. We arrived at Petersburg on the eighteenth day of April.

"In this eventful campaign, the regiment, in every engagement, bore itself with conspicuous gallantry. The conduct of the officers, in every instance, was such as to elicit the praise of every one. Adjutant James T. Clancy, throughout the whole campaign, rendered me most efficient service. His conduct in the action of April fifth called forth the commendation of Major General Crook and several of his staff. On that day, while gallantly charging with a detachment of the regiment, he received a painful sabre wound in the hand. He declined to leave the field in this and subsequent battles. Great credit is due to Captain Hughes for our final success in the afternoon engagement of April fifth. On the sixth of April, First Lieutenant Thomas H. Ford received a wound in the left breast by a glancing shot, prohibiting the use of his bridle arm and the wearing of a sabre belt, but he remained with and took an active part in all the battles of the regiment.

"The following non-commissioned officers and private received medals of honor from the Secretary of War for gallantry in the campaign: First Sergeant George W. Stewart, Company E; Sergeant Aaron B. Tompkins, Company G; Sergeant David Southard, Company C; Color Sergeant Charles Wilson; Sergeant William Porter, of Company H; Sergeant Charles Titus, of Company H; Sergeant John Wilson, of Company L; Corporal William B. Hooper, of Company L, and Private Christian Straele, of Company I. In these medals of honor the soldier received a token which is of more value than anything else which could be given him, as they stamp the recipient a brave, faithful soldier, a name to be honored and revered.

"Sergeant-Major William T. Allen; Sergeant Samuel Walton, Company A; Sergeants Charles Krouselmire and John Tinney, Company B; Sergeants William R. Branson, Culver Marshall and Chester Merritt, of Company C; Sergeant John H. Warner, Company D; Sergeants John Shields, William Russell and John Fogarty, Company E; Sergeants Michael Williams and Edward F. Wenner, of Company G; Sergeants John Brochbank and William Hudson, and Corporal Philip Klespie, Company H; Corporals Joseph Marsh and Francis Brown, and Sergeants George W. McPeek, Aaron H. White, William S. Booth and William H. Powell, of Company K; Sergeant William Stout, and Corporals John McKinney and James Brady, Company L; Sergeants John Dane and James S. Tillman, and Corporal William B. Easton, of Company M, are all worthy of mention. They are well known in the regiment for their good conduct in this memorable campaign.

"We remained in camp near Petersburg until the morning of the twenty-fourth of April, when, in connection with the cavalry corps, we took up our line of march toward Danville, Va., to operate against the rebel General Johnston's army. After a march of five days we reached Boston Bridge Station, on the Richmond and Danville Railroad, when we learned that Johnston had surrendered his army to General Sherman. We encamped there for the night, and on the following morning commenced our return march for Petersburg, arriving there on the third day of May.

"The regiment was not engaged during this march. In this as well as in the previous campaigns, we are indebted to Lieutenant Robert Henry, of Company A of this regiment, and aid-de-camp to Brevet Major-General

Davies, for many good services he rendered the regiment. In all engagements of the regiment, when possible, he was sure to be with us, and with his courage and zeal, won the admiration of both officers and men.

"On the morning of May tenth we broke camp and commenced our march for Alexandria, via Richmond and the Orange and Alexandria Railroad. We arrived at Alexandria on the morning of the sixteenth of May. On the twenty-first we marched to Bladensburg, Maryland. On the twenty-second we had the pleasure of receiving our State colors. On the twenty-third we took part in the grand review at Washington. The regiment was complimented by many for the neat uniform, dress, and soldierly appearance of its officers and men, and its precision in marching."

The regiment was mustered out of the service at Vienna, Virginia, July 24th, 1865, by Lieutenant P. L. Lee, A. C. M., Department Washington, D. C. Leaving Washington about noon, the veterans reached Trenton at six o'clock, evening, and were met by a large concourse of citizens, who gave them a hearty welcome. The ladies at the "Soldiers' Rest" had a plentiful supper in waiting, and the regiment was regaled with all the substantials and delicacies that liberality could provide. After the men had satisfied their hunger, Hon, W. S. Johnson, Secretary of State, made a brief and appropriate address, bidding them welcome to their homes, and expressing the debt of gratitude due them for the bravery they had shown and the sacrifices they had endured in behalf of their own State and in defence of the nation. The speech was received with hearty cheers. They afterwards accepted of an invitation to an entertainment provided for them at Bechtel Hall. The regiment numbered about eight hundred men, in good health and condition.

CHAPTER XIX.

LIST OF ACTIONS IN WHICH THE FIRST NEW JERSEY CAVALRY PARTICIPATED FROM ITS ORGANIZATION IN 1861 UNTIL DISCHARGED IN 1865.

1. Pohick Church, Va., December 29, 1861.
2. Pohick Creek, Va., January 15, 1862.
3. Seddons' Farm, Va., May 1, 1862.
4. Gray's Farm, Va., May 9, 1862.
5. Strasburg, Va., June 1, 1862.
6. Woodstock, Va., June 2, 1862.
7. Harrisonburg, Va., June 6, 1862.
8. Cross Keys, Va., June 8, 1862.
9. Madison Court House, Va., July 27, 1862.
10. Barnett's Ford, (Rapidan,) Va., July 29, 1862.
11. Barnett's Ford, (Rapidan,) Va., August 4, 1862.
12. Barnett's Ford (Rapidan,) Va., August 7, 1862.
13. Rappahannock Station, Va., August 18, 1862.
14. Cedar Mountain, Va,, August 19, 1862.
15. Rappahannock Station, Va., August 20, 1862.
16. Warrenton, Va., August 23, 1862.
17. Waterloo Ford, (Rappahannock,) Va., August 24, 1862.
18. Snicker's Gap, Va., August 28, 1862.
19. Second Bull Run, Va., August 29, 1862.
20. Second Bull Run, Va., August 30, 1862.
21. Chantilly, Va., September 1, 1862.
22. Warrenton, Va., September 24, 1862.
23. Aldie, Va., October 31, 1862.
24. Port Conoway, Va., November 19, 1862.
25. Fredericksburg, Va., December 11, 1862.

26. Fredericksburg, Va., December 13, 1862.
27. Rappahannock Station, Va., April 7, 1863.
28. Stoneman's Raid, Va., April 30, 1863.
29. Rappahannock Station and Kelly's Ford, Va., May 19, 1863.
30. Brandy Station, Va., June 9, 1863.
31. Aldie, Va., June 17, 1863.
32. Middleburg, Va., June 19, 1863.
33. Upperville, Va., June 21, 1863.
34. Westminster, Md., June 30, 1863.
35. Gettysburg, Penna., July 2, 1863.
36. Gettysburg, Penna., July 3, 1863.
37. Emmettsburg, Md., July 4, 1863.
38. Emmettsburg, Md., July 6, 1863.
39. Tettersburg, Penna., July 7, 1863.
40. Cavetown, Md., July 8, 1863.
41. Harper's Ferry, Va., July 14, 1863.
42. Sheppardstown, Md., July 16, 1863.
43. Berryville, Va., July 31, 1863.
44. Salem, Va., August 15, 1863.
45. White Plains, Va., August 16, 1863.
46. Sulphur Springs, Va., October 12, 1863.
47. Bristow Station, Va., October 14, 1863.
48. Mine Run, Va., November 27, 1863.
49. Parker's Store, Va., November 29, 1863.
50. Custer's Raid, Va., February 18, 1864.
51. Ravenna River, Va., February 21, 1864.
52. Ely's Ford, (Rapidan,) Va., May 3, 1864.
53. Todd's Tavern, Va., May 5, 1864.
54. Todd's Tavern, Va., May 7, 1864.
55. Sheridan's Raid, Va., May 9, 1864.
56. Beaver Dam Station, Va., May 10, 1864.
57. Yellow Tavern, Va., May 11, 1864.
58. Fortifications of Richmond, Va., May 12, 1864.
59. Ashland Station, Va., May 11, 1864.
60. Church of the Messiah, Va., May 21, 1864.
61. North Anna River, Va., May 24, 1864.
62. Hawes' Shop, Va., May 28, 1864.

63. Emmons's Church, Va., May 29, 1864.
64. Cold Harbor, Va., June 1, 1864.
65. Gaines' Mills, Va., June 2, 1864.
66. Chickahominy River, Va., June 2, 1864.
67. Bottom's Bridge, Va., June 4, 1864.
68. Bottom's Bridge, Va., June 5, 1864.
69. Pamunkey River, Va., June 8, 1864.
70. Trevillyan Station, Va., June 12, 1864.
71. White House, Va., June 20, 1864.
72. White House, Va., June 21, 1864.
73. St. Mary's Church, Va., June 24, 1864.
74. Rear of Petersburg, Va., June 29, 1864.
75. West of Petersburg, Va., July 12, 1864.
76. Malvern Hill, Va., July 28, 1864.
77. Malvern Hill, Va., July 30, 1864.
78. Malvern Hill, Va., August 14, 1864.
79. Charles City Court House, Va., August 16, 1864.
80. Charles City Cross Roads, Va., August 17, 1864.
81. Reams Station, Va., August 26, 1864.
82. Malvern Hill, Va., September 5, 1864.
83. Charles City, Va., September 11, 1864.
84. Jerusalem Plank Road, Va., September 17, 1864.
85. Reams Station, Va., September 29, 1864.
86. Reams Station, Va., September 30, 1864.
87. Vaughn Road, Va., October 1, 1864.
88. Boydton Road, Va., October 6, 1864.
89. Stony Creek, Va., November 27, 1864.
90. Bellefield Station, Va., December 9, 1864.
91. Dinwiddie Court House, Va., February 6, 1865.
92. Hatcher's Run, Va., February 7, 1865.
93. Five Forks, Va., March 31, 1865.
94. Jettersville, Va., April 5, 1865.
95. Sailor's Creek, Va., April 6, 1865.
96. Farmville, Va., April 7, 1865.
97. Appomattox Court House, Va., April 9, 1865.

APPENDIX:

FIELD AND STAFF FIRST CAVALRY REGIMENT, N. J. VOLS.

William Halsted, Colonel.
Percy Wyndham, Colonel.
John W. Kester, Capt. Co. E, Lieut. Col., Colonel.
Hugh L. Janeway, Capt. Co. L, Major, Lieut. Col., Colonel.
Myron H. Beaumont, Major, Lieut. Col., Colonel.
Julius H. Alexander, Lieut. Colonel.
Joseph Karge, Lieut. Colonel.
Virgil Broderick Capt. Co. K, Major, Lieut. Colonel.
Walter R. Robbins, Capt. Co. G, Major, Lieut. Col.
Henry C Halsted, Major.
Ivins D. Jones, Capt. Co. C, Major.
Alexander M. Cummings, Major.
John Shelmire, Capt. Co. A, Major.
Henry W. Sawyer, Capt. Co. K, Major.
James H. Hart, Capt. Co. A, Major.
William Harper, Capt. Co. E, Major.
William H. Hick, Capt. Co. L, Major.
William E. Morford, Adjutant.
Brock Carroll, Adjutant.
Myer Asch, Adjutant, Capt. Co. H.
Marcus L. W. Kitchen, Adjutant, Capt. Co. A.
Charles H. McKinstry, 2d Lieut. Co K, Adjutant.
James T. Clancy, 2d Lieut. Co. F, Adjutant, Capt. Co. B.
Benjamin B. Halsted, Quartermaster.
Allen Dale, Com. Sergeant, Quartermaster.
Edwin R. Blaker, 1st Lieut. Co. E, Quartermaster.
William W. James, Quartermaster.
Algernon Walton, Sergeant Co. A, Commissary.
Aaron P. Irons, Q. M.'s Sergeant, Commissary.
Charles W. Camp, Commissary.
William C. Conover, Commissary.
William W. L. Phillips, Surgeon.
Wm. S. Willes, Asst. Surg., Surgeon.
Ferdinand V. Dayton, Asst. Surgeon.
John W. Blackfan, " "
Samuel Powell, " "
Samuel Jones, Hospital Stew'd, Asst. Surgeon.
Stephen W. Van Duyn, Asst. Surgeon.
Henry R. Pyne, Chaplain.

NON-COMMISSIONED STAFF.

William Logan, Private Co. C, Serg't Major.
Thomas S. Cox, Serg't Major, Serg't Co. K.
William P. Logan, Serg't Major.
Cortland Inglin, Corp'l Co. D, Serg't Major, 2d Lieut. Co. F.
Robert B. Canse, Serg't Co. H, Serg't Major, 2d Lieut. Co. G.
Cephas Ross, Serg't Co. A, Serg't Major.
James Dalziel, Serg't Co. B, Serg't Major, 2d Lieut. Co. B.
Charles A. Rowand, Private Co. C, Serg't Major.
William T. Allen, Serg't Co. I, Serg't Major, 2d Lieut. Co. E.
Edward F. Wenner, Q. M's Serg't Co. G, Serg't Major.
Edwin R. Blaker, Q. M's Serg't, 2d Lieut. Co. I.
Charles H. McKinstry Private Co. A, Q. M's Serg't, 2d Lieut. Co. L.
Aaron P. Irons, Serg't Co. F, Q M's Serg't, Commissary.
James M. Stradling, Com. Serg't Co. D, Q. M's Serg't.
Charles P. Thompson, Com. Serg't, Q. M's Serg't, Quartermaster.
Allen Dale, Com. Serg't.
Charles Beans, Serg't Co. A, Com. Serg't.
John R. Morrell, Private Co. A, Com. Serg't.

Joseph P. Meyer, Private Co. I, Saddler Serg't.
Tracy E. Waller, Hospital Steward.
Wm. M. Shaw, Serg't Co. A, Hospital Steward, 2d Lieut. Co. F.
William Hallowell, Serg't Co. A, Hospital Steward.
Reuben B Cole, Private Co. A, Hospital Steward.
Joseph P. Turner, Private Co. H, Vet. Surgeon.
George Applegate, Farrier Co. H, Vet. Surgeon.
Charles H. Wendell, Bugler Co. E, Chief Bugler.
Michael Keefe, Bugler Co. L, Chief Bugler.
Thomas S. Heffren, Private Co. B, Chief Bugler.

BATTALION NON-COMMISSIONED STAFF.

FIRST BATTALION.

Robert Newberg, Serg't Co. E, Serg't Major.
John L. McFarland, Q. M's Serg't Co. E, Q. M's Serg't.
David J. Walton, Corp'l Co. A, Q. M's Serg't.
Lewis Oldfield, Saddler Co. A, Saddler Serg't.
Abraham Morley, Bugler Co. E, Chief Bugler.
Smith Wright, Farrier Co. L, Vet. Surgeon.

SECOND BATTALION.

Lewis Raincar, Serg't Co. F, Serg't Major.
Lemuel Fisher, 1st Serg't Co. I, Q. M's Serg't.
Jonathan Goble, Q. M's Serg't Co. F, Com. Serg't.
Richard Wilson, Vet. Surgeon Co. C, Vet. Surgeon.

THIRD BATTALION.

Samuel Craig, Serg't Major.
Franklin Hammell, Serg't Co. H, Q. M's Serg't.
Isaac Newning, Private Co. B, Com. Serg't.
Peter H. Suydam, Saddler Co. H, Saddler Serg't.
Charles Niles, Private Co. M, Farrier.
William H. Barnhart, Bugler Co. E, Chief Bugler.

DIED.

Virgil Broderick,
Hugh L. Janeway,
John Shelm re,
James H. Hart,
Algernon Walton,
Samuel Powell.

COMPANY A.

John Shelmire, Captain, Major.
James H. Hart, Captain, Major.
Samuel Craig, 1st Lieut. Co. H, Captain.
Jacob R. Sackett, 1st Lieut, Capt. Co. M.
John Hobensack, Serg't, 2d Lieut., 1st Lieut.
William Wyncoop, 1st Serg't, 2d Lieut., 1st Lieut., Capt. Co. C.
George A. Bowne, 2d Lieut. Co. B, 1st Lieut., Capt. Co. M.
Gilbert J. Johnson, 2d Lieut. Co. C, 1st Lieut., Capt. Co. L.
Edward H. Parry, Serg't, 2d Lieut., 1st Lieut. Co. D.
Theodore Michenor, Private, Serg't, 2d Lieut.
Robert Henry, Private Co. C, 2d Lieut.
Joshua P. Kirk, Corp'l, 1st Serg't.
Sam'l Walton, Private, Corp'l, Serg't, 1st Serg't.
Algernon Walton, Serg't., Reg'l Com.
John T. Marple, Corp'l, Serg't.
Cephas Ross, Private, Corp'l, Serg't, Serg't Major.
Edwin Twinning, Serg't.
George K. Roberts, Corp'l, Serg't.
William M. Shaw, Private, Serg't, Hospital Steward.
William Hallowell, Corp'l, Serg't, Hospital Steward.
Charles Beans, Private, Serg't, Reg't Com. Serg't.
Harrison Megargee, Private, Corp'l, Serg't.
John D. Williams, Private, Corp'l, Serg't, 2d Lieut. Co. B.
Albert W. Terry, Private, Corp'l, Serg't.
James D. Walton, Private, Corp'l, Serg't.
Ephraim M. Croasdale, Priv., Serg't.
Charles E. Wilson, Private, Serg't.
Michael Keefe, Chief Bugler, Serg't.
James Grimes, Private, Corp'l, Serg't.
Arthur Shook, Private, Corp'l, Serg't.
John F. Buck, Private, Corp'l, Serg't.
Thomas J. Hellings, Private, Corp'l.
David J. Walton, Corp'l, Q. M's Serg't.
Washington M. Raisner, Private, Corp'l.
Charles Holman, Private Co. I, Corp'l.
Michael Sullivan, Private Co. B, Corp'l.
William Miller, Private, Corp'l.
William C. R. Batten, Private, Corp'l.
Edwin Cramner, Priv. Co. G, Corp'l.
Thomas Ford, Private Co. G, Corp'l.
James F. Long, Private, Corp'l.
Michael Collen, Private Co. G, Corp'l.
John Schoedler, Private, Bugler.
Thomas Holford, Private Co. C, Bugler.
Charles Myers, Blacksmith.
Lewis Oldfield, Saddler Serg't 1st Bat.
Lewis Boissett, Private, Farrier.
William A. Ackerly, Private.
Kinsey C. Allen, "
James E. Austin, "
John Barker, "
James S. Barnard, "
William P. Barnes, "
Edward Beans, "
Charles Beecher, "
James Bloomer, "
Francis Borden, "
Joshua Boyles, "
Oliver L. Bross, "
William E. Brown, "
John H. Bush, "
Henry Cash, "
Solomon Clark, "
Charles R. Coffman, "
Reuben B. Cole, "
John Coleman, "
John D. Cooper, "
Francis Cornell, "
John H. Craven, "
Thomas M. Croasdale, "
James Davenport, "
Mortimer M. Dease, "
John R. Devlin, "
Robert S. Darling, "
William H Embrey, "
John H. Ferrous, Private, Q. M's Serg't.
Richard G. Fletcher, Private.
Jacob R. Giegor, "
William Gillen, "
Theodore F. Grey, "
Rush Griffith, Farrier, Private.
John Gunn, Private.
John H. Gunn, "
Jesse Haff, "
Henry Hagerman, "
Jacob Hart, "
Frank E. Hatch, "
Alexander Hornbeck, "
David W. Howell, "
Gilbert Hunter, "
James W. Ingersoll, "
Harrison Johnson, Private, Serg't, Private.
Jonathan Johnson, Private.
Thomas B. Jordan, "
Patrick King, "

Elwood Knowles, Private.
Joseph H. Lambert, "
William Leonard, "
Joseph Levis, "
William H. Lockwood, "
Joseph Lock, "
John G. Losey, "
William C. Lower, "
Alexander McAffe, "
John McGuire, "
Charles McKinstry, Private, Reg't'l Q. M's Serg't.
Benjamin Messinger, Private.
Lewis B Moorehouse, "
Isaiah Morgan, "
John R. Morrell, Private, Reg't'l Com. Serg't.
James Murray, Private.
Thomas Nice, "
John O'Grady, "
Samuel Paugh, "
Theodore Radcliff, Private, Serg't, Private.
Irving C. Rand, Private.
Michael Riley, "
Jesse Rubencamp, "
Lawrence Rush, Private, Bugler, Private.
Robert Savercool, Private.
Joshua Schaffer, "
Charles J. Shelmire, Private, Corp'l, Wagon Master, Private.
Henry V. Slugg, Private.
Edward Smith, "
William A. Sterling, "
James Stoltz, "
Joseph D. Strader, "
Daniel Sweeny, "
William Taggart, "
David P. Thompson, "
George W. Todd, "
Edwin D. Totten, "
David Van Blarcon, "
William Van Pelt, "
Alfred Walton, "
William Webb, "
Washington W. Weeks, "
Daniel L. Williams, "
Augustus Winterholder, "
Paul P. Winslow, "
Alfred Winters, "
William E. Weller, "
Albert D. Young, "
Ebenezer Young, "

DISCHARGED.

John C. Hobensack, Serg't.
Isaac Jarrett, Private Co. K, Corp'l, Serg't.
Theodore Johnson, Corp'l.
Charles B. Chandler, Private.
Ralph Eastwood, "
John Habnell, "
George O. Miller, "
Joseph Mitchell, Private.
William Montgomery, "
Peter Peterson, "
John Peze, "
Samuel Phillips, "
John H. Sullivan, "
Wilson Teats, "

TRANSFERRED.

Charles B. Perkinpine, Corp'l.
James Welsh, Private.

DIED.

Edmund Scott, Corp'l, Serg't.
Herman Z. Beans, Private, Corp'l, Serg't.
John Black, Private.
James Conn, "
Elias P. Hall, "
Charles B Hart, "
Michael Heilman, "
Franz Heldwin, "
Francis Jagleman, "
Benjamin Jess, "
Franklin Jones, "
Jonathan Jones, "
Henry Laagley, "
Francis Lewis, "
Andrew J. Love, "
Moses W. Lukens, Private.
Thomas O'Brien, "
Charles T. Parry, "
Randolph Radcliff, "
Richard Scribner, "
James Shaw, "
Barnard Smith, "
Henry Smith, "
Charles Somers, "
William C. Stout, "
William Trauger, "
Harvey Tomlinson, "
Daniel Ward, "
William C. Weeks, "
James M. Williams, "

DESERTED.

Elias R. Bennett, Private, Serg't.
George Wallace, Private, Corp'l.
James Conrad, Private, Bugler.
James Black, Private.
James Boyle, "
Edward Brown, "
John B. Cridland, "
John Crossley. "
George W. Daily, "
Adam Fichter, "
Henry Ford, "
Lewis Frey, "
Patrick Gilligan, "
George Goff, "
Charles Hardt, "
Thomas Hartley, "
William Horney, "
Wm. H. Houtdington, "
John Keenan, "
Lewis Knopp, "
John J. Krane, "
Nathan T. Kulp, "
James S. Lefausheur, Private.
Lewis Lock, "
Michael Mathews, "
Charles Maynard, "
Richard McKinley, "
Joseph Messersmith, "
Robert Mitchell, "
John O'Brien, "
Jackson Potter, "
Mahlon Scott, "
Edward Shay, "
James Smith, "
John Stout, "
John Taylor, "
Charles Thompson, "
Henry Tie, "
Henry Varn, "
Thomas Walsh, "
Charles Wilson, "
Daniel Young, "
Isaac B. Zanes, "

UNACCOUNTED FOR.

David Barry, Private.
William Birney, "
George Brown. "
Nathan J. Carey, "
John Carlton, "
William Clark, "
James W. Collins, "
Joseph Cooper, "
James H. Courtenay, "
James Devlin, "
John P. Dillon, "
Patrick Donohue, "
Franklin Edmundson, "
John Farrell, "
Terrence Gorman, "
Charles Green, "
Peter Hauferman, "
Patrick Harvey, Private.
Joseph Hill, "
Korine Hochesion, "
John C. Johnson, "
Joseph Lanning, "
William Lee, "
Peter Logan, "
George Mead, "
Alfred Miller, "
John Miller, "
Joel M. Minnerly, "
Charles Myer, "
Theodore Scott, "
Oscar Tooker, "
John Wiele, "
Samuel H. Wilson, "

COMPANY B.

Richard C. Lewis, Captain.
Horace W. Bristol, 1st Lieut. Co. M, Captain.
Francis B. Allibone, 1st Lieut. Co. L, Captain.
James F. Clancy, Adjutant, Captain.
William Frampton, 1st Lieut.
Harry Jones, 1st Serg't Co. E, 2d Lieut., 1st Lieut.
Richard Hamilton, Serg't Co. C, 1st Lieut.
James Tomkinson, 2d Lieut.
Joseph O'Harris, 1st Serg't, 2d Lieut.
John Hobensack, Serg't Co. A, 2d Lieut., 1st Lieut. Co. A.
Voorhees Dye, 1st Serg't Co. L, 2d Lieut., 1st Lieut. Co. L.
George A. Bowne, Serg't Co. I, 2d Lieut., 1st Lieut. Co. A.
James Dalziel, Serg't Major, 2d Lieut., 1st Lieut. Co. L.
John D. Williams, Serg't Co. A, 2d Lieut., 1st Lieut. Co. H.
Loraine C. Hurtt, Serg't, 1st Serg't.
Charles Krouselmire, Private, 1st Serg't.
John Clark, Private, Serg't, 1st Serg't.
John Williams, Private Co. G, Q. M's Serg't.
John Lawson, Private, Com. Serg't.
William F. Strock, Private, Corp'l, Serg't.
Richard P. Forman, Private, Serg't.
John Kane, Corp'l, Serg't.

Arnold Vanderveer, Private Co. H, Serg't.
John Tynon, Private, Serg't.
John McDade, Private, Serg't.
William H. Wilson, Private Co. H, Serg't., 2d Lieut. Co. G.
William Akroyd, Bugler, Corp'l.
Alex. Cummings, Private, Corp'l.
Daniel B. Risley, Private, Corp'l.
John W. Conover, Private Co. G, Corp'l.
Elias Slack, Private Co. A, Corp'l.
Thomas Henderson, Private, Corp'l.
Philip Ray, Private Co. E, 1st Serg't, Private, Corp'l.
Daniel Sullivan, Private, Corp'l.
James Skinner, Private, Bugler.
Charles McCully, Private, Bugler.
Isaac Meyers, Private, Blacksmith.
Isaac Johnson, Private, Farrier.
Michael Durning, Private Co. I, Saddler.
Samuel V. Adams, Private.
Steward Apgar, Priv., Corp'l, Priv.
James S. Baker, Private.
Michael Bauer, "
John Binder, "
Samuel Birch, "
James Bogert, "
Patrick Broderick, "
James Brown, "
John Brownmiller, "
Thomas J. Cahoe, "
Jacob Casler, "
James Clark, "
George S. Cole, "
Michael Conners, "
William H. Conover, "
Adolph Copisicus, "
Peter Craft, "
Charles W. Davis, "
Amos Featheralf, "
George Fenton, "
John Fitzgibbons, "
Charles B. Fowler, "
John W. France, "
William Glendower, "
Marcus Goodman, "
George Heaney, Saddler, Private. Private.
Thomas S. Heffren, Private, Chief Bugler.
Henry Huber, Private.
Levi Inscho, Private.
Gustavus A. Jackson, "
Eli M. Johnson, "
Jacob E. Johnson, "
William Joules, "
Michael Keep, "
Andrew Klainman, "
John Lawrence, "
James R. Mathews, "
Patrick McAnoy, "
Henry McClellan, "
John Mesner, "
Christian Milier, "
James Morgan, "
Jacob Moritz, "
Francis Murphy, Serg't, Private.
James Murphy, Private.
Jacob Newbold, "
Isaac Newning, Private, Com. Serg't.
James O'Neal, Private.
William H. Palmer, "
John Quinn, "
Aaron H. Rake, "
Whitfield Riker, "
William S. Ruple, "
William Schenck, "
Enoch Shaw, "
John Small, "
Charles Smith, "
Philip Smith, "
Charles Stephens, "
Joseph Stephens, "
James Stiles, "
Peter Stratton, "
Charles Taylor, "
John Thomas, "
Isban Van Hise, "
James Vaughn, "
Jacob Vreeland, "
Theodore Vreeland, "
Peter Wall, "
John Welsh, "
Morgan Welsh, "
John White, "
David C. Whitehead, "
Benjamin Wiles, "
John Williams, "
Richard Williams, "
George W. Willis, "
George Wilson, "
Bernard Winn, "
Daniel Winters, "

DISCHARGED.

Smighton P. Crossman, Private, 1st Serg't.
Peter P. Rink, Serg't.
Austin E. Vanarsdale, Private, Serg't.
Martin Murphy, Corp'l.
Christopher Pomeroy, Corp'l.
John H. W. Seeds, Farrier.
Charles Adams, Private.
Jeremiah Carroll, Corp'l, Private.
George Crowther, Blacksmith, Private.
Henry Danford, Private.
Frederick Gilder, Corp'l, Serg't, Private.

Abraham P. Griggs, Serg't, Private.
Richard Grimes, Private.
George F. Hulshizer, "
Daniel W. Ingersall, "
Patrick Keary, "
Henry Lake, "
Samuel McGann, "
William McGinn, "
David McPherson, "
John A. Meeker, "
James Mills, Private.
Jacob Moore, "
Thomas Mylan, "
Mark C. Price, "
Jacob Smith, "
Thomas Smith, "
Samuel Thomas, "
William Tindle, "
James Toole, "

TRANSFERRED.

Edwin S. Bishop, Private.
John Crooks, "
Antone Frecaut, Private.
Thomas Sampson, "

DIED.

George V. Ege, Serg't.
Charles Page, Private, Serg't.
Henry Alton, Private, Corp'l.
Samuel H. Woodruff, Bugler.
John A. Thomas, Private, Saddler.
Gideon L. Adams, Private.
James C. Barker, "
William B. ecroft, "
John G. Bergfels, Private, Corp'l, Serg't.
George Burren, Private.
John Connolly, "
Joseph Cunningham, "
Alexander Gibson, "
Hugh Gilbraith, Private.
Archibald Hammill, "
William Hitchens, "
James Holt, "
Joseph Howard, "
Charles Kell, "
Thomas Kerr, "
Conrad Klineman, "
Samuel Percival, "
John C. Pownall, "
Jacob Robinson, "
Ransom Shoemaker, "
William Thiel, "
Samuel Tindle, "

DESERTED.

John O'Donnell, Private, Serg't.
Henry Robinson, Private, Corp'l.
John Leonard, Corp'l.
Edward Baker, Private.
Ab'm Barrowclough, "
Daniel Barton, "
Henry Bolton, "
James Boone, "
Peter Brady, "
William Brevier, "
Cyrus F. Bugbee, "
Edward Burke, "
William Castleton, Corp'l, Private.
Henry Christie, Private.
James Clifford, "
William Clough, "
Michael Connelly, "
Solomon Conover, "
William Cupe, "
Robert Curry, "
Thomas Curry, "
John C. Donald, "
Hugh Doran, "
John Eagan, "
William H. Fenton, "
Thomas Glenn, Private.
Henry Goodwin, "
Henry Grand, "
John W. Harman, "
Charles Harrington, "
George Hoff, "
Samuel Hoff, "
Joseph Hurst, "
Michael Madigan, "
Thomas McFarland, "
John Murphy, "
Terence Riley, "
Harmon Smith, "
James Stokes, Private, Corp'l.
John Sweeney, Private.
Arnold Vanetman, "
Peter S. Van Hess, "
Francis Wells, "
William N. Werner, "
James G. West, Bugler, 1st Serg't Co. G, Private.
John White, Private.
Thomas White, "
William Wood, Corp'l, "
Henry Zeakel, "

UNACCOUNTED FOR.

George Adams,	Private.	John Morgan,	Private.
Henry M. Bartlett,	"	Edwin Mulhall,	"
James Burns,	"	Joseph Shaman,	"
James Burt,	"	John Smith, (1)	"
Francis Dean,	"	John Smith, (2)	"
John Eidepentz,	"	John Sullivan (1)	"
James Johnson,	"	John Sullivan, (2)	"
Edwin Jones	"	George Taylor,	"
John Kelly, (1)	"	Henry Thomas,	"
John Kelly, (2)	"	Andrew Thompson,	"
William Kelly,	"	Sydney Thompson,	"
Bernard Kiernad,	"	John Wall,	"
John King,	"	William Walsh,	"
Thomas McGrath,	"		

COMPANY C.

Ivins D. Jones, Captain, Major.
John L. Tash, 1st Lieut., Captain.
William W. Gray, 2d Lieut., 1st Lieut., Captain.
William Wynkoop, 1st Lieut. Co. A, Captain.
William Hughes, 1st Lieut. Co. K, Captain.
William Harper, 2d Lieut., 1st Lieut., Captain Co. E.
Samuel C. Lame Serg't, 2d Lieut. Co. E 1st Lieut.
Jeremiah P. Brower, 2d Lieut. Co. M, 1st Lieut, Captain Co. D.
Charles Watts, Private, Corp'l, Serg't, 1st Serg't, 2d Lieut. Co. E, 1st Lieut.
John H. Morris, Private Co. H, 2d Lieut.
Isaac Rogers, 1st Serg't, 2d Lieut.
Gilbert J. Johnson, Serg't Co. G, 2d Lieut., 1st Lieut. Co. A.
Louis Fohs, 1st Serg't Co. H, 2d Lieut.
William Patterson, Corp., 1st Serg't.
William Branson, Private, Corp., 1st Serg't.
Joseph Voorhees, Private, Serg', Q. M's Serg't.
Robert Patterson, Corp'l, Com. Serg't.
Culver Marshall, Private Co. F, Q. M's Serg't.
Richard Hamilton, Serg't, 1st Lieut. Co. B.
James F. Clancy, Private, Serg't, 2d Lieut. Co. F.
Joseph Voorhees, Private, Serg't
Geo. Wispert, Private, Corp'l, Serg't.
Charles Shion, Corp'l, Serg't.
Isaac Simons, Private, Corp'l, Serg't.
Thomas McParlan, Serg't
Samuel R. Gordon, Private, Corp., Sergeant.
Cornelius Shahan, Private, Sergeant.
James McNeil, Private, Serg't.
Arthur Cooner, Private, Corp'l, Serg't.
David Southard, Private, Corp'l, Serg't.
Charles F. Patterson, Corp'l.
Albert Cox, Private, Corp l.
Jacob Miller, Private, Corp'l.
Harvey Adams, Private, Corp'l.
George W. Hole, Private, Corp'l.
John Akins, Private, Corp'l.
John Sloan, Private Co. F., Corp'l.
Chester Merritt, Private, Corp'l.
William Clark, Private, Corp l.
Levi Heaton, Private, Corp l.
Miles Downey, Private, Corp'l.
John Metcalf, Private, Corp'l.
Aaron Swain, Bugler.
Isaiah Smith, Private, Bugler.
James Cafferty, Private, Farrier.
William Green, Private, Farrier.
James Lindley, Private, Blacksmith.
Geo. C. Davis, Private, Blacksmith.
Thomas J. Emlin, Saddler.
George Wehler, Private, Saddler.
Richard Wilson, Vet. Surgeon.

Barzilla Allen,	Private.
Frederick Amthor,	"
William Arey,	"
Isaac Aten,	"
Henry Bigle,	"
Charles H. Bishop,	"
Henry Bolliger,	"
John P. Brown,	"
Lewis Buckman,	"
John Carlin,	"
John Chamberlain,	"
Garrett S. Cole,	"
John M. Conrow,	"
Richard H. Cox,	"
Samuel Cox, Private, Bugler.	
Louis Courtois,	Private.
William K. Crawford,	"
Oliver D. Cromell,	"
John Cuningham,	"
William Davis,	"

Peter Duffy,	Private.
Charles Eggling,	"
John C. Emerson,	"
George Emlin,	"
Terrence Farrell,	"
William Fitzsimmons,	"
Frank Gardner,	"
Benjamin Gaskill,	"
Benjamin Gaunt,	"
Frederick Gentner,	"
William Glenn,	"
Robert Given,	"
Alfred Green,	"
William M. Griffin,	"
Richard C. Haines,	"
William P. Haines,	"
Cyrus F. Hale,	"
James Harrington,	"
William Heally,	"
Robert Henry,	"
Michael Hoover,	"
Peter Horn,	"
James Jones,	"
Charles Kane,	"
Jonathan D. Kinney,	"
John Kramer,	"
Joseph Lehman,	"
Fred Lowen,	"
Francis Lynch,	"
Michael McCarthy,	"
James McDonald,	Private.
Samuel McGowan,	"
Charles McFeely,	"
John McKinnon,	"
John McSloy,	"
John F. Moore, Serg't,	Private.
William Moran,	Private.
Thomas Nealy,	"
William Newcomb,	"
John W. Newman,	"
George Penn,	"
James Peterson,	"
Thomas Pittman,	"
David Rathburn,	"
Aaron Ruber,	"
Jacob Schaffer,	"
William Scott,	"
John Severns,	"
Carl Otto Shultz,	"
William Sickenger,	"
Charles E. Smith,	"
Frederick Smith,	"
Elias D. Taylor,	"
George Thompson,	"
Erasmus B. Webb,	"
Thomas Williams,	"
Charles Wilson,	"
Joseph Worth, Corp'l, Serg't,	Private.
Parker C. Worth, Corp'l,	Private.

DISCHARGED.

James McAnney, Serg't.	
William Closson, Serg't.	
Edwin Wood, Blacksmith.	
John Brown,	Private.
John Cline,	"
William Davenport,	"
John Delaney,	"
Lewis R. Fischer,	"
Samuel Fletcher,	"
Christopher Gaffney,	"
Jacob Gfrocher,	"
James Grindrod,	"
Lvins Grover,	"
John Holzkneath,	"
George W. Hubbs,	"
Henry Jamison,	Private.
Peter Kearge,	"
Thomas Launing,	"
Louis Leipsett,	"
William B. Logan,	"
William McElhenny,	"
Ellis Newman,	"
John Parker,	"
Courtland Patterson,	"
John B. Plum,	"
Rudolph Schroder,	"
James Simons,	"
Benjamin Watts,	"
Isaac Wilson,	"
Henry Yost,	"

TRANSFERRED.

Thomas Crossin,	Private.
Thomas Lampson,	"
Charles H. Newman,	"
Thomas Taylor.	Private.
John Winterhalter,	"

DIED.

Charles A. Douglass, Private Co. A, 1st Serg't.	
Merrick Arundale,	Private.
George Bauer,	"
Thomas Boyle,	"
William Claypole,	"
Max Lewi,	Private.
William McCune,	"
Daniel Roche,	"
William R. Smith, Corp'l,	Private.
Jonathan Stewart,	Private.

DESERTED.

Charles Beldin, Private.
Thomas H. Bell, "
William Bogarth, "
James Brown, "
Owen Byrne, "
Shreve H. Carter, "
Stephen R. Champion, "
Jesse Cheeseman, "
George Clark, "
Charles Co'e, "
Richard Dalton, "
Charles A. Davis, "
John Davis, "
Joseph D. Dempsey, "
Charles Dubois, "
James Dunlavey, "
Benjamin F. Graves, "
Charles Howart, "
James C. Hughes, "
Jules Jalaber, "
James Johnson, "
John J. Johnson, "
Michael Kelly, "
Carpenter Koombs, "
George W. Lewis, Private.
James A. Leonard, "
Louis Marais, "
John Mattha's, "
John McCabe, "
James McMann, "
John Mortimer, "
George B. Morton, "
James O'Brien, "
John R. Poole, "
James Robinson, "
Charles A. Rowand, Private, Serg't Maj., Private.
Frank Sackriter, "
David Scratt, "
George Shepley, "
Henry Smith, "
William Stunn, "
William Weller, "
Charles L. Wheeler, "
James W. Willis, "
Charles Winters, "
Charles Wood, "

UNACCOUNTED FOR.

Henry Antler, Private.
Frederick Bark, "
John Dwier, "
John Ford. "
Franz Haker, "
John Morgan, Private.
Henry Newman, "
Felix Prude Homme, "
Louis Rochel, "
John Ryan, "
Charles Schultz, "
William Sladon, "
James Smith, (1) "
Thomas Lynch, Private.
Marco M's ena, "
John Mayer, "
John Mee, "
Edward Miller, "
James Smith, (2) Private.
Samuel Smith, "
George Souer, "
Isaac Updike, "
John Williams, "
Robert Wilson, "
Charles Wolf, "

COMPANY D.

Robert N. Boyd, Captain, Major.
Jeremiah P. Brower, 1st Lieut. Co. C, Captain.
John Worsley, 1st Lieut.
Henry W. Sawyer, 2d Lieut., 1st Lieut., Captain Co. K.
P. Penn Gaskell, 2d Lieut., 1st Lieut., Captain Co. F.
Edward H. Parry, 2d Lieut. Co. A, 1st Lieut.
Thomas H. Ford. Private, Corp'l, Serg't, 2d Lieut., 1st Lieut., Captain Co. E.
William H. Wilson, 2d Lieut. Co. G, 1st Lieut.
Edward E. Jemison, 1st Serg't Co. E, 2d Lieut., 1st Lieut. Co. I.
Samuel Craig, Serg't Co. L, 2d Lieut.
James Mettler, Private, Corp'l, Serg't, 1st Serg't, 2d Lieut.
John H. Warner, Corp'l, Serg't, 1st Serg't.
Charles P. Thompson, Private, Corp'l, Com. Serg't, Reg'l Q. M's Serg't.
William Hampton, Private, Q. M's Serg't.
James M. Stradling, Corp'l, Com. Serg't, Reg'l Q. M's Serg't.
Thomas Yocum, Private, Corp'l, Com. Serg't.
John J. Kennedy, Private, Serg't, 1st Serg't.
George L. Sawtell, Private, Serg't.
Harry L. Gillmore, Hospital Stew'd, Serg't, Q. M's Serg't.
James Dean, Private, Serg't.
Samuel H Etchell, Private, Serg't.
Amos Smith, Private, Serg't.
Daniel T. Reed, Private, Serg't.
Archibald Lee, Private, Corp'l.

William Morley, Private, Corp'l.
William Hughes, Private, Corp'l, 2d Lieut. Co. K.
Samuel B. Carter, Private, Corp'l.
George W. Cox, Private, Corp'l.
Charles Schnrig, Private, Corp'l.
John C. Garwood, Private Co. G, Corp'l.
William J. Miller, Private, Corp'l.
James H. Donohue, Private Co. C, Corp'l.
Geo. W. Koster, Private Co. K, Corp'l.
Chas. Beecroft, Private Co. B, Corp'l.
Henry C. Probasco, Private, Corp'l.
Jeremiah B. Wheeler, Private Co. G, Corp'l.
Christian Werths, Private, Corp'l, Bugler.
Lewis Stevens, Blacksmith.
Joseph Crane, Saddler.
Frederick Adams, Private Co. A, Saddler.
Daniel Sailor, Private, Farrier.
Philip Sharwick, Wagoner.
Octave Antonio, Private.
William C. Armstrong, "
Lawrence Ayres, "
James Bell, "
George Bird, "
John W. Brown, "
John Brant, "
Isaiah Buchanan, "
James H. Burke "
George Chappell, "
Henry Chappell, "
James Charlesworth, "
William Conner, "
Joseph J. Cook, "
John Cunningham, "
Thomas DeCourcey, Private Co, A, Q. M's Serg't, Private.
John T. Dulaney, Private.
George W. Dunfee, "
John Evans, "
Charles Fornst, "
Watson Frankenfield, "
Charles George, "
James Gillen, "
Louis Gilley, "
Thomas Graney, "
James Green, "
George W. Haines, "
Patrick Harfford, "
John P. Hart, "
John Heiley, "
Daniel E. Hogbin, "
George L. Holland, Private.
Henry Holm, "
Alfred L. Holmer, "
Robert H. Howell, "
Charles Hulmes, Private, Corp'l, Private.
Thomas G. Ireland, Corp'l, Private.
Albert Jaggars, Private.
William H. Jaggers, "
John Kelso, "
David Lane, Private.
Henry Latterette, "
Peter Lavere, "
Charles Lepec, "
John Lewis, "
Patrick Maher, "
Samuel McGowan, "
Patrick McGrath, "
James McNeil, "
Martin Miller, "
Frederick Morley, Corp'l, Serg't, Private.
Isaac C. Nicholson, Private.
Thomas Palmer, "
Carl Pendert, "
James Pettis, "
John C. Raak, "
Alexander Randall, "
William Randolph, "
Christopher Renneeson, "
Charles Robinson, "
John Roemer, Priv., Corp'l, Priv.
Edward Rush, Private.
Michael Ryan, Private.
Theodore Schramm, "
Charles Shields, "
Charles Smith, (2) "
John Smith, "
Peter Smith, Corp'l, Private.
Thomas Smith, Private.
William Smith, "
Patrick Stack, "
James E. Stackhouse, "
Peter Steim, "
Joseph Teets, "
Wm. H. Thompson, "
Stephen Titus, "
Stephen H. Vanderveer, Private, Corp'l, Private.
Peter Vardey, Private.
Caleb L. Warner, "
James Warren, "
Frederick Weyer, "
Alexander Williams, "
Thomas P. Wood, "
William A. Yeager, "

DISCHARGED.

Edward H. Allen, Private.
George Brown, "
Peter Dailey, "
George Engenoch, Private.
August Lang, "
Richard Lloyd, "

Elias Richards,	Private.	Thomas Sumner,	Private.
William F. Robbins,	"	Abraham Van Hise,	"
Frederick Schaffer,	"	Charles Weigold,	"
Ralph Stones,	"		

TRANSFERRED.

Henry Butler,	Private.	Henry R. Fancher,	Private.
Albert Dickson,	"	Robert Updyke,	"

DIED.

James P. Vandergrift, Serg't.
Thomas H. Nutt, Corp'l, Serg't.
Charles G. Marseilles, Bugler, Corp'l, Serg't.
John W. Somers Bugler.
George Jones, Blacksmith.

Henry Austin,	Private.	Morris Levy,	Private.
Cornelius Baker,	"	Franz J. Leshner,	"
Samuel G. Darrow,	"	John McDermott,	"
John H. Burkhardt,	"	Robert Montgomery,	"
Joseph Kershaw,	"	Thomas B Murphy,	"
		Jeremiah Northrap,	"
		John H. Reynolds,	"
		Charles Tash,	"
		James S. Teets,	"
		Lewis P. Vandergrift,	"
		Edward Wilcox,	"

DESERTED.

Thomas E. Brady, Serg't, Private.

John H. Burton,	Private.	David Miller,	Private
Charles Choleman,	"	Charles Moore,	"
Robert Conway,	"	Peter Morris,	"
Henry Craymore,	"	George Neff,	"
Peter Donley,	"	Patrick O'Brien,	"
Ephraim Ellison,	"	Leopold Opper,	"
Edward Gordon,	"	Charles F. Peterson,	"
Thomas Gordon,	"	John Robbins,	"
Robert Herman,	"	John N. Smith,	"
Charles Johnson,	"	James Thompson,	"
Abraham Latterrette,	"	Joseph Walters,	"
James Lloyd,	"	Andrew Wesley,	"
George Lotteg,	"	James Williams,	"
Anthony Mason,	"	John Williams,	"
Adam Meyers,	"	George Wood,	"

UNACCOUNTED FOR.

Charles Blair,	Private.	Frederick Miller,	Private.
John Caton,	"	William Moore,	"
John Cook,	"	Lawrence Owens,	"
Patrick Dougherty,	"	James P. Reilly,	"
David Guelting,	"	James B Robinson,	"
Alexander La Baiez,	"	Thomas Smith,	"
John Louer,	"	George W. Thomas,	"
Charles Miller,	"	Joseph L. Walker,	"

COMPANY E.

John W. Kester, Captain, Lieut. Col.
William Harper, 1st Lieut. Co. C, Captain, Major, Brevet Major.
Thomas H. Ford, 1st Lieut. Co. D, Captain.
Patton Jones York, 1st Lieut., Capt. Co. I.
Harry Jones, 1st Serg't, 2d Lieut. Co. B, 1st Lieut.
Edwin R. Blaker, 2d Lieut. Co. I, 1st Lieut., R. Q. M.
William Wynkoop, 2d Lieut. Co. A, 1st Lieut.
John Hobensack, 1st Lieut., Capt. Co. F,
Robert B. Canse, 2d Lieut. Co. G, 1st Lieut., Capt. Co. G.

Edward Gaskill, 2d Lieut. Co. G, 1st Lieut.
Francis B. Allibone, 2d Lieut., 1st Lieut. Co. L.
Alexander Stewart, 1st Serg't Co. H, 2d Lieut.
Samuel C. Lane, Serg't Co. C., 2d Lieut., 1st Lieut. Co. C.
Daniel McIntyre, 1st Serg't Co. I, 2d Lieut.
Charles Watts, 1st Serg't Co. C, 2d Lieut.
William T. Allen, Serg't Major, 2d Lieut.
Edward E. Jemison, Serg't, 1st Serg't, 2d Lieut. Co. D.
Joseph Kelly, Private, Corp'l. Serg't, 1st Serg't, 2d Lieut. Co. K.
George K. Stewart, Private, Corp'l, Serg't, 1st Serg't.
John L. McFarland, Q. M. Serg't.
Alfred R. Vail, Private, Corp'l, Q. M. Serg't.
William Russell, Private, Corp'l, Com. Serg't.
Robert Newberg, Corp'l, Serg't, Serg't Major.
Edward L. Williams, Serg't.
Robert P. Ewing, Private, Serg't.
John Shield, Private, Corp'l, Serg't.
Hugh Green, Corp'l, Serg't.
John Fogarty, Private, Serg't.
Robert Williams, Private, Corp'l, Serg't.
Theodore L. Clement, Private, Corp'l, Serg't.
John Burke, Private, Serg't.
Wm. H. Anderson, Private, Corp'l.
John S. Griffith, Private, Corp'l.
Benjamin S. Hovis, Private, Corp'l.
Albert Wilkinson, Private, Co. G., Corp'l.
Snowden M. Preston, Private, Corp'l.
Griffith Jones, Private Co. F, Corp'l.
Ernest V. Schneider, Private Co. I, Corp'l.
John Miller, Private, Corp'l.
Josiah F. Eastblack, Private, Corp'l.
Charles H. Wendell, Bugler, Chief Bugler.
William H. Barnhart, Bugler, Chief Bugler 3d Bat.
James B. Ellis, Corp'l, Bugler.
Abraham Morley, Bugler, Chief Bugler 1st Bat.
Isaac Dilks, Wagoner.
William Nuneviller, Saddler.
Henry Harris, Blacksmith.
Abraham M. Preston, Farrier.
Michael Clement, Private, Farrier.
Richard K. Allen, Private.
John Anderson, Private.
David S. Barr, Corp'l, Private.

Chas. F. Bachterlie, Private.
Hugo Brentyman, "
Oliver E. Brown, "
James Burke, "
Sylvester B. Carr, "
Henry H. Chamberlain, "
William N. Clark, "
Isaac Cohen, "
Peter Coon, "
Joseph Crawford, "
Charles A. Dansbury, "
Hudson Decker, "
John De Grote, "
John Eberlie, "
Lewis Edell, "
Thomas Elliott, "
Ephraim B. Fithain, Blacksmith, Private.
Wesley W. Foe, Private.
Amariah Foster, "
Bernard Francis, "
Bernard Gaffney, "
William Gledhill, "
Patrick Green "
Barnabas K. Hall, "
Stephen Hall, "
Judson Hand, "
Samuel Helms, "
Samuel R. Hiler, "
John H. Jones, "
John Kirby, "
John Kline, "
Christian Krahl, "
William H. Lambert, "
Charles Lamblack, "
Thomas H. Locke, "
Peter Lynch, "
Frank Marden, "
Christopher Martin, "
William Moir, "
Dedrick Moore, "
Richard Morgan, "
Frank Morris, "
Joseph Mosbaker, "
Thomas Murray, "
John Nash, "
John Nelson, Private, Corp'l, Private.
John O'Brien, Private.
Henry Rash, "
Maskell C. Reeves, "
John Riley, "
Simeon Ringdolph, "
Charles P. Roberts, "
Walter G. Rogers, "
Henry Sanders, "
Thaddeus Schofield, "
Joseph R. Sharp, "
Enoch F. Sheppard, "
Morgan Shinn, "
William Shuster, "
Hudson W. Smith, "
Miller Smith, "
John Steppenfield, "

Michael Sullivan, Private.
John Tinney, "
George Townly, "
Frederick Trullender, Private, Reg'l Armorer.
Amos Vail, "
Amzy Waer, "

Thomas R. Ward, Private.
Nelson Washer, "
George W. White, "
Samuel Williams, "
Rogers Wray, "
James Young, "
Thomas A. Zeak, "

DISCHARGED.

William B. Ewing, Serg't.
Timothy L. Middleton, Serg't.
James Van Hise, Corp'l, Serg't.
John Marshall, Corp'l.
John Anderson, Private.
Robert Anderson, "
Robert R. Atchinson, "
Henry Baldwin, "
Horace Ely, "
Louis R. Fisher, "
William D. Fowler, "
John Green, "
Andrew Hill, "

Charles Monroe, Private.
William B. Reeves, "
Smith Reynolds, "
Smith Robinson, "
Joseph Schubert, "
Joseph H. Steward, "
Thomas Tobin, "
Augustus Tolksdolph, "
John Van Cott, "
Isaac Van Hise, "
Charles R. Walton, "
John Workman, "

TRANSFERRED.

James Cisco, Private.
Charles B. Fisher, "

John Lantherboren, Private.
Lionel N. McKenzie, "

DIED.

Joseph R. Reed, Priv., Com. Serg't, 1st Serg't.
William D. Likes, Private, Corp'l, Serg't.
George H. Fowler, Corp'l Serg't.
James H. Palmatier, Private, Serg't.
Amos L. Stockton, Private, Serg't.
Charles F. Atkinson, Private.
Joseph Dunfee, "
Charles A. Fowler, "
Charles B. Fowler, "
Bernard Goodbread, "
Asa Hawk, "

Edward Jordan, Private.
Martin Kizer, "
Charles Layton, "
George Malcomb, "
William McKenna, "
George T. Roulson, "
William R. Shoars, "
Lemuel O. Smith, "
William Smith, Corp'l, Private.
John Wandell, Private.
Hamilton Williams, "
Abner Wood, "
Erward Zeak, "

DESERTED.

John B. Ayres, Private.
Apollo M. Brewer, "
Michael Burns, "
John Campbell, "
George Carson, "
Edmund Fivey, "
William B. Fowler, "
David Hankins, "
Charles R. Harris, "
Samuel Henderson, "
Jerry Herron, "
James Hink, "
David Hinkley, "
Charles Holmes, "
Peter W. Hoopler, "

William H. Layton, Private.
Michael Logan, "
Daniel McCormick, "
Michael McNight, "
Martin Murphy, "
John O'Brien, "
Augustus Roback, "
James Robinson, "
James Rogers, "
James Smith, "
George Subers, "
John Sullivan, "
Wheaton N. Watson, "
Jacob Young, "
Charles Zeak, "

UNACCOUNTED FOR.

Lawrence Brady.	Private.	George Kitson,	Priva'c.
Edward Burrs,	"	Henry Lake,	"
George W. Clark,	"	Elias Rochello.	"
George Comstock,	"	William Sullivan,	"
John Duvell,	"	Frank Taylor,	"
William Fox,	"	John Thompson,	"
William Hogard,	"	James Wall,	"
Patrick Kelley,	"		

COMPANY F.

John H. Lucas, Captain.
P. Penn Gaskell, 1st Lieut. Co. D, Captain.
John Hobensack, 1st Lieut. Co. E, Captain.
Moses W. Maulsbury, 1st Lieut., Captain Co. M.
John Kinsley, 1st Serg't, 2d Lieut. Co. H, 1st Lieut., Cap'. Co. M.
William M. Shaw, Hospital Stew'd, 2d Lieut., 1st Lieut.
Lawrence Fay, Private, Corp'l, 1st Serg't, 2d Lieut., 1st Lieut.
Aaron L. Robins, 2d Lieut.
Jacob H. Hoffman, 2d Lieut.
Cortland Inglin, Serg't Major, 2d Lieut., 1st Lieut. Co. G.
James F. Clancy, Serg't Co. C, 2d Lient., Adjutant.
Carrell Carty, Serg't, 1st Serg't, 2d Lieut. Co. L.
Amos L. Poinsett, Private, Corp'l, 1st Serg't.
Charles H. Buck, Corp'l, Com. Serg't, Q. M's Serg't.
Jonathan Goble, Q. M's Serg't., Com. Serg't 2d Bat.
Robert Burns, Private, Com. Serg't.
Lewis Rainear, Serg't, Serg't Major 2d Bat.
Aaron P. Irons, Serg't, Reg'l Q. M's Serg't.
Jos. F. Thibeaudean, Corp'l, Serg't.
Ridgway S. Asay, Private, Corp'l, Serg't.
John McBu'r, Private, Serg't.
Joseph B. Clayton, Private, Corp'l, Serg't.
Benjamin F. Toms, Serg't.
Cyrus E. Cook, Private, Serg't.
Richard Skirm, Private, Corp'l.
Edward P. Adams, Corp'l.
Edward McGlasky, Private, Corp'l.
Thomas Gouldy, Private, Corp'l.
John Charles, Private, Corp'l.
Charles Cadott, Private, Corp'l.
Leander Murphy, Blacksmith.
Jacob B. Hopper, Private, Saddler.
James Cliver, Private, Farrier.
John D. Adams, Private.

Joseph Allen,	Private.
Jacob Allison,	"
John Allison,	"
George Anderson,	"
William Anderson,	"
James H. Bergen,	"
George H. Blair,	"
William A. Brown,	"
John Burchill,	"
Edward Cannon,	"
Alfred Capps,	"
Philip Carman,	"
Charles S. Clark,	"
Daniel Cliver,	"
James Cookson,	"
Thomas Cross,	"
William Curley,	"
John C. Dants,	"
John Deitsel,	"
George Dohm,	"
Richard Doremus,	"
Joseph Duncan,	"
Albert Emmons,	"
David H. Emmons,	"
Edward Frederick,	"
Theodore Freund,	"
Samuel Gallway,	"
Moses Garthwaite,	"
Christian Gerber,	"
John Giberson,	"
Charles Goldberg.	"
Franklin Goodman,	"
James H. Graham,	"
Edward Grover,	"
John Grover,	"
George A. Hammond,	"
Eden G. Harvey,	"
Henry Haneman,	"
Adolphus Hill,	"
Harman Hoft,	"
Peter Hohman,	"
Augustus Horn,	"
Henry Howe,	"
John B. Hutt,	Priv., Corp'l, Priv.
Barzilla P. Irons,	Private.
Alfred Johnson,	"
James L. Johnson,	"
William J. Johnson,	"
John Kinney,	"
John Lanler,	"

Ph'lip Lee, Private.
Joseph F. Lemon, "
William Lewis, "
Thomas Luker. "
George B. Malsbury, "
John Mason, "
Solomon Mason, "
William H. May, "
Samuel McGlaskey, "
James S. McKeivy, "
John Miller, "
Nathan Moore, "
Henry Morris, "
Alfred Nelson, "
John Phillips, "
Albe t N. Pratt, "
Joseph D. Proud, "
Thomas Rainear, "
W lliam Reed, (1) "

Franc's Rowland, Private, Corp'l, Private.
Thomas Russell, Private.
Howard Ryan, "
Freder'ck Shaffer, "
William Scott, "
Gotleib Schultz, "
Christian Seibert, "
Samuel Sheppard, "
Edward Sherman, "
Job Simons. "
Lowrenz Skibnskil, "
Randelph Snell, "
Henry Stahal, "
Israel Talmadge, "
Jefferson Thompson, "
Charles Turpin, "
John A. Vauderhoof, "
George Wilson, "

DISCHARGED.

Charles H. Wardell, Corp'l, Q. M's Serg't.
Abner P. Zelly, Corp'l, Serg't.
Alfred Matthews, Bugler.
William Law, Bugler.
Townsend Cox, Farrier.
Charles P. Adams, Private.
John H. Adams, "
James R. Applegate, "
Alexander Bethune, "
Elisha Boger, "
Charles A. Buffin, "

Gershom Craft, Private.
Elisha Decker, "
John C. Fay, "
Charles C. Green, "
Nathan Long, "
Oliver Monroe, "
Charles H. Phillips, "
Lew's Ritter, "
William Rose, "
Sydney Snable, "
Samuel Whitehouse, "

TRANSFERRED.

Henry Lamb, Private.

DIED.

Samuel Rainoar, Corp'l, Serg't.
William Conrow, Corp'l.
George Sweeney, Private, Corp'l.
Israel R. Applegate, Private.
George Bishop, "
William Doremus, "
Bartine Fifer, "
James H. Gallway, "
Joel W. A. Groves, "
Henry Haft, "

Peter W. Hooner, Private.
John B. Hovencamp, "
Charles Long, "
Elisha Luker, "
Joseph Miller, "
John Mills, "
Theodore A. Palmer, "
Orlando B. Snell, "
Samuel Van Buskirk, "
Lewis Ward, "

DESERTED.

James Bryant, Private.
John B. Campbell, "
John Freedlin, "
William Herbert, "
Charles Jones, "
Major McGlasky, "
Benjamin Morton, "

William Page, Private
Thomas Rogers, "
William Schaffer, "
John A. Wagener, "
Edward Wells, "
John W. Worths, "

UNACCOUNTED FOR.

Michael Hoffman, Wagoner.
Joseph Adams, Private.
Joseph Akirt, "
John Cody, "
Thomas Hart, "
William Kennard, Private.
James Smith, "
William Tobin, "
Thomas A. Waters, "

COMPANY G.

John H. Smith, Captain.
Henry E. Clark, Captain.
Walter R. Robbins, Private, 2d Lieut., 1st Lieut., Captain, Major.
Robert B. Canse, Serg't Major, 2d Lieut., 1st Lieut. Co. E, Captain.
George W. Wardell, 1st Lieut.
Cortland Inglin, 2d Lieut. Co. F, 1st Lieut
Peter A. Bertholf, 2d Lieut.
Gerald Weston, "
Richard Colwell, "
Alexander Stewart, "
Edward Gaskill, 1st Serg't Co. E, 2d Lieut., 1st Lieut. Co. E.
William H. Wilson, Serg't Co. B, 2d Lieut., 1st Lieut. Co. E.
Jeremiah P. Brower, Private. 1st Serg't, 2d Lieut. Co. M.
Maitland Gardner, Corp'l, Serg't, 1st Serg't.
Gilbert S. Johnson, Private, Corp'l, Serg't, 1st Ser'gt, 2d Lieut. Co. C.
Philip Gundell, Private, Corp'l, 1st Serg't, 2d Lieut. Co. L.
Aaron B. Tompkins, Priv., 1st Serg't.
Richard Darmstadt, Priv., Corp'l, Q. M's Serg't, 2d Lieut. Co. I.
Edward F. Wenner, Private Co. L, Corp'l, Serg't, Q. M's Serg't, Serg't Major.
Frederick Greenwood, Private, Q. M's Serg't.
John Farrell, Private, Corp'l, Com. Serg't.
Michael Williams, Private, Corp'l, Serg't, Com. Serg't.
Britton Height, Serg't.
Borden Joline, Private, Corp'l, Serg't.
Jacob V. Co lies, Private, Corp'l, Com. Serg't, Serg't.
John Disbrow, Corp'l, Serg't.
James McKeon, Private, Serg't.
Frederick Brenner, Private, Corp'l, Serg't.
John W. Smith, Corp'l.
Hutchings Brown, Private, Corp'l.
Richard Lawrence, Private, Corp'l.
James H. Stubbs, Private, Corp'l.
Henry C. Maps, Private, Corp'l.
Gustavus Haberguan, Private, Corp'l.
Thomas Bird, Private Co. M, Corp'l.
Edward Shook, Private, Corp'l.
Ira S. DeHart, Private Co. I, Corp'l.
James Anderson, Bugler.
John Schnider, Bugler.
John Raepple, Private, Farrier.
William Crotty, Saddler.
Michael McGinn, Blacksmith.
Joseph Decker, Private, Wagoner.
Minian Alexander, Private.
William Andog, "
Samuel Anderson, "
Thomas Beadshelder, "
George Beam, "
Frederick Bemberg, "
Michael Bergen, "
Samuel Booth, "
Thomas Burrell, "
James Burns, "
King Campbell, "
Peter B. Carman, "
Theodore C. Casterline, "
Joseph Chamberlain, "
Wm. M. Chamberlain, "
James Chambers, "
Thomas Clifford, "
Thomas Conklin, "
Michael Connery, "
Edward W. Cox, "
Michael Devlin, "
Thomas Donnelly, "
George R. Eldridge, "
Isaac S. Eldridge, "
Edward H. Ely, "
Sylvanus Emmons, "
Frederick Esais, "
John Finnegan, Priv., Serg't, Corp'l, Private.
Jonas C. Gillson, Corp'l, Private.
Jordan Green, Corp'l, Private.
John Hall, Private.
William P. Hall, Private, Corp'l, Private
William H. Harley, Private.
Henry Housell, "
Jesse Howland, "
Warren C. Hursh, "
William B. Imbley, "
William Jardin, "
Charles S. Jones, "
James D Jones, "
Morgan Jones, "
Rudolph Kaiser, "
Frederick Krause, Private, Farrier, Private.

Joseph K. Lanning, Private.
Henry Linne, "
James H. Lloyd, "
Thomas C. Lovett, "
James Maps, "
Moses H. McCormick, "
George R. Miller, "
Jacob Miller, "
John Montgomery, "
Edward Morris, "
John Morris, Private, Serg't, Private.
John B. Morris, Private.
Lewis Obendofer, "
John O'Brien, "
James Radcliff, "
William Reed, (2) "
Rudolph Richner, "
Morris H. Rogers, Corp'l, Private.
William Rogers, Bugler, Private.
Thomas B. Schaffer, Private.
Albert Schoel, "
William Siback, "
Jacob Skillman, "
John J. Tabor, Serg't, Private.
John Thomas, Private.
Peter Vogel, "
Peter Walker, "
Valentine Weber, "
William A. Wilder, "
Ignatz Wirtz, "
Horton Wood, "
James Wood, Farrier, Private.
George Woodey, Private.
Charles M. Wooley, "
William H. Yeaton, Private, Corp'l, Private.

DISCHARGED.

James Hankins, Corp'l, Com. Serg't.
Cornelius Abrams, Private.
Jacob Bodenweiser, "
John M. Britton, "
Walter Brown, "
John W. Clayhance, "
John Conover, "
Joseph Covert, Saddler, Private
Ezra Curtis, Private.
James R. Ehert, "
Nicholas Gulick, "
Francis Harring, "
William Heminover, "
Wm. C. Hendrickson, "
Charles R. Holmes, "
Samuel Jones, Private.
Thomas Karry, "
Kasper Keiser, "
John Kelly, "
Peter Kelly, Private, Corp'l, 1st Serg't, Private.
Michael Kitts, Private.
Patrick Lynch, "
John H. Magonegal, "
Thomas Rafferty, "
James S. Reed, "
Benno Schroeder, "
Lyman H. Stone, "
Joseph Storms, "
Francis Taylor, "
Charles Winch, "

TRANSFERRED.

Matthias Babcock, Private.
Jacob Clemmens, "
Jacob Harr, Private.
Abraham F. Randolph, Private.

DIED.

James W. Haywood, Corp'l, Q. M's Serg't.
John Skillman, Q. M's Serg't.
George Martin, Private, Com. Serg't.
Francis T. Martin, Serg't.
Augustus Ringleb, Private, Corp'l.
John Bennett, Private.
Jacob Brower, "
Thomas Burleigh, "
Nicholas Connery, "
Samuel Corlies, "
Thomas Elson, "
Nicholas Emory, "
Robert Falke, "
John Ferguson, Private.
James Franklin, "
John Guyer, "
George Howard, "
Lewis Munzie, "
Charles Netzeel, "
George Phillipson, "
Marshall Summers, "
Benjamin Tuttle, "
John R. Vanderveer, Corp'l, Private.
Allen L. West, Private.
William Wilson, "
Joseph Wirtz, "

DESERTED.

John C. Allen, Private.
George Bittner, "
Lewis Contry, "
Charles F. Cook, "
George Covert, "
Frederick Ever, "
William Farber, "
Daniel Fell, "
Felix Frascari, "
Charles Hemmens, "
Augustus Hoover, "
Michael Hoy, "
Franklin Johnson, "
Daniel Keefe, "
James King, "
Henry Lange, "
Michael Landy, "
John Lee, "
Martin Lowry, "
John McDonald, "
Thomas McDonald, Private.
Andrew McNeil, Private.
Mitchell E. Mead, Bugler, Private.
Frederick Mondreff, Private.
Christian Minger, "
James Nixon, "
James L. Polen, "
Thomas Raywood, "
John Ritter, "
George Root, "
Jacob Schmelser, "
Charles Schultz, "
George Seaton, "
Richard Shuttleworth, "
Joseph Swartz, "
Charles Thomas, "
Samuel Tiele, "
Alonzo Wambough, "
John Wilson, "
Charles Wright, "

UNACCOUNTED FOR.

William Barry, Private.
Charles R. Clark, "
John Evans, "
Charles Fuchs, "
James Hughes, "
John E. Kelley, Private.
Edward Salsbury, "
Decatur Simpson, "
John Smith, "
Lyman H. Stone, "

COMPANY H.

Henry C. Perley, Capt.
Myer Asch, Adj't., Capt.
Joseph Billy, 2d Lieut. Co. E, 1st Lieut., Capt.
William T. Inman, 1st Lieut.
James H. Hart, 2d Lieut. Co. A, 1st Lieut., Capt. Co. M.
Joseph Brooks, Serg't Co. K, 1st Lieut., Capt. Co. K.
Samuel Craig, 2d Lieut. Co. L, 1st Lieut., Capt. Co. A
John D. Williams, 2d Lieut. Co. B, 1st Lieut.
Henry S. Stull, Q. M. Serg't Co. I, 2d Lieut.
John Kinsley, 1st Serg't Co. F, 2d Lieut., 1st Lieut. Co. F.
Hyde Crocker, 1st Serg't Co. M,, 2d Lieut.
Alexander Stewart, 1st Serg't, 2d Lieut. Co. E.
Louis Fohs, Corp'l, Serg't, 1st Serg't, 2d Lieut. Co. C.
John Brockbank, Private, Corp'l, 1st Serg't.
William Hudson, Priv., Corp'l, Com. Serg't, 1st Serg't.
Franklin Hamell, Serg't., Q. M. Serg't 3d Bat.
Dan'l Predmore, Corp'l, Priv., Serg't
Henry Werner, Corp'l, Serg't, 2d Lieut. Co. K.
Robert B. Canse, Corp'l, Serg't, Serg't Major.
Charles Titus, Private, Corp'l, Serg't.
James Devine, Private, Corp'l, Serg t.
George Reeder, Priv., Corp'l, Serg't.
Andrew Kerr, Private, Serg't.
William Porter, Priv. Corp'l, Serg't.
David Fleming, Priv., Corp l, Serg't.
John Corcoran, Priv., Corp'l, Serg't.
Daniel Hatelan, Private, Corp'l.
Cornelius Bailey, Corp'l, Priv., Corp'l.
Patrick Kelly, Privaet, Corp'l.
John Husted, Private, Corp'l.
Philip Klespies, Private, Corp'l.
John A. Dunn, Private, Corp'l.
Benjamin B. Murphy, Private Co. M. Corp'l.
David Castimore, Private Co. E, Corp'l.
Rudolph Rupp, Private, Bugler.
Peter H. Suydam, Saddler, Saddler Serg't.
August Smith, Private, Saddler.
Abram Lawrence, Corp'l, Private, Blacksmith.
George Applegate, Farrier, Vet. Surg.

William Acker, Private.
Joseph Allegar, Priv., Corp'l, Priv.
William Alston, Private.
James M. Auld, "
Rudolph Bergman, "
Charles Bills, "
Patrick Brennan, "
George Brust, "
John Bush, "
James Carden, Priv., Corp'l, Priv.
Leonard Christ, Private.
John Colhepp, "
Thomas Connell, "
John Corcoran, "
Chester F. Dewy, "
Alfred B. Dunham, "
Edward Dunham, "
Julius Erbe, "
John Farrell, "
John Feaster, "
Douglass E. Grey, "
Balthaser Gross, "
Peter Hadley, "
John Hagan, "
Pyatt Hardy, "
David Hart, "
Peter Hartz, "
Theodore Heickle, "
John Henry, "
Charles Hinckley, "
Thomas Hipwell, "
Ralph Hoagland, "
Joseph Holbrook, "
William H. Jackson, "
William Jewell, "
Lewis R. Johnson, "
Walter Kelly, "
Henry B. Labar, "
William H. Labar, "
John Letts, "
Julius Linke, "
William J. Loderick, "
Joseph Lowrey, Private.
William C. Lundy, "
Timothy Mahoney, "
Jerry McGerrin, "
John McLaughlin, "
Jonathan Mescrole, "
John Miller, "
Lawrence L. Moore, "
John H. Morris, Private, 2d Lieut. Co. C.
Cornelius Murphy, Private.
Robert Murray, "
Joseph Nicholson, "
John Oakes, "
John Oliver, "
Charles A. Parden, "
John Plum, "
George E. Porter, "
Frank Riley, "
George Riley, "
John H. Riley, "
Edward Roof, "
Alexander Roth, "
Moses Ryer, "
Louis A. Schafer, "
Henry H. Schureman, "
Charles Simms, "
Charles Smith (1) "
George S. Snable, "
Sanford Snover, "
Theodore Snyder, "
Paul Sweitzer, "
Chase Taylor, "
Joseph P. Turner, Private, Vet. Surg.
Peter Vannote, Priv., Corp'l, Priv.
Thomas Walsh, Private.
Charles Wells, "
Leonard F. Whitebeck, "
Edward Whitcraft, "
Jonathan S. Wilson, "
Thomas Wilson, "
John J. Wolfinger, "

DISCHARGED.

Henry S. Whitfield, Serg't.
Charles Marcks, Serg't.
James Lawrence, Corp'l, Serg't.
Joseph E. Layton, Corp'l, Serg't.
Peter D. Warner, Private, Corp'l.
Jacob Shulthise, Bug'er.
Charles Abrams, Private.
Luther Calloway, "
Jesse C. Davison, "
John Ectel, "
Amos Garis, "
John M. Hoagland, "
John Kohler, Private.
Charles W. Marks, "
Abraham Merrick, "
Abraham Quick, "
Stephen Sass, "
George Sifert, "
Stephen Sndyer, "
William Stevens, "
Stephen Suydam, "
William Thatcher, "
John Van Etten, Corp'l, Priv.

TRANSFERRED.

James McLaughlin, Private, Corp'l.
Henry Sinker, Corp'l, Priv.
George W. Smith (2), Private.

DIED.

Joseph Hodapp, Priv., Corp'l, Serg't.
Edward Anderson, Private, Corp'l.
John A. Schaffer, Private, Corp'l.
Garret Anderson, Private.
Leo Carr, "
George B. Cole, "
Oscar Condit, "
Charles Darrone, "
William T. Estell, "
William B. Fenton, "
Nicholas Fallar, "
Thomas Foster, Private.
James Malone, "
James McClellan, "
John R. McNulty, "
Ralph Miller, "
George Quick, "
Samuel A. Thomas, "
Christopher Voorhees, "
Israel Ward, "
Robert Whitehead, "
Charles D. Wilson, "

DESERTED.

George A. Rosback, Serg't.
Robert Sidner, Blacksmith.
James Bahan, Private.
John Brown, "
Samuel Brown, "
Daniel Cane, "
Philip Cusick, "
Michael Eagan, "
Patrick Dunn, "
James Fullom, "
William Glenn, "
Brock Grant, "
Anthony Herbert, "
William Holliday, "
Halsted Humphrey, "
George Johnson, "
John Kipp. "
Christopher Krams, "
John Lauer, "
William Lauer, "
Francis Lavalle, "
John Leckner, Private.
George Letts, "
John Lyons, "
Patrick Murphy, "
William Nichols, "
Benjamin Norman, "
James O'Brien, "
Robert Peters, "
William Rappleyea, "
James Reiley, "
Daniel Reinheimer, Bugler, Private,
John Schafer, Private.
George Schneck, "
Charles H. Shaw, "
Thomas H. Smith, "
William Smith, "
Anthony Van Hise, "
John Vollmer, "
Luke Walters, "
John Webster, "

UNACCOUNTED FOR.

Patrick Benson, Private.
James Carr, "
Philip H. Cyphers, "
Michael Danoghy, "
Michael Donovan, "
Henry Gobat, "
Martin Hollingsworth, "
James Jamp, "
James Mathewall, "
Anton Meller, Private.
Martin Nevin, "
Daniel Shaw, "
Charles H. Sharp, "
William Snyder, "
Valere Verhurst, "
Aaron Weiss, "
John Williams, "
George Worthington, "

COMPANY I.

Benjamin W. Jones, Captain.
P. Jones Yorke, 1st Lieut. Co. E, Captain.
Garrett V. Beekman, 1st Lieut. Co. M, Captain.
James C Hunt, 1st Lieut.
William W. Wurts, 1st Lieut.
Edward E. Jemison, 2d Lieut. Co. D, 1st Lieut.
Birdsall Cornell, Serg't Co. K, 2d Lieut., 1st Lieut.
Frederick Schall, Private, Serg't, 2d Lieut., 1st Lieut.
Edward Field, 2d Lieut.
Edw'd R. Blaker, Reg'l Q. M's Serg't, 2d Lieut., 1st Lieut. Co. E.
Cornelius G. Van Reypen 2d Lieut.
John W. Bellis, Serg't Co. M, 2d Lieut.
Richard Darmstadt, Q. M's Serg't Co. G, 2d Lieut.
Lemuel Fisher, 1st Serg't, Q. M's Serg't 2d Bat.

Daniel McIntyre, Serg't, 1st Serg't, 2d Lieut. Co. E.
Andrew Post, Private, Corp'l, Serg't, 1st Serg't.
Henry S. Stull, Q. M's Serg't, 2d Lieut. Co. H.
Owen Handcock, Private, Serg't, Q. M's Serg't.
Robert Wohlfarth, Private, Corp'l, Serg't, Com. Serg't.
George A. Bowne, Corp'l, Serg't, 2d Lieut. Co. B.
William T. Allen, Private, Serg't, Serg't Major.
Achard Johnson, Private, Corp'l, Serg't.
Edward M. Myers, Private, Corp'l, Serg't.
Henry H. Covert, Private, Serg't.
Abram R. Harris, Private, Serg't.
Abraham S. Sutphin, Private, Serg't.
Charles B. Dowdley, Corp'l, Private, Corp'l.
Francis W. Reeder, Private, Corp'l.
Louis Hopp, Private, Cor'pl.
Alexander Todd, Private, Corp'l.
William Dougherty, Private, Corp'l.
John S. Carman, Private, Corp'l.
Hugh McGreehan, Private Co. L, Corp'l.
William Looby, Private, Corp'l.
William Vandergrift, Private, Corp'l.
George Spendler, Private, Corp'l.
Nicholas McCardle, Bugler.
Charles Dross, Private, Corp'l, Private, Saddler.
George N. Griffith, Farrier.
David K. Reeder, Blacksmith.
George W. Adair, Private.
Henry Alves, "
Peter Apple, "
Jacob August, "
George Barnes, "
John Bassing, "
William T. Beyer, "
Conrad Birkenbush, "
John V. D. Bogart, "
Levi Bolton, "
Peter Brannin, Private, Corp'l, Private.
Patrick Burns, Private.
Andrew Butcher, "
Edward Clark, "
Henry Cliver, "
Thomas Connor, "
James Cooper, Priv., Serg't, Private.
Ferdinand Cruse, Private, Corp'l, Private.
William W. Cushing, Private.
Michael Dalton, "
Benjamin C. Davis, "
Horatio N. Davis, Jr., "
Edward Denman, "
John N. Errickson, "
Herman Fleischaner, "
Ebenezer M. Gammie, "
Michael Garrity, "
Charles Garribaldi, "
Christian Green, "
John Hacker, "
John P. Hackman, "
Peter Helf, "
Frederick W. Henry, "
Charles Honig, "
Henry Horseman, "
Peter Hoover, "
Elias A. Hunt, "
James Keefe, "
John Kennigan, "
Martin Layman, "
Charles Lentz, "
Henry D. Mades, "
Joseph D. Mayer, Saddler Serg't.
Thomas McAllister, Private.
Frank Morris, "
William Nugent, "
Nicholas Rick, "
Edwin Robbins, "
Patrick Ryan, "
Albert Scharf, "
Christian Schmalbrack, "
Albert Schmidt, "
Charles Shepperd, "
Christian F. Sluter, "
Henry Smith, "
James Smith, "
Leonard Smith, "
William Steinman, "
Christian Straele, "
John S. Sullivan, "
William Talbot, "
Ernest Thornman, "
John Tinsley, "
Armenius Trisch, "
John V. N. Vanarsdale, "
Oscar Van Zeder, "
John Waltz, "
George H. Weeden, "
Henry Werle, "
Alexander Wilkinson, "
John Williamson, "
William C. Wilson, "
William W. Wilson, "
George H. Wolfel, "

DISCHARGED.

Napoleon B. Adams, Serg't, Q. M. Serg't.
Edward M. Richardson, Corporal.
Abram M. Voorhees, Corporal.
James B. Story, Corporal.
William Kelly, "
Francis W. Downs, "
John Anderson, Private.

Thomas Brotherton, Private.
Thomas Brownley, "
Bowman F. Cisco, "
James Donalson, "
Thomas Dooley, "
Charles Earley, Serg't, Priv.
John Fanning, Private.
Bartolett Flatley, "
Michael Herbert, "
John Horton, "
Charles L. Jackson, "
Richard Lacey, Private.
Edward McCardle, "
Timothy Miller, "
Albert Obert, "
Frederick W. Pohlman, "
James Proud, "
Benjamin W. Reeves, "
John J. Sifke, "
John Skelton, "
David Steurer, "

TRANSFERRED.

Xavier Abt, Private.
George W. Freeland, "
Thomas Jones, Private.
Joseph Thomas, "

DIED.

Nathan P. Fisher, Serg't.
John Edwards, Serg't.
Warren Rutan, Serg't.
John Emley, Corporal.
George Kelley, Private, Corp'l.
Lewis Rappleyea, Private, Corp'l.
Owen McCabe, Priv. Co. D, Corp'l.
Jacob F. Vanderslici, Bugler.
David Brink, Private.
John Glenn, "
Philip Hann, "
Henry Higgins, "
Jonathan Hunt, "
Samuel H. Manning, Private.
Amos Matchett. "
John Matthew, "
Henry Meyer, "
William Paddock, "
Isaac W. Reeves, "
William H. Ribbons, "
Abram Stryker, "
Ludwick Suckoo, "
John Tooley, "
James Toorney, "
Holloway W. Woolverton, Private.

DESERTED.

Jarvis Ball, Private.
James H. Bluett, "
Samuel Carr, "
William Conroy, "
Martin Corby, "
John Denecours, "
John T. Dougherty, "
Leon Equey, "
Daniel F. Foley, "
Ebenezer Francis, "
Michael Gangwich, "
James H. Hasbruck, "
Charles Hofer, "
George Holcomb, "
William Jenkins, "
Michael Kelly, "
John Lambert, "
David Lanceburg, "
James Lovett, "
Samuel McKinstry, "
Alexander McNider, "
John Merryman, Private.
Michael Michel, "
John Morgan, "
George Morris, "
James Murphy, "
Daniel Murphy, "
Merritt Myers, "
Adolphus Newman, "
Alfred Oehring, "
Fred Orthon, "
Edward Palmer, "
Charles Rathner, "
Andrew Regan, "
Benjamin Romaine, "
Henry Schmidt, "
John Schneider, "
Herman Sieger, "
Alexander Spencer, "
August Strause, "
John Taylor, "
Frank Walters, "

UNACCOUNTED FOR.

Matthias Bauer, Private.
John Callaghan, "
William Charlton, "
Charles H. Conlin, "
James Conlin, "
Garrett Dehan, "
Thomas Flinn, "
George Frank, Private.
Charles Frei, "
Patrick Geary, "
Pastorini Giovanni, "
Arthur Gough, "
Ernest Haller, "
Lewis Heminger, "

Albert Huber, Private.
James Hughes, "
Peter Lynch, "
James Mack, "
Carl Marshall, "
Henry Miller, "
Charles Morgan, "
Jacob Moser, Private.
William Ott, "
William Reed, "
Charles Simpson, "
John Sullivan, "
Alexis Tournier, "
John Woods, "

COMPANY K.

Virgil Brodrick, Captain, Major.
Henry W. Sawyer, 1st Lieut. Co. D, Captain, Major.
Joseph Brooks Corp'l, Serg't, 1st Lieut. Co. H, Captain.
Thomas H. Ford, Captain.
Thomas R. Haines, 1st Lieut., Captain Co. M.
C. Benjamin Young, 1st Lieut.
William H. Hick, 1st Lieut., Captain Co. L.
William Hughes, Corp'l Co. D, 2d Lieut., 1st Lieut, Captain Co. C.
John Fowler, 2d Lieut.
William M. Hazen, Com. Serg't Co. L, 2d Lieut.
Joseph Killy, 1st Serg't Co. E, 2d Lieut. 1st Lieut. Co. H.
Henry Werner, Serg't Co. H. 2d Lieut.
Henry Darris, 1st Serg't.
George W. McPeek, Private, Serg't, 1st Serg't.
David Smith, Corp'l, Serg't, Q. M. Serg't.
Robert J. Seeley, Private Co. I, Q. M. Serg't.
Lemon Canfield, Priv., Corp'l, Serg't, Com. Sergt'.
Robert Tuthill Private, Corp'l, Serg't.
Thomas S. Cox, Serg't Major, Serg't, 2d Lieut. Co. M.
Birdsall Cornell, Serg't, 2d Lieut. Co. I.
Samuel Craig, Private, Serg't.
Henry Heater, Private, Corp'l, Serg't.
John M. Hendershot, Private, Corp'l, Serg't.
Lawrence McKinney, Bugler, Serg't.
Aaron H. White, Private, Corp'l, Serg't.
William Rea, Private, Serg't.
William S. Booth, Private, Serg't.
Thomas J. Lewis, Private, Serg't, Private, Serg't.
William H. Powell, Private Co. A, Serg't.
Nathaniel Martin, Private, Corp'l.
Seth W. Slate, Private, Corp'l.
Charles Hoffman, Private, Corp'l.
Thomas Sheridan, Private Co. H, Corp'l.
David X. Gardner, Private Co. A, Corp'l.
John E. Ford, Private, Corp'l.
William Sheridan, Private, Corp'l.
John Meyers, Private, Corp'l.
James E. Vanderbelt, Private, Corp'l.
Joseph Green, Private, Bugler.
Joseph Marsh, Private, Bugler.
William Robinson, Saddler.
Andrew T. Titus, Farrier.
Peter B. Babcock, Private, Blacksmith.
Charles Ackerson, Private.
William Ascherle, "
George M. Baird, "
John Baldwin, "
John J. Banta, "
William Barrett, "
Conover L. Bedell, "
Thomas Belfield, "
Charles Blake, "
Nathan Bostwick, "
Bernard Bradley, "
John L. Brenning, "
Oliver Bronson, "
Francis Brown, "
Nathan E. Carhuff, "
Michael Carr, "
Frederick S. Cole, "
William H. Cook, "
William Copeland, "
Joseph Corby, "
James Cornelius, "
Eli Curtis, "
John Dalzell, "
John Darris, "
William H. Davenport, "
James DeWitt, "
John Devlin, "
John Dwyer, "
Charles H. Eaton, "
James H. Edgerton, Private, Corp'l, Private.
Henry W. Edsall, Private.
William B. Eldridge, "
Hiram Everman, "
Joseph Everman, "
John P. Fitzgerald, "
Thomas A. Fountain, "
Nelson E. Hagerty, "
Marcus A. Hamilton, "
John Hanley, "

Dennis Hart, Private.
Mark Hendershot, "
John Hollman, "
Abram P. Hopper, "
William Howell, "
James Jackson, "
George M. Jenkins, "
John Jenkinson, "
Andrew Johnson, "
William Kelly, "
Patrick Kennedy, "
Lewis Kimble, "
Henry Koopman, "
Cornelius Lacoste, Private, Corp'l, Private.
John D. Loveszy, Private.
James Maloney, "
Robert J. McClure, "
Michael McConnell, "
Richard McGough, "
William McGovern, "
Francis McKnight, "
Jonas B. McMullen, Wagoner, Priv.
Jeremiah B. McPeek, Private, Corp'l, Private.
Michael Mee, Private.
Daniel Mott, "
Patrick Murphy, "
Jasper T. Owens, "
Alfred Philhour, "
William S. Phillips, Private.
William J. Pierson, "
John Predmore, "
William Predmore, "
Cornelius Reagan, "
Samuel Rubenstine, "
Mahlon Rochelle, Corp'l, Private.
Daniel Rogers, Private.
Jacob Roth, "
Christopher Search, "
George Shaw, "
Edward Smith, "
Thomas Smith, "
Thomas G. Smith, "
William Snediker, "
John Snyder, "
Joseph E. Stoll, Serg't, Private
John Terhune, Private,
James Thompson, "
Jacob D. Vanderhoof, "
Wm. D. Vanderhoof, "
Jeffrey C. Walton, "
John L. Warbasse, "
Francis Ward, "
Peter Washer, "
George Williams, "
John W. Wilson, "
George E Wood, "
Arthur H. Yetman, "
Jacob P. Youmans, "

DISCHARGED.

Charles C. Morgan, Corp'l, Serg't.
John E. F. Cleghorn, Private.
Cornelius Conover, "
Enos Conter, "
Isaac Dickerson, "
Joseph L. Doty, "
John Heater, "
Henry H. Henyon, "
Whitfield Larue, "
John Leonard, Private.
Charles C. Moran, "
Mordecai Mott, Corp'l, Private,
Henry Potts. Private.
Thomas Rafferty, "
Caleb Sergeant, "
Christopher Townsend, "
Frederick C. Winter, "

TRANSFERRED.

Reuben B. Arthur, Private.
Joseph Barkman, "
Albert G. Fowler, "
Joseph W. Holly, Private.
Joseph W. Turner, "

DIED.

Richard Decker, Priv., Corp'l, Serg't.
Henry P. Cook, Priv., Corp'l, Serg't.
Jacob Dickerson, Priv., Corp'l, Serg't.
Joseph C. McWilliams, Priv., Corp'l.
Michael Callaghan, Private, Corp'l.
Daniel McCarty, Blacksmith.
George W. Ayre, Private.
William Baker, "
David Boyles, "
James Brisnahan, "
Peter Burns, "
Andy Cammell, "
John Carnes, "
Walter E. Conklin, "
John Cotter, "
Philip A. Decker, Private.
Charles Ebner, "
Theodore Edwards, "
George Flood, "
Michael Folliard, "
Richard Hawk, "
John Hermes, "
John Hobson, "
William Hubbard, "
Edward Ichler, "
Charles N. Lyons, Priv., Corp'l, Priv.
David Lyons, Private.
John Paugh, "
Caleb J. Rude, "
Wilson S. White, "

DESERTED.

John Thompson, Private, Serg't.
Peter Henyon, Private, Corp'l.
John Bird, Private.
Elias Crill, "
John Decker, "
Harrison A. Doty, "
Joseph L. Drake, "
James H. Gibbs, "
George Hayes, "
Malvin G. Hutalan, "
Frederick Leech, "
John Livingstone, Private.
William Mackenn, "
John McDonald, "
William Porter, "
Andrew J. Quick, Corp'l, Private.
Jacob H. Simonson, Private.
John Thompson (2), "
John Fiddaback, "
Isaiah Utter, "
William Van Scoten, "
Charles Wilson, "

UNACCOUNTED FOR.

Theodore F. Brooks, Private.
John Brawer, "
John Buzzell, "
Milton R. Buzzell, "
John H. Chadsey, "
John Clark, "
Michael Crowe, "
George Davidson, "
Charles Devats, "
Augustus Gerhardt, "
John W. Heintz, "
Francis Henry, "
William Herbert, "
William H. Hill, "
Peter Hughes, "
Charles Hussler, "
James Kelly, "
William McCabe, Private.
James McGuire, "
John McKee, "
Charles Meyers, "
John Mitchell, "
John J. Moore, "
Frank Nichols, "
Michael R. Nolan, "
William O'Neil, "
Edward Ring, "
Martin Ryan, "
Joseph Schmidt, "
Carl Schulzendorf, "
John A. Segon, "
Stephen Smith, "
George Somers, "
Henry Winans, "

COMPANY L.

William W. Taylor, Captain.
Hugh H. Janeway, 1st Lieut., Capt., Major.
William H. Hick, 1st Lieut. Co. K, Captain, Private, Captain, Major.
Gilbert J. Johnson, 1st Lieut. Co. A, Captain.
Francis B. Allibone, 2d Lieut. Co. E, 1st Lieut., Captain, Co. B.
Voorhees Dye, 2d Lieut. Co, B, 1st Lieut.
James Dalziel, 2d Lieut. Co. B, 1st Lieut.
Peter H. Langstaff, 2d Lieut.
Garrett V. Beekman, 1st Serg't, 2d Lieut., 1st Lieut. Co. M.
Charles H. McKinstry, Reg. Q. M. Serg't, 2d Lieut., Adjutant.
Samuel Craig, 2d Lieut., 1st Lieut. Co. H.
Carrel Carty, 1st Serg't Co. F, 2d Lieut., 1st Lieut. Co. M.
Philip Grundell, 1st Serg't Co. G, 2d Lieut.
William R. Stout, Private, Corp'l, Serg't, 1st Serg't.
William B. Hooper, Private Co. M, Q. M. Serg't.
Lewis A. McIntosh, Private, Q. M. Serg't.
William M. Hazen, Serg't, Com. Serg't, 2d Lieut. Co. K.
William H. Field, Private, Corp'l, Com. Serg't.
Asher Wardell, Private, Corp'l, Serg't.
Adolphus Weitfle, Private, Serg't.
George Schoonover, Private, Corp'l, Serg't.
William Douglass, Private, Corp'l, Serg't.
John S. Shinn, Private, Serg't.
Albert Powell, "
James Pointer, "
John Wilson, Private Co. I, Serg't.
Benj. C. Pullen, Private, Corp'l.
Edward L. Harris, "
William Curran, "
Joseph W. Bonnell, Private Co. I, Corp'l.
John M. Leadley, Private, Corp'l.
Theodore Irwin, "
John McKenna, "
Thomas Harvey, "
James Brady, "
Michael Keefe, Bugler, Chief Bugler.
Frederick Jones, Private, Bugler.
William H. Clifton, Private Co. H, Bugler.
James Watts, Private Co. K, Music'n.
Edward McGuire, Blacksmith.

Geo. W. Marsh. Private, Blacksmith.
Smith Wright, Farrier.
Matthew D. Conover, Farrier.
Cornelius Gallagher, Priv., Vet. Sur.
John H. Anderson, Private.
Isaiah Applegate, "
James Avoy, "
Louis Baner, "
Joseph Bertholf, "
Willis Blake, "
Ellis S. Bloomfield, Jr., "
Francis Boner, "
William Boner, "
James Boyd, "
Alfred Brenner, "
Oscar W. Brockhoff, "
Michael Brown, "
William Buckter, "
Ephraim Case, "
John C. Clevinger, Serg't, Private.
Alexander Conklin, "
Daniel Cronin, "
James J. Crouch, "
David Davis, "
Charles E. Dennis, "
Patrick C. Dolan. "
George Duffield, "
Jeremiah Duyer, "
Thomas Emley, "
William Evans, "
William W. Evans, "
John Finch, "
Michael Flynn, "
Joseph Fox. "
Reuben Gahart, "
Francis Gallagher, "
Charles L. Glazier, Corp., Serg't, Priv.
John W. Green, Private.
Daniel Hagerty, "
Joseph H. Hall, "
Horace E. Hamilton, "
Frederick Helmlinger, "
Thomas Hennessee, "
Joseph L. Hill, "
Alfred W. Horn, "
Jerome Hulitt, "
Nelson T. Hunt, "
Hubert Hursch, "
John Hustwait, "
Ebenezer B. Jackson, Private.
John Jacobs, "
Jas. M. Johnson, Priv., Corp'l, Serg't,
Michael Kiesel, Private. [Priv.
Philip Kiesel, "
Nathan T. Kunkle, "
James Lahey, "
Edward Lane, "
Charles Lange, "
Patrick Lawless, "
Henry Loring, "
John Mahoney, "
David Martin, "
William Matthews, "
Samuel McCombs, "
Marcus Miller "
William Mowerson, "
Michael Murphy, "
John Nolan, "
Patrick Ohair, "
Harrison Parent, "
August Pfausteil, "
John Porter, "
William Prime, "
William H. Pullen, "
Henry Richard, "
Henry Rigit, "
Charles A. Roberts, "
James Robinson, "
Jacob Rogers, Private, Corp'l, Priv.
Francis Sage, Private.
Peter Saunt, Private, Corp'l, Priv.
Charles Sheppard, Private.
John Shilling, "
John Shufeldt, "
William Sigler, "
Michael Sullivan, "
Daniel P. Taylor, "
Gustavus D. Tonkin, "
John Traynor, "
Gotleib Trupert, "
William Van Geison, "
Benjamin Wagoner, "
Stewart A. Walters, "
Thomas White, "
Abraham Whitlock, "
Charles T. Williams, "
James Wilson, "
Isaac Wood, "
Joseph Worthly, "
Alexander Yard, "
Henry Zimmer, "
Jacob Zimmerman, "

DISCHARGED.

William H. Brown, Corp'l.
Milton G. Horton, "
William H. Butler, Saddler.
Charles A. Anderson, Private.
Elijah Benson, "
William Blomell, "
Samuel Carr, "
Henry W. DeCamp, "
Ferdinand Deifle, "
Edward Gallagher, "
Charles Haskart, "
William Henry, "
Frederick Hughes, "
John Kelly, "
David Longstreet, "
James McCormick, "
Philip Miranda, "
David Morrison, "
Amos Rockhill, "
William W. Titus, "
James Van Hise, "
David H. Wilson, "

DIED.

Henry Kulthau, Corp'l, Serg't, 1st Serg't.
John J. Bray, Private, Q. M. Serg't.
Lewis D. Hughes, Private, Com. Serg't.
Uriah Curtis, Serg't.
William H. Wight, Private, Corp'l, Serg't.
Joseph B. Starker, Corp'l.
Robert Gravatt, "
George Patterson, Private, Corp'l.
Chas. T. Cowperthwait, " "
James Brown, " "
George W. Adams, Private.
Louis Bassit, "
Michael Britton, "
John Cowan, Jr., "
Michael Downing, "
John H. Horner, "
Zachariah C. Maloney, "
Patrick McCormick, "
Michael Riley, Sr., "
John G. Soden, "
Christian Stock, "
John L. Thornell, "
Leonard S. Vosbergh, "

DESERTED.

Robert Milligan, Corp'l.
John E. Andrews, Private.
Thomas Bahnos, "
William Beker, "
William Buckby, "
George Carroll, "
John Clark, "
John Corbit, "
John Cowan, "
Lewis Crackburn, "
Dennis Cunningham, "
Joshua DeWitt, "
Jules Dusart, "
Thomas Elyea, "
Geo. P. Emley, Corp'l, Serg't, Priv.
Henry M. Foster, Private.
Edward Greenfield, "
John Hancock, "
John Harvey, Private.
Charles Jefferson, "
John Lane, "
Barnard C. Lanth, "
George W. Lyming, "
James McNamara, "
John Meagan, "
Patrick Meagan, Bugler, Private.
Jacob D. Mase, Private.
John Murphy, "
James O'Neal, "
Richard Pease, "
Richard Reagan, "
Michael Riley, Jr., "
George Salt, "
Henry Travers, "
Charles Walters, "
John Zabriskie, "

UNACCOUNTED FOR.

John C. Baker, Private.
Thomas Bleason, "
William Brannon, "
John Brooks, "
John C. Clark, "
John Haakel, "
Gregory P. Harrington, "
James Hedden, "
William Hendrickson, "
Anton Herman, "
John Kelly, "
Edward Kennedy, Private.
Peter Lob, "
Lorenzo Mood, "
John Moore, "
Daniel Mulligan, "
William O'Brien, "
Frank Richmond, "
John Smock, "
Peter Stout, "
James Thompson, "
William R. Williams, "

COMPANY M.

John P. Fowler, Captain.
Thomas R. Haines, 1st Lieut. Co, K, Capt.
Jacob R. Sackett, 1st Lieut. Co. A, Capt.
James H. Hart, 1st Lieut. Co. H, Capt.
Moses M. Maulsbury, 1st Lieut. Co. F, Capt.
John Kinsley, 1st Lieut. Co. F, Capt.
George A. Bowne, 1st Lieut. Co. A, Capt.
Horace W. Bristol, 1st Lieut., Capt. Co. B.
Harry Jones, 1st Lieut.
Garrett V Beekman, 2d Lieut. Co. L, 1st Lieut., Capt. Co. I.
Thomas S. Cox, Serg't Co. K, 2d Lieut., 1st Lieut.
Carrel Carty, 2d Lieut. Co. L, 1st Lt.

Samuel Warbasse, 2d Lieut.
Jeremiah P. Brower, 1st Serg't, 2d Lieut., 1st Lieut. Co. C.
Alanson Austin, 2d Lieut.
Samuel A. Wood, Serg't, 1st Serg't, 2d Lieut.
Hyde Crocker, 1st Serg't, 2d Lieut. Co. H.
Emerson C. Thompson, Priv., 1st S'gt.
James M. Tillman, Private, Corp'l, Serg't, Q. M. Serg't.
Robert K. Adams, Serg't, Com. Serg't.
Wm. L. Kirk, Private Corp'l, Serg't.
John W. Bellows, Private, Serg't, 2d Lieut. Co. I.
John H. Dane Private, Corp'l, Serg't.
Madison W. Coleman, Corp'l, Private, Serg't.
Jacob J. Showles, Private, Serg't.
William F. Payne, Private, Serg't.
Stockton Hurd, Private, Corpl, Serg't.
Conrad Schantz, Private, Corp'l, Serg't.
James G. Hornbeck, Private, Corp'l.
James E. Gunderman, Private, Corpl.
John B. Easton, Private Co. L, Corp'l.
John Van Blarcom, Private, Corp'l.
Harrison Beemer, Private, Corp'l.
John H. Elston, Private, Serg't, Private, Corp'l.
Dedrick Lasson, Private Co. L, Corp'l,
Peter Belcher, Bugler.
James Bishop, Private, Bugler.
Abel B. Snow, Private Bugler.
Peter Dolan, Farrier, Blacksmith.
Abner W. Rickart, Private, Blacksmith.
Isaac McPeek, Private, Farrier.
Barney Ayers, Private.
George Ball, "
William T. Bateman, "
William Berrigan, "
Charles W. Bishop, "
Thomas Boyd, "
David Braner, "
Charles W. Burnham, "
James Campbell, "
Terence Cassidy "
Charles H. Collver, "
John L. Conklin, "
Aaron R. Cool, "
Thomas Coyle, "
Joseph M. Creamer, "
Peter Cyphers, "
Philip Cyphers, "
George M. Davis, "
Samuel Decker, "
Patrick Delaney, "
Jacob M. Drew, "
James Doyle, "
Martin Eagan, "
William Earl, "
Joseph H. Ellis, "
Levi Ellis, "
Daniel Everman, Private.
Jesse L. Fairchild, "
Lucien H. Fairchild, "
Robert J Fitzgibbons, "
William H. Ford, "
William Germath, "
Wilson C. Gunn, "
Cunningham Hales, "
Silas W. Hance, "
Manche Hoffman, "
Aaron J. Hornbeck, "
George W. Hornbeck, "
Charles Hulmes, "
Robert B. Kinsey, "
John J. Kotziel, "
James H. Linley, Private, Corp'l, Private.
James T. Lockhard, Private.
Michael Loffery, "
Daniel Lyons, "
William McGann, "
Michael Maloney, "
John J. Martin, "
Daniel Maxwell, "
Baltus P. Melick, "
Henry S. Montonye, "
Thomas J. Morrow, "
Martin Mould, "
Edward M. Nevins, "
John S Nichols, "
Charles Niles, Priv., Farrier, 3d Bat.
Thomas P. Norman, Private.
Joseph H. North, "
William Osborne, "
Sydney Polley, "
Lewis P. Post, "
Charles Price, "
Winfield S. Reed, "
Christian Renner, "
George W. Ross, "
John Rusk, "
Patrick G. Ryan, "
Nathan Slavacool, "
John E. Schmidt, "
Henry Shoars, "
John Smith, "
Sydney V. Snavel, "
Timothy Stack, "
Henry Straway, "
John Terry, "
Edward S. Tillman, "
Robert D. Toner, "
Edward S. Tracy, "
Martin V. B. Van Horn, "
Eugene Van Ness, "
Horace Van Order, "
Tracy E. Waller, Priv., Hosp'l Stew'd.
Lewis Westbrook, "
Smith Winans, "
Frederick Winnecke, "
Ezra D. Wintermute, "
Jacob Winters, "
Charles Worst, "

DISCHARGED.

Andrew J. Edsall, Serg't.
Robert J. Anderson, Blacksmith.
Samuel Angell, Private.
Stacey Brown, "
William E. Bryant, "
William Clawson, "
George W. Doland, "
William Everman, "
Felix R. Gardner, "
James H. Garland, "
Benjamin Kithcart, Corp'l, Priv.
Robert S. Lane, Corp'l, Priv.
David Lott, Private.
John Parliment, "
John J. Rieley, "
James W. Roys, Serg't, Priv.
John W. Schroth, Private.
Isaac Seeds, "
Andrew J. Shuler, "
Theodore Smith, "
Warren S. Smith, "
Charles S. Wheelwright, Private.

TRANSFERRED.

George Van Inwegin, Private, Serg't.
Daniel P. Shultz, Private, Corp'l.
George R. Dart, Corp'l.
Charles Williams, (1) Saddler.
Lewis Cane, Private.
James J. Crowe, "
Jacob McCann, Private.
William D. Reed, "
John Ross, "
Frank Schmidt, "
Charles Williams, (2) "

DIED.

David Dean, Private, Corp'l.
Solomon Bensley, Private.
August Bloom, "
John Cassimore, "
Joseph B. Conklin, "
David Cooper, "
John H. Douglass, "
James Everman, "
Thomas Goss, "
William Kern, Private
Arthur D. Potter, "
John F. Pratt, "
Joseph Shumm, "
David Titus, "
Andrew J. Utt, "
Isaac Van Atten, "
Henry M. Wyant, "
William H. Wyant, "

DESERTED.

William T. Ayres, Serg't, Private.
William Bayles, Private.
John Brown, "
Miles Burke, "
Henry Cruesdale, "
Henry Degraw, "
Francis Dow, "
Benjamin H. Edsall, Corp'l, Private.
Charles Harrison, Private,
Horace Happaugh, "
Andrew Jackson, "
John Kennedy, "
Morris Klein, "
Jeremiah Lambert, "
Simon M. Lewis, Corp'l., Private,
Michael Mack, Private,
John McCauley, "
John McCormick, "
Joseph Minton, Corp'l, Private,
Joseph Myers, Private.
Michael O'Hara, "
John M. Ray, "
Joseph Rozencrantz, "
George F. Seaver, "
Isaac Stein, "
James Stray, "
Charles Summers, "
Frank C. Summers, "
Frederick Thorpe, "
Floyd Tuthill, "
John H. Westbrook, "
Samuel Whitmore, "
John Wilson, "
Edward R. Worrell, "
Samuel Yard, "
Joseph Zeck, "

UNACCOUNTED FOR.

John W. Brown, Private.
Joseph Budsworth, "
Ira Crum, "
William Dougherty, "
Charles Foster, "
Frank Haskell, "
George Hayes, "
Charles Hudson, "
Alexander John, "
William Jones, Private.
John A. Madou, "
George Martin, "
Kohl Matthew, "
Daniel McCabe, "
Philip H. Remington, "
John Smith, "
Francisco Suaser, "
Joseph Terry, "

www.ingramcontent.com/pod-product-compliance
Lightning Source LLC
Chambersburg PA
CBHW021803110726
47902CB00006B/1626

* 9 7 8 3 3 3 7 8 1 4 5 9 5 *